T0076794

"*The Business of We* is for anyone who is committed to creating a welcoming and productive work environment for all. With more than twenty years' experience managing culture gaps in the workplace, Laura Kriska impressively offers practical steps for bridging these gaps—whether they're related to age, race, nationality, ethnicity, or any factor of identity."

—Jenna Fischer
Actor and Producer/Host of the podcast *Office Ladies*

"There has never been a more important time for Laura Kriska's WE-building tools. As a leader in a global company, I have seen the positive impact these strategies have on promoting connection among people of different backgrounds. This is an important book for our increasingly diverse global marketplace."

—Yasuyuki Sugiura,
Former President of Mitsubishi Corporation America

"As a biotech executive working across borders, I recognize the challenge of managing a culturally diverse workforce. Laura Kriska has nailed it with this timely book. Take the time to read, highlight, and dog-ear the wisdom of these pages. You will learn how to take simple actions to turn *Us versus Them* people into an enlightened team of WE!"

—Anthony Sun,
MD, Chairman and Chief Executive Officer of Zentalis

"I have watched Laura Kriska's career since she began working at Honda thirty-five years ago. I don't know anyone who knows more about building a WE culture than Laura."

—Scott Whitlock,
Former Executive Vice President of
Honda of America Manufacturing, Inc.

"I have known Laura Kriska for twenty-five years and watched as her curiosity and insights have built a purposeful career in bridging culture gaps. As a leader for a globally diverse company, I know that building connections across differences is a key factor for success in the twenty-first century."

—Larry Fitzgibbon,
Cofounder and CEO of Tastemade

"I highly recommend *The Business of We* for any organization embarking on the thoughtful journey of self-discovery to strengthen its commitment to inclusion, diversity, equity, and access. I've known Laura Kriska for more than twenty-five years, and she is a charismatic leader with outstanding international business and consulting credentials. These tools have been invaluable to me as the leader of a nonprofit organization focused on the double bottom line of financial sustainability and community impact."

—Bruce A. Harkey,
President and CEO of Franklin Park
Conservatory and Botanical Gardens

THE
BUSINESS
OF

LAURA KRISKA

HarperCollins
Leadership

AN IMPRINT OF HarperCollins

Published by HarperCollins Leadership, an imprint of HarperCollins
Focus LLC.

Any internet addresses, phone numbers, or company or product
information printed in this book are offered as a resource and are not
intended in any way to be or to imply an endorsement by HarperCollins
Leadership, nor does HarperCollins Leadership vouch for the existence,
content, or services of these sites, phone numbers, companies,
or products beyond the life of this book.

ISBN 978-1-4002-1681-9 (eBook)
ISBN 978-1-4002-1680-2 (Paperback)

Library of Congress Control Number: 2020944830

Printed in the United States of America
20 21 22 23 LSC 10 9 8 7 6 5 4 3 2 1

To the original WE-builders who have supported
me on my path: Shige Yoshida, Sally and Brian
Kriska, and Masa Iino.

To protect my clients, I have changed names and masked industry-specific information. In some cases, I altered information by combining situations, condensing timelines, and modifying storylines to maintain confidentiality and to clearly express specific concepts.

"Overall, we've managed to move toward a more inclusive understanding of ourselves and acceptance of each other. Historically, though, we have wavered and are currently at a crossroads: Are we going to advance toward a broader definition of 'we' or will we retreat to a narrower one?"

—Richard Blanco, *How to Love a Country*

CONTENTS

INTRODUCTION

DAVID LETTERMAN TRAVELED with his colleague Tom Keaney to India in 2016 to participate in an episode of the Nat Geo TV show *Years of Living Dangerously*. Neither had been to India before, but they were excited about the project and eager to do well. At their request, I prepared a two-page document with basic cultural information for them to use as a reference for their trip. For example, in India, cows are considered sacred, cricket is the most popular sport, and business cards are used much more extensively than in the United States. I'm not an authority on India, but I am an expert in knowing how cultural data impacts the way people work, especially when there is a wide and deep divide. As American professionals going to work in India, they would inevitably encounter many cultural differences. Whenever someone from one culture ventures into another for work or play, there will be unexpected situations. By educating themselves in advance, they could prevent some typical "ugly American" encounters, like trying to order a beef hamburger in Mumbai. But more than just avoiding problems, I wanted them to leverage cultural data into positive outcomes, just as I have instructed thousands of other global professionals to do throughout my career.

My own experience managing culture gaps in the workplace started in the 1990s with my first job after college, in Honda Motor Company's Tokyo headquarters, where I was the only American woman working among thousands of Japanese colleagues. I was born in Tokyo to missionary parents but returned to the United States at age two, so I had no memory of those early years in Japan. My formative years were spent in a very white community in the Midwest, surrounded by people who looked, sounded, and prayed like I did.

Despite my homogeneous hometown and because of my parents' adventurous spirit, I grew up with a strong attachment to Japan. During college, I was able to spend a year studying in Tokyo and learning to speak the language. So, when I got that job at Honda as an assistant to a senior executive, I thought I had hit the first-job jackpot.

But the culture shock started for me on my very first day of work. I had put a lot of thought into how I would make my first professional impression and showed up wearing a brand-new designer suit. You can imagine my disappointment when I was given a used blue polyester uniform to put on—a uniform that was *only* for women, and for *all* women in the company.

I worked with ten Japanese "office ladies"—all lovely and young and single. We supported the forty directors of the company by serving tea, cleaning ashtrays, and sharpening pencils. Despite my strong desire to be part of the team, I just didn't fit in. The way I looked, the way I spoke Japanese, my unintentional failure to follow the rules—both written and unwritten—caused an *Us versus Them* dynamic. I was definitely, and conspicuously, the only *them*.

As a twenty-two-year-old, I was not aware of the many cultural norms that impacted my daily life. This inability to anticipate inevitable cultural differences caused problems in the ways I built relationships, communicated with colleagues, and worked as part of a team. I wrote about my many failures, and a few success stories, in my first book, *The Accidental Office Lady.*

One reason I had difficulty anticipating differences is that many cultural norms are invisible. Without spending time with other people, building trust, and learning about their cultural norms, it is easy to misinterpret what you see. For example, years ago, during my first week as an exchange student in Japan, I was invited to have a meal at a fellow exchange student's home with his host family. During the meal, my friend stuck his chopsticks upright into his rice and excused himself from the table for a moment. The host family froze. Everyone silently stared at the red lacquer chopsticks sticking straight up from a mound of white rice. It was clear that everyone was upset, but I did not understand why. Then, after a moment, the host mother reached over to his bowl, pulled the chopsticks out of the rice, and placed them on the table. There was a palpable sigh of relief as though she had corrected a grave mistake. And, as I later learned, she had. The only time chopsticks are placed upright in a bowl of rice is during funeral rituals in Japan.

Like many people, I thought that culture differences were present only when someone like David Letterman traveled to India or when I went to work in Japan. What I didn't know then is that culture differences are everywhere. Defining culture simply by variations in customs between foreign countries is much too narrow.

Every human has a cultural identity made up of many factors including the country where a person grew up. A cultural identity is based on gender, gender identity, race, sexual orientation, ethnicity, body type, family structure, religion, physical ability, socioeconomic class, education, occupation, skills, neurodiversity, life experience, and more. These identity characteristics intersect in every person in different ways, which means that our identities are complex and ever changing. Any one of these factors or a combination of factors can become the basis of a culture gap.

For more than twenty years, I worked with organizations in various industries on four continents. No matter where or with whom I worked, I inevitably encountered *Us versus Them* divisions. On a business trip to Brazil, I listened as people in Sao Paolo, referred to as Paulistanos, talked about their colleagues in Rio, referred to as Cariocas, as though they were rivals. Paulistanos saw themselves as hardworking and described Cariocas as interested only in going to the beach. Cariocas viewed the Paulistanos as overly uptight and demanding. The comments reminded me of an encounter a few weeks earlier on a business trip to Houston when I had made the mistake of suggesting that Houston and Dallas were similar. The folks in Houston set me straight right away. "We are not Dallas!" one woman claimed emphatically.

In my work with thousands of professionals, I saw that *Us versus Them* divides were defined not only by geography but by internal structures: sales versus marketing; front office versus back office; management versus non-management. *Us versus Them* divides were defined by any and all factors of identity, including age, gender, race, sexual orientation, religion, and more. I saw how these gaps impacted employees, customers, B2B partners, and supplier relationships. Boomers versus Millennials. Black versus white. Christian versus Muslim.

Every professional in every organization deals with multiple *Us versus Them* dynamics. The trick is figuring out which of these divides are harmless and which have the potential to negatively impact business and the people in business. If the gap is big and the job is important, then taking action is wise even if you are one of the most recognized names in America. David Letterman, for his part, did not assume he was above cultural adaptation and prepared well. He recognized the need to adjust to a different culture. Among other culturally excellent strategies he employed during his trip, he brought tailor-made business cards that he presented to Indian officials, including Prime Minister Narendra Modi.

Even gestures that seem small and inexpensive can make a big impact. A client in Indonesia prevented an escalating conflict between Christian and Muslim employees who refused to eat together in a shared company cafeteria after a Christian worker used the microwave to heat pork on a ceramic plate. With the purchase of paper plates and an additional $50 microwave, to prevent mixing Halal food with non-Halal food, the employees gathered in the cafeteria together once again. Another client in Brazil eased tensions between employees from the countryside and city folks with a gathering to watch soccer and eat potluck. A client in rural Illinois closed the language gap between management from China and U.S. factory workers with a free language app downloaded to every smartphone.

Over the years, my work expanded from bridging the U.S.-versus-Japan divide to closing any *Us versus Them* gap. In 2018, I was invited to give a TEDx talk in New York City on "How Small Gestures Can Bridge the Gap Between Us and Them." In the talk, I shared examples of what I call WE-building—engaging in actions that close *Us versus Them* gaps. For example, I have witnessed how the simple act of saying another person's name correctly or using one word in another person's language can transform a first introduction from forgettable to memorable.

Small gestures are the starting point for fundamental change in the way people relate to one another, especially when people look or sound different from each another. But small gestures alone are not enough to effect change. They simply begin a process of closing *Us versus Them* gaps. As we will see throughout the book, a small gesture is only meaningful when it is followed by actions—actions that require time, resources, and effort. Without substantive actions, a gesture that initially signified solidarity and connection with another person becomes an empty, superficial, and performative act.

Some small gestures are so profound, they have the power to radically transform a single moment. Following the murder of George Floyd by a police officer in Minneapolis, there was great turmoil around the country. Police, National Guard, and other law enforcement clashed with protestors in all fifty states. In the midst of violence and tense *Us versus Them* standoffs between citizens and law enforcement, a few leaders made a gesture that de-escalated conflict and, at least for that moment, created a shared experience that had the capacity to alter the trajectory of the situation.

It was the same gesture that Colin Kaepernick made to protest racial injustice, police brutality, and systemic oppression of Black people.[1] He knelt. His gesture initially caused controversy and outrage among some, but four years later this simple gesture became an act of solidarity between two groups literally standing in opposition to each other: law enforcement versus protestors. A small gesture, like taking a knee, can be game-changing in the moment, but a single act is never enough to close gaps.

In Santa Cruz, California, the police chief, Andy Mills, and Mayor Justin Cummings took a knee with protesters. The highest-ranking uniformed member of the New York City Police Department, Terence Monahan, took a knee with protestors, as did leaders in cities from Coral Gables, Florida, to Portland, Oregon.[2] One young activist in Trenton, New Jersey, described the impact of officers taking a knee and why he protested. "This whole thing is to incite that type of change where we can get one of them to show empathy and become one of us."[3]

Unfortunately, most law enforcement around the country did not de-escalate in the early days of the protests, most notably in Washington, DC, and later in Portland, OR.[4] In many places, there appeared to be no effort to close the gap between law enforcement and protestors. In those places, many people were hurt and some were killed.[5]

Small WE-building gestures are the starting point for change, especially for people who want to close *Us versus Them* gaps but don't know how to start. I've met well-meaning people from various backgrounds who genuinely wish to connect across difference but do not know how to start. Their worry over doing or saying something wrong outweighs their impulse to act or speak. But remaining silent and avoiding actions are no longer acceptable.

Just as surely as I knew David Letterman would encounter cultural differences when he traveled to film a TV episode in India, I know that every American will encounter consequential gaps in their workplaces and in their lives. For example, as a result of the Black Lives Matter protests, many white Americans were awakened to a racial gap they have long ignored or did not truly understand. Other gaps may be related to business or geography or any of the many factors that make up a person's identity. When these gaps go unrecognized, problems can result, such as marginalization of talented employees. Miscommunication, poor teamwork, complaints, lost revenue, and even lawsuits can occur. The *Us versus Them* mindset is outdated and harmful because our marketplace and our workplaces are increasingly diverse and interconnected.

This book provides a proven three-step process for closing *Us versus Them* gaps in your workplace. We'll look closely at these steps throughout the book.

1. Foster **Awareness**
2. Self-**Assess**
3. Take **Action**

This three-step approach has helped thousands of professionals successfully navigate issues in their workplaces. It has encouraged them to develop awareness of cultural gaps throughout their organizations, and it has provided them with the tools to assess their own role in *Us and Them* dynamics. Most importantly, it has inspired thousands of professionals to take action to close the gaps.

In today's increasingly diverse and deeply interdependent world, developing a WE-mindset will generate positive outcomes. This is true no matter what *Us versus Them* gap you are facing.

You may be newly committed to racial justice but do not know where to start.

You may be managing an international project.

You may have a group of subordinates of different ethnicities.

You may be targeting customers from a different country.

You may have colleagues who are twenty years younger, or older, than you.

You may have B2B partners who speak a different first language.

You may be dealing with a longstanding interdepartmental division.

Whatever your *Us versus Them* gap, this book will provide solutions that will increase productivity, enhance engagement, improve policies, help you reduce complaints, and avoid legal problems. I've used the three-step approach in a wide range of situations to help people achieve their desired outcomes. I even helped one diverse group win the Indy 500!

The Business of We offers tools, success stories, and inspiration to help you take action at a time when an *Us versus Them* mindset is more counterproductive than it's ever been. As the COVID-19 pandemic has made clear, we are a deeply interconnected global community. A cough in Wuhan reverberated around the globe, impacting the health of Italian grandmothers and Iranian health ministers alike.

The pandemic accelerated *Us versus Them* behavior in some. Anxiety and uncertainty caused fearful behaviors like overt anti-Asian discrimination, hoarding important medical supplies, and even fighting over toilet paper. The disproportional negative impact of the virus on communities of color demonstrated centuries of inequality within the health-care industry.[6]

But the pandemic also brought out WE behavior that prioritized the common good, like wearing facemasks to protect others and manufacturers shifting production to create protective equipment and ventilators. The international scientific community embraced a WE approach by broadly sharing research and abandoning competitive practices like keeping laboratory findings secret.[7] Global leaders who chose collaboration and cooperation over competition and division were more successful in protecting the lives of their citizens.[8]

Fearful, protectionist actions are not a viable long-term solution. Our ability to thrive in the twenty-first century will depend on our ability to collaborate broadly. The diverse nature of business in nearly every sector of our economy requires cooperation across differences of many kinds, whether we are fighting a pandemic, working toward racial justice, or building a diverse organizational team.

My life's work has been to close the gaps between *Us* and *Them* using this three-step approach in organizations with various divides across multiple borders. My goal is to inspire others to narrow whatever gaps exist in their lives. This book is written to help you develop a WE-mindset so that together we can create a more productive, inclusive, and welcoming environment for all.

WE-building Rules

1. Be genuine in your commitment to narrow a specific *Us versus Them* gap in order to create a safer, more welcoming, and productive environment for all.

2. Acknowledge that dominant cultural norms exist and are privileged over other norms.

3. Be open to new norms of inclusion based on common factors that promote a broad definition of WE.

4. Set aside negative stereotypes and practices that perpetuate gaps including use of language, attitude, and behavior.

5. Recognize that face-to-face encounters are an essential method for gathering accurate data (visible and invisible) about another person or cultural group.

6. Be open to engaging in face-to-face interactions of increasing depth across differences of gender, race, age, ethnicity, nationality, religion, sexual orientation, socio-economic class, ability, and other factors even if these encounters are uncomfortable or difficult.

7. Seek opportunities to engage in face-to-face interactions across *Us versus Them* gaps.

8. Reflect humbly and honestly on your own life experience in order to better understand your assumptions and biases that inform *Us versus Them* gaps.

9. Be accountable to others and follow through with any WE-building commitments you voluntarily make.

10. Support and encourage others in their WE-building efforts.

FRAMING THE

ORGANIZATIONAL

CHALLENGE

1

DIVERSITY CAN BE DIVISIVE

A Growing Problem in a Culturally Varied Organization

DIVERSITY HAS BEEN PART of the American dialogue for more than fifty years, but protests in support of Black Lives Matter combined with disproportional impact of the COVID-19 virus on communities of color inspired overdue and urgent attention unlike any in my lifetime. During the past five decades, we have seen a dramatic increase in the number of diversity and inclusion directors, as well as conferences and publications devoted to the topic. Yet most organizations still don't have an integrated and diverse workforce. They lack effective programs that enhance inclusion, despite the increasingly varied population. Many organizations' responses to employee diversity issues have been superficial, reactive, and not effective.

It's no wonder, then, that tensions between various groups of employees remain high and hurt organizational efforts to create high-functioning teams or to produce synergies among employees from different countries, races, or generations. At best, organizations struggle with integrating diverse employees onto

teams. At worst, they're the target of lawsuits and negative publicity that affect their stock prices, their hiring and retention
capability, and their employee morale and productivity.

Most business leaders recognize that these problems exist,
but they don't always see how extensive or damaging the effects
are. It's telling that few companies openly acknowledged issues
of racial disparity until Black Lives Matter protests swept the
country. In response, many of America's largest and most influential corporations, including Walmart, Amazon, Apple, General Motors, and YouTube, made public statements denouncing
racism and calling for justice.[1] Some companies made dona-
tions; others committed to new policies. Even NFL Commissioner Roger Goodell, who had openly criticized Colin
Kaepernick, posted a public apology saying that he and the NFL
had been wrong for not listening earlier to players who had protested police brutality toward Black people.[2]

As we will see throughout the book, organizations often take
action to close gaps only in reaction to negative publicity, a lawsuit, or public demand. As such, their efforts to address diversity
are rushed, costly, and orchestrated to quell criticism rather
than address underlying issues. There is a better, proactive, less
costly approach and it starts with examining who is in charge.

Organizations are grappling with many types of cross-
cultural issues because so often there is a homogeneous group
in power—I call it *the home team*. The home team norms of communication and behavior become the standard by which all
people in the organization are measured. Employees who identify with the home team have an advantage but are often unaware of it. Until those on the home team engage in
self-reflection and understand their role in any specific *Us versus
Them* gap, diversity will be viewed as a problem to be solved
rather than a strength to be leveraged toward successful
outcomes.

Everyone agrees that cooperation can be a powerful tool
in business and in life. Working with others can lead to

accomplishments that no single human, no matter how talented, can achieve on his or her own. Michael Jordan, one of the most talented and successful athletes of all time, knew that as a singular player his contributions could make the difference in games. He famously said, "There is no 'I' in team, but there is in win."[3] In the popular ESPN documentary series *The Last Dance*, however, even Jordan revealed that he alone could not achieve the greatness he desired, which was to win NBA championship titles. "Talent wins games, but teamwork and intelligence wins championships."[4]

WE-building is more than cooperation. WE-building is working together across differences. It is seeing difference as an opportunity, not a barrier, to learn and to expand. WE-builders do not subscribe to superficial stereotypes or pretend that differences do not exist. Instead, WE-builders see that differences are real and must be acknowledged. They look at difference not as good and bad or better or worse, but as predictable outcomes of growing up in different environments. WE-building is the deliberate choice to close any gap between people who are separated by geography, language, generation, ethnicity, race, religion, or any factor that divides.

Diversity in the workplace has increased, as it should, to reflect changing demographics. But skills among those on the home team to see and to recognize difference elude many people, including leaders. Knowing how to close gaps remains a mystery to many of us. Instead of trying to understand difference, many people default to magical thinking that proximity to those who are different will be enough to bridge the vast divides that exist in everyday life. WE-building provides a specific, much-needed process for building lasting connection with those who are different—those who speak a different first language, worship in a different faith, or see a different reflection when they look in the mirror. WE-building is a proven methodology that can help anyone close a gap that gets in the way of their ability to communicate and to build trust successfully.

This book provides a three-step process for bridging any gap. While the process is simple, the commitment needed to create real change is not. Concrete action and accountability is an essential part of the process for closing *Us versus Them* gaps. It will take time and effort. But when people work together across differences and take action to close gaps, amazing things can result.

In this book, I will share stories about companies that created profitable new revenue streams, reduced supplier costs, and shortened approval processes—and all because leaders and employees from different backgrounds closed *Us versus Them* gaps. If they can do it, so can you.

———

The workplace is growing more diverse, and it is mission critical to acknowledge this.

———

GOOD PEOPLE, BAD COMMUNICATION

Cultural damage occurs because people completely misunderstand and misperceive what is actually happening. Lack of familiarity with people who aren't members of their own social group causes anxiety and fear, triggering them to think and behave in ways they would consider ridiculous or unacceptable if the tables were turned.

Esther was employed at a New Jersey bank for three years and had performed at a high level. She was always prepared and on time for work. Having grown up in Haiti, she spoke English with a slight accent. One day a supervisor noticed a problem with some missing data from a customer. He pointed it out to Esther, but she told him that she didn't know anything about it. The bank took customer issues very seriously and soon one of the bank's vice presidents was fuming about the missing data. "Someone must know where it is!" he exclaimed. The vice president then privately questioned each of the six employees in Esther's department in his office. When it was Esther's turn, she went to the office and answered every question honestly and directly. However, as she had been raised to do in the presence of any authority figure, she kept her eyes down and did not look directly at the vice president when she spoke. Her supervisor approached her later that day to say that the vice president had concluded that Esther was lying. "He said you didn't look at him," the supervisor told her. "That made him think you had something to hide."

Esther explained to her supervisor that in Haiti she had been taught to show respect for her parents and others who were older by never looking them in the eye. Fortunately, her supervisor believed Esther and was able to explain the cultural misunderstanding to the vice president.

Large organizations today have hundreds or even thousands of Esthers—people whose backgrounds differ from what the home team considers the norm. Instead of recognizing that there is a dominant culture within the organization, leaders inside organizations may inadvertently make critical mistakes like firing a great employee. Instead of seeing an opportunity to understand an employee who comes from a different cultural background, many home team leaders might think they understand Esther, believing that they've helped her learn the company culture and that she has adapted to it. Visibly, that may be true. But invisible messages are being sent or perceived with every encounter. We need to foster greater understanding of these invisible pieces of information. If we don't, managers will fail to grasp why an employee like Esther acts the way she does and may make false assumptions about what her actions signify.

A PAINFULLY SLOW, EVOLVING CONSCIOUSNESS

How did we get to this place, where we're becoming more enlightened about fostering diversity yet still unable to tap into the value such diversity offers? Let's look at the problem within a historical context.

Bridging cultural difference has always been a workplace requirement, but for many decades in the United States and Europe, the dominant cultural norm has been narrow and closely aligned with white, male culture. This is a generalization and of course there have been exceptions, but even a cursory glance at a list of C-suite executives demonstrates that white men ruled and continue to do so.

It is important to note that just because people share identity factors like gender and race does not automatically mean that they will get along. But when the people leading and working in an organization share defining identity factors, many norms of behavior and unspoken values are aligned. These norms are then accepted as correct and become the default to which others are expected to follow.

The demographics of the American workplace began to change permanently after the Civil Rights Act of 1964 when women, African Americans, and other minorities joined, not only as laborers or clerical staff, but as professionals who became managers and leaders. These non-white males influenced standards of day-to-day workplace behavior through various means. When spoken or unspoken requests for change were not heeded, lawsuits and new rules forced new standards. As a result, the dominant standards of white male culture began to erode and cultural norms began to shift. For example, the TV show *Mad Men* portrays life in an advertising agency in the 1960s and early 1970s, and the contrast between our current #MeToo norms and what was then considered normal office behavior toward women is striking.

The Immigration Act of 1965 triggered what would become a fifty-year trend of increasing immigration, often called the Fourth Wave, bringing people from around the world into our workplaces. Reducing international trade barriers in the 1980s and 1990s introduced more global diversity into the U.S.

workplace through emerging markets, global outsourcing, mergers, and acquisitions. This Fourth Wave peaked in 2002 with 12.2 million people coming from more than twenty different countries, each with different ethnic, religious, and other cultural norms, now part of the fabric of modern American society.

Each of these slow-moving but powerful trends increased cultural diversity in the U.S. workforce, and started to push "home teams" to reassess what was considered acceptable behavior. But still, awareness of workplace diversity grew slowly in the early twenty-first century with uninspiring results. The combination of video evidence and viral transmission of discriminatory practices brought new clarity to the issue. Video of two black men removed from a Philadelphia Starbucks in April of 2018 caused outrage. Thousands of riveting #MeToo stories shared by recognizable female names has heightened the consciousness about discrimination and harassment of women in the workplace. But it was the swift and powerful impact of the Black Lives Matter protests that sparked accountability among corporate leaders unlike anything that came before it. For the first time, many home team leaders finally seemed to be able to see and name problems. Silence and resistance in the face of such obvious oppression were no longer options for most business leaders. Not everyone handled it well.

REAL-WORLD CONSEQUENCES

CrossFit is a successful fitness company with annual revenue estimated by *Forbes* to be $4 billion.[5] CEO Greg Glassman caused big trouble with a racially insensitive tweet following the death of George Floyd and inappropriate comments during a company Zoom call in which he allegedly said, "We're not mourning for George Floyd."[6] His silence in response to Black Lives Matter protests was criticized. Within days of his tweet and comments, affiliate gyms cut ties with CrossFit, and sponsors like Reebok announced that they would end their licensing agreement with the company. Glassman tweeted a public apology, but it was not enough to repair the damage he had caused. Within days, Glassman resigned from the company.

Companies like Uber and others have experienced the real costs of customer, employee, or investor outrage when they see evidence of failure to embrace diversity and to create welcoming workplaces. Uber's CEO, Travis Kalanick, resigned over allegations that he fostered a toxic workplace where sexual harassment and bullying were tolerated.[7]

It took less than two months for Jeffrey Whitman, owner of Uriah Heating & Cooling & Refrigeration to feel the full impact of this kind of rejection. On July 3, 2018, Whitman was driving on Route 71 in Columbus, Ohio, and got so angry at another driver for allegedly cutting him off in traffic that he followed this driver, an African American man named Charles Lovett, to his home. Whitman, who is white, proceeded to verbally assault Lovett by calling him horrible names repeatedly. Lovett shot a video of the racist tirade as Whitman sat in his work van, which clearly displayed the company name and information, including his state contractor license number. Lovett can be heard calmly telling Whitman that he will report his behavior to the state. The next day when confronted by television reporters, Whitman made no apology and seemed genuinely surprised that his behavior had drawn so much attention. But within two days the backlash against Uriah Heating had taken its toll. "I'll never work in Columbus again," Whitman told a local newspaper.[8] Whitman lost his accreditation with the Better Business Bureau and officially closed his business one month later.

In the last decade, a growing number of women and people from other minority groups have assumed leadership roles in every sector of society, including powerful positions in politics and industry. In 2018, Rashida Tlaib (MI) and Ilhan Omar (MN) became the first Muslim women elected to the U.S. Congress. In 2018, Ravinder Bhalla was sworn in as Hoboken, New Jersey's first Sikh mayor. On January 3, 2019, the most diverse class in history was sworn in to the 116th U.S. Congress. This class has more gender, gender-identity, sexual-orientation, race, religious, and ethnic diversity than ever before seen in the halls of Congress. The number of leaders of color at Fortune 500 companies has dropped in recent years, but the C-suite is growing more diverse. The list currently includes CEOs Marvin Ellison at Lowe's, Kenneth Frazier at Merck, Roger Ferguson Jr. at TIAA, René Jones at M&T Bank, Jide Zeitlin at Tapestry, Ramon Laguarta at PepsiCo, and Joey Wat at Yum China.[9] Increased representation in positions of power by those who have historically been the targets of discrimination will result in more meaningful consequences for those who continue with old unacceptable behaviors. ABC Entertainment Group President Channing Dungey, who in 2016 became the first Black president of a major broadcast TV network, made the decision to cancel the show *Roseanne* after its star made an offensive and racist tweet.

Everyone's consciousness has been raised when it comes to diversity, especially following Black Lives Matter protests. What we need now is to act on a simple truth that more people are willing to admit today than in the past: we've all felt like outsiders at some point in our lives, like one of *them*. This recognition provides powerful insight, and can lead to bridging gaps and finding solutions.

I have heard thousands of stories in which people felt unwelcome, not included, and even unsafe. These firsthand experiences happen to everyone, regardless of race, religion, sex/gender identity, or ethnicity. Some of these encounters are inconsequential; others are life-changing. None of them are forgettable.

———

Everyone has felt like a *them*.

———

For instance, here are personal statements of feeling like a *them* collected from a few of the many participants in my trainings over the years:

> "In high school, I played golf and all the cool kids played baseball."
> "I was an only child and all my friends had siblings."
> "I emmigrated from Hong Kong when I was twelve and the other kids made fun of my food and my accent."
> "I was the only Muslim in my middle school."

Here are a few business examples:

> "I'm the only woman on the trading floor."
> "I work with people who have an Ivy League education and I don't."
> "I am the only gay manager in an automobile manufacturing factory."
> "I am the only Black senior vice president in an executive suite filled with white people."

Recognizing these differences is a start; refusing to accept the subordinate status they imply is the next step. But these are individual responses. Organizational leaders need to be aware that their companies have to do things differently if they want to succeed in an increasingly diverse world.

MISTAKES AND MISCONCEPTIONS

It's not as if diversity is a secret. It's not as if business leaders have completely overlooked the cross-cultural issues that exist in their organizations. Nonetheless, until recently, most companies failed to respond appropriately or effectively.

If you're a senior leader, you may read this and think to yourself, "Wait a second. We've invested significant resources in diversity. We've prioritized recruitment and hiring of diverse staff. We've launched training programs designed to help people learn how to work with others from different backgrounds. We've established a code of conduct that makes it clear we will not tolerate any discrimination based on factors such as sex/gender identity, country of origin, religion, race, or age. What else can we do?"

A lot. These programs and policies are better than nothing. But they rarely offer an opportunity to address our own complicity in perpetuating the culture gaps that arise when people from different backgrounds work together. Programs designed to check off a compliance box do not foster self-reflection. As journalist and author Pamela Newkirk wrote in her prescient book, *Diversity, Inc.*, "Despite decades of deliberation and multibillion dollar initiatives, many are still pondering and gesturing rather than meaningfully increasing diversity."[10]

The two most important factors needed to bridge any gap successfully are free: honest self-reflection and a genuine willingness to actively build trust with others. Fostering connection between people from different backgrounds requires face-to-face interactions of increasing depth over time, including online and virtual interactions where connection in person is not possible. If these requirements are met, almost any gap can be narrowed.

Rather than addressing these *Us versus Them* issues head-on and with confidence, leaders of many global organizations tiptoe around cultural differences (especially race, sex/gender identity, and ethnicity). Otherwise talented, experienced, and thoughtful leaders rely on proximity as a panacea. They assume that having people from different backgrounds working together in offices and on teams will magically reduce tension, misunderstandings, and conflict.

Proximity to people different from ourselves is not enough to bridge gaps.

Leaders convince themselves that they are cross-culturally intelligent enterprises until an event helps them see the truth. One of the few major companies that addressed racism in a public and comprehensive way prior to the Black Lives Matter protests was Starbucks after the arrest of Rashon Nelson and Donte Robinson at a Philadelphia Starbucks in April 2018. The store manager, a white woman, called 911 only two minutes after the men arrived for a business meeting. She falsely claimed that they were trespassing. A bystander captured video of the police arresting the two men and it went viral.

In the days following this episode, the company faced increasing criticism. Less than two months later, Starbucks closed more than eight thousand retail stores in the United States for a half-day of racial bias training, which experts estimate cost the company $12 million in lost revenue.[11]

It's not just U.S. companies that fail to be proactive. I've worked extensively with Japanese companies operating outside of Japan, and the dominant culture for all of these companies has been Japanese and male. In some of these companies—organizations with enormous resources, deep knowledge of their industries, and a strong wish to succeed in the U.S. marketplace—it was a lawsuit or formal complaint that motivated meaningful change in the way they hired women, minorities, and managed other cross-cultural gaps.

Online training has become an increasingly popular response to diversity. And it can be a good starting place for learning about other cultural groups. But while it's a convenient method of acquiring knowledge on a specific subject, and proved a critical tool during the COVID-19 pandemic, its virtual reality is no permanent substitute for face-to-face interactions. Online resources are fine to help employees learn historical information about a specific cultural group, but they must be carefully designed in order to address the substantive work of building trusting relationships. The difference between online culture training and in-person training is like the difference between reading about dieting and working with a nutritionist. Online training may provide an extrinsic understanding of what needs to happen, but it does not often catalyze the intrinsic shifts that result in real behavioral change.

LEADERSHIP

Building bridges across cultural difference in the workplace requires emotional bravery and stamina from leaders—the kind that can seem scary and overwhelming to otherwise confident and skillful people. In order to begin to bridge any significant *Us and Them* gap, especially if you are part of the dominant culture, you must look honestly and unflinchingly at your choices. Real change requires firsthand experience with the *them* culture. Engaging in firsthand encounters can be challenging and will require courage, because the result may not be what you expected or hoped for. The action you take to bridge gaps may even cause interpersonal conflict. But without taking some risks, there can be no meaningful change. Shedding one's protective armor in order to narrow an *Us and Them* gap can be difficult. Managers need to exhibit courage and encourage their employees to do likewise.

Helping people learn to work effectively across various boundaries is not a quick fix. A diversity day or onetime workshop is a simplistic approach to complex problems. These issues—interpersonal conflict, complaints, unwanted turnover, social media catastrophe, public relations damage, business failure, and lawsuits—are a result of decades of slow-moving institutional and social change that has now reached a twenty-first-century tipping point.

Be aware that you're running up against problems that are the manifestation of years of narrow thinking by the dominant culture. Smart, twenty-first-century leaders are starting to see that successfully managing cultural diversity must be prioritized. It will require a commitment of resources and time to get it right.

STUMBLING INTO CULTURAL GAPS

While some companies run into problems because they have deeply biased executives behaving badly—harassing women, refusing to hire minorities, and so on—the majority are not malicious, but victims of their lack of awareness. When organizations experience cross-cultural catastrophes, they are often unexpected events: the people in charge didn't see the gaps between *Us and Them* and plunged headlong into disaster.

Luxury brand Dolce & Gabbana, one of the most successful fashion companies in the world, got its start in Milan, Italy, in 1986 when young designers Domenico Dolce and Stefano Gabbana introduced their first full collection. They called the collection "Real Women," in part because they lacked the funds to pay professional models and had to recruit female friends to be in the fashion show. It was reported that the designers had so few resources that they even brought a bedsheet from home to use as a stage curtain.[12]

Their trajectory to success happened quickly over the following years. The company opened its first showroom in Milan in 1987. They expanded overseas to Japan in 1989 and then to the United States in 1990. Menswear, children's clothes, shoes, perfume, and lingerie were added to their line. In 1994, the company profit grew from $50 million to $125 million. In 2003, they opened a store in Hong Kong and revenue reached $523 million.

By 2018, D&G was widely recognized as a global success story, but perhaps they had paid too little attention to cultural data and the increased diversity of their customer base. They planned their biggest fashion show ever in Shanghai for November 21, 2018. After months of preparation, a significant financial investment, and the involvement of thousands of people (fashion models, celebrities, backstage support), they released three short online videos to promote the show. The videos caused a social media sensation—but not in the way D&G had hoped.

D&G later claimed that the videos, featuring a Chinese woman trying to eat Italian food with chopsticks, were meant to be humorous. But they were widely viewed as insensitive by millions of Chinese people who represent a third of the world's growing luxury market—the very people that D&G wanted to attract. The videos were followed by insulting Instagram posts by Stefano Gabbana, which D&G would later claim were hacked.[13] The fallout was swift and costly—the fashion show was canceled and most online retailers in China removed D&G merchandise from their sites. Despite a hastily organized #DG-LovesChina campaign and public apology, celebrities and customers across China criticized the company and some even uploaded videos of themselves burning D&G goods.[14] Experts estimate that it will take years for D&G to repair the damage—years when D&G will have a diminished role in the estimated $7 billion Chinese luxury-brand market.[15]

Did Dolce & Gabbana have any Chinese colleagues on their promotional team? Did they test the promotional videos with Chinese consumers? Did dominant Italian cultural norms determine that the "humorous" videos would achieve the business goal?

These are hindsight questions, but they should have been asked early in the process. D&G opened its first Chinese store in 2003 and had logged fifteen years in the Chinese market before making this cultural error. Clearly, being there isn't the same as being aware. A #DGLovesChina twitter campaign does not translate into the ability to form meaningful connections with people outside your own tribe.

If D&G had strong, open relationships with Chinese colleagues, it is likely that some of those colleagues would have expressed concern over the videos. If D&G had paid attention to cultural data, they would have learned that the videos would not be a successful promotional tool. If they had listened to Chinese voices, they could have anticipated that many Chinese consumers would find the videos insulting.

It's entirely possible that one of D&G's Chinese colleagues suggested that the videos could be a problem. It is probable, however, that this colleague was not included in the decision-making process, and that was a mistake. If this individual had been part of the decisionmaking team, their opinion would not only be heard but heeded.

The best way to avoid cultural catastrophe is to first assume your viewpoint, your standards of "right," may not be the same as other people's norms. Check your view with others. This is the starting point for bridging any *Us and Them* culture gap. You don't have to like or agree with other cultural norms, but you must understand them in order to leverage this data toward your goals.

Cultural Data—A Mission-Critical Tool

In 2004, General James Mattis had a very big goal—establish stability in al-Anbar province during a tumultuous period of fighting. Mattis led the First Marine Division to al-Anbar with this goal in mind, and he armed his experienced Marines with all the necessary tools—including food, water, weapons, and cultural data.

Marines were given training on Iraqi culture and history, and they were taught rudimentary Arabic. General Mattis even issued specific orders including "no wearing of sunglasses when speaking with Iraqi people" because it was considered rude.[16] He also encouraged his Marines to grow mustaches because it would make them seem more familiar to Iraqi civilians.

It took several years, during which time there were successes and serious failures. But through collective efforts of many leaders and individuals using all of the resources available, including cultural data, the Marines were successful in their effort to restore order to al-Anbar province.

A year later, in 2005, General Mattis increased access to cultural data as a military tool throughout the Marine Corps by establishing the Center for Advanced Operational Culture

Learning (CAOCL).[17] Pre-deployment training programs covered three specific topics including language, regional expertise, and culture.[18] However, as of July 2020, a decision was made to divest from CAOCL "so as to invest in areas of higher priority." Fortunately, some functions of the center will be retained under Marine Corps University.

Whether a gap is about ethnicity, race, religion, or any number of important identity factors, organizations need to:

● Accept that many definitions of "right" exist.
● Understand that their default definition is narrow and may differ from other ideas of "right."
● Grasp the difference between the traditional organizational view of "right" and another view of "right."

In this way, companies can make culturally informed choices. We'll talk about this process in much more detail later, but for now, I will introduce the first tool—the WE-building Cross-Cultural Continuum. The chart below provides a framework for understanding the WE-building premise, which is that failure to consider cultural data about a person or another group can have a negative impact. Actively gathering and considering cultural

CROSS-CULTURAL CONTINUUM

NEGATIVE CULTURAL IMPACT			POSITIVE CULTURAL IMPACT		
GAME-CHANGING	CONSEQUENTIAL	INCONSEQUENTIAL	INCONSEQUENTIAL	CONSEQUENTIAL	GAME-CHANGING
Significant, long-term negative outcome.	Measurable negative outcome.	Not meaningful enough to cause measurable negative outcome.	Not meaningful enough to cause measurable positive outcome.	Measurable positive outcome.	Significant, long-term positive outcome.
Damage caused is difficult or impossible to repair. Some permanent damage is done.	Time required rebuilding goodwill and trust. Money spent on solutions. Formal apology necessary.	Resources are not impacted. Register a moment of confusion.	Resources are not impacted. Register a moment of connection or clarity.	Achieve improved communication and relationships. Trust and goodwill established.	Achieve excellent communication and teamwork in culturally diverse group.

FIGURE 1

data about a person or another group can have a positive impact. The goal of WE-building is to leverage cultural data toward positive outcomes and business goals. *Us versus Them* behavior can have either inconsequential, consequential, or game-changing impacts. WE-building can also have inconsequential, consequential, or game-changing impacts (see Figure 1).

If we look at the stories in this chapter, we can categorize them as follows: Esther's encounter with her boss was a negative, consequential situation. Starbucks, CrossFit, and Dolce & Gabbana's catastrophe in China were all negative game-changing situations. General Mattis, on the other hand, falls into the positive game-changing category.

Misunderstanding and Miscommunication

Here is an inconsequential example on a micro-level of how cross-cultural misunderstandings arise. A sign on the office wall of an Atlanta-based energy company—let's call it PL for short—triggered a panic. Charlie Walker had worked there for ten years, and a large Chinese conglomerate had acquired PL six months earlier. Charlie and other veteran employees were worried because the energy market has always been volatile, and everyone knew that M&A often meant employee layoffs. There was a lot of uncertainty among local employees. Until Charlie walked into the office one Friday, he had not heard anything specific but assumed the ax was coming for some of the locally hired Americans.

PL had been started by an entrepreneur fifteen years previously. Since then it had grown from ten employees to over two hundred, with offices around the country. It was a company with a casual, seat-of-your-pants culture that operated quickly and without a lot of rules. People wore jeans to work, and to celebrate a big success, the boss would bring out bottles of Jack Daniel's.

Since the acquisition, a dozen Chinese staff had shown up in Atlanta taking over desks and working long hours. The causal culture began to change with more regulations and reporting required by the new parent company. A Chinese man, Mr. Fan, was sent from headquarters to head up PL's operations. Mr. Fan spent nearly all of his time in his office and seemed to work from early morning to late at night.

When Charlie walked through the hall on Friday morning, he noticed a series of signs printed in Chinese characters, with an arrow pointing toward the conference room. The only thing Charlie could understand on the sign was the room number where the most important meetings took place including a handful of times when lawyers had come to handle sensitive employment situations.

"This is it," Charlie thought to himself. "The layoffs are going to start." It was the only explanation Charlie could think of when he saw signs written in Chinese. There were no smart-phones or translation apps at the time so he was left to imagine the worst. "They are trying to hide this," Charlie said to his colleague Steve. "Why else would the signs be written only in Chinese?" Steve told Cheryl, who consulted with Pam, and be-fore they knew it, most of the local staff were convinced that the pink slips were coming at any moment.

Then a small group of Chinese businessmen in suits were ushered into the office and marched down the hall to the con-ference room. Rumors started spreading that a team of lawyers was in the conference room preparing for the layoffs. Later that morning, Mr. Fan sent Charlie an email asking him to meet at eleven. Charlie went to see Mr. Fan convinced he was about to be fired. Instead, Mr. Fan asked if Charlie would be willing to head up a new initiative. It quickly became obvious that Mr. Fan wasn't interested in firing Charlie or anyone else. In fact, Mr. Fan mentioned that they might need to hire more people if the initiative went well.

At the end of the meeting, Charlie paused and asked Mr. Fan about the Chinese signs in the hall. "They directed the outside auditors toward the conference room they are using today," he explained.

OVERCOMING *US VERSUS THEM* MINDSETS

Traditionally, business organizations have been psychologically closed to "outsiders." There was the "old boy's network." There was the management group composed solely of white Protestant men who went to Ivy League schools. There was the law firm where everyone was a blue blood. While these organizations sometimes employed people who were different from themselves, they usually were segregated by job type/title.

For years, companies could prosper despite this *Us versus Them* mentality. Now, in a global business world where diversity is a critical business asset and cross-cultural teams are crucial, this mentality can be destructive. Nonetheless, this type of mindset has a strong hold on company cultures. Many talented professionals like to consider themselves worldly and open-minded, yet their organizations are, as CrossFit's Greg Glassman discovered, one tweet away from cultural catastrophe.

Preeminent law firm Paul Weiss in New York learned this in December 2018 when it proudly announced the firm's new partner class on LinkedIn—with a photo of eleven white men and one white woman.[19] Despite being one of the more diverse law firms in the United States, they scrambled to quell fierce online criticism, especially after 170 General Counsels signed an open letter to big law firms stating they would prioritize working with firms that are committed to diversity and inclusion.[20]

INEFFICIENCIES

It was almost Christmas when I visited the Houston branch of a large international oil and gas company. As I walked on to the twenty-second-floor office, I saw one open office with about fifty desks, each with low dividers. I immediately noticed that this open space felt like it was separated into two distinct cultures. On one side of the office were colorful holiday cards, Christmas trees, and even electric lights decorating various desks. The other side of the office was austere—not a red or green decoration or any indication of personalization to be found. This unadorned section was the Japanese-speaking side, and typical of the office spaces where I had worked in Japan early in my career. There were none of the family photos or sports team paraphernalia that often mark the workplaces in U.S. companies. About twenty-five English-speaking employees sat on the decorated side of the office. These employees provided service to English-speaking corporate customers. The Japanese-speaking side provided service to Japanese corporate clients in the United States.

For many years, the rigid separation between Japanese and English made business sense and was easy to maintain. But now it was causing trouble with international clients in Europe and South America. The rigid *Us and Them* culture meant that there was almost no communication between employees of the same company who sat in the same room. As a result, the two sides ended up competing for new business. Rather than communicate and cooperate on behalf of the whole Houston office, the English-speaking side would unknowingly put themselves in direct competition with the Japanese-speaking side. Not only did this diminish the company's competitive capacity, it made the whole company look bad in front of potential customers.

BENIGN IGNORANCE

The *Us versus Them* mentality isn't usually the result of overt racism, sexism, or ageism—at least not consciously. Instead, many business leaders—especially those over the age of fifty— are victims of their upbringing. They've been socialized into seeing cross-cultural issues through a narrow lens rather than the wide-angle view that encourages inclusive policies, programs, and personal growth.

From the time I began working as a cultural consultant to Japanese companies in 1997, I encountered talented and hardworking professionals who I enjoyed working with immensely.

But many of them were inherently ill-prepared to work with non-Japanese people. These were top-level graduates of Japan's best universities working in Fortune 500 companies. They were the carefully selected top performers who had come to the United States to work for a period of time, usually three to five years. Because almost all of these people had spent their lives living and working in a very homogeneous country, they had very little interaction with people different from themselves.

They wanted to be successful while working in the United States. None of them wanted problems or intended to cause difficulties. But their lack of first-person experience with non-Japanese people made it very hard. They all labored under the illusion that working side by side with U.S. colleagues would be enough to bridge the gaps between themselves and people from a different culture. In actuality, working in the same building offered proximity. Proximity is good but it's not enough to build trust. Trust develops over time and is a result of deliberate interpersonal effort.

One of the most insidious aspects of *Us versus Them* mindsets is that we are often taught to ignore or not name our differences. This is especially true in the United States for white people over age fifty—including me. Born after the Civil Rights Act of 1964 and raised to be culturally polite, I've been taught to avoid calling attention to racial or ethnic differences. While this may have been a well-intentioned message, it doesn't prepare us to acknowledge and confront factors that can divide us. And it does not help people to come to terms with their own complicity in dynamics that perpetuate unfair practices in the workplace. Many older white Americans care about creating racial equality but they don't know how because they have been conditioned not to think deeply about it.

An unspoken yet lasting message among white people in the post-1964 Civil Rights era was do not discuss race. I never did. I subscribed to the "we're all human" attitude, which, by definition, overlooks the significance of racial, religious, and other cultural differences.

People like Howard Schultz, founder of Starbucks, clearly care about closing gaps between *Us and Them*. The problem, though, is that he's been acculturated in such a way that his strategy for closing the gaps has been awkward and naïve. During a CNN interview in February 2019, during his brief presidential run, Schultz claimed, "I don't see color."[21]

In March, 2015, Starbucks launched Race Together, an effort to address race relations.[22] Schultz was sincere in his response to tragic events, including the killing of Michael Brown in Ferguson, Missouri, in 2014. "I cannot be a bystander," Schultz was quoted as saying repeatedly in discussions at Starbucks.[23] After a series of successful in-house forums on race where Starbucks employees and board members shared and learned from one another, Schultz decided to expand this effort, believing, as the campaign claimed, that "conversation has the power to change hearts and minds."

While the instinct to try to connect and facilitate deeper understanding through honest discussion was a laudable goal, Race Together was a failure because it operated on the simplistic assumption that baristas could start conversations with customers about race and heal the wounds.[24] Conversations are a good starting point, but conversations with strangers about race are not enough to create systemic change. *Us versus Them* mindsets are complex and rooted in decades of societal and familial messages, making it impossible for superficial approaches to have any meaningful impact. This is why the impact made by law enforcement officers who knelt in response to Black Lives Matter protestors is fleeting. This is why there is deep skepticism in response to the many polished statements of solidarity from corporate America. Small gestures must be followed by meaningful actions that lead to structural and intrapersonal change.

The first action for people like Howard Schultz and other well-meaning white people is to reflect on our own firsthand experience with other cultural groups. Listening and learning provides a framework for understanding how each of us fits in to and perpetuates any specific *Us versus Them* dynamic.

RECOGNIZING WHAT WORKS AND WHAT DOESN'T

Organizations have made mistakes when attempting to manage cross-cultural issues. It is a complex topic for most businesses, and it takes time and testing to figure out best practices. But the time has come to recognize and avoid the following mistakes:

- Putting your head in the sand and hoping that diversity-related conflicts will somehow disappear.
- Continuing to live the same non-diverse life but hoping for different results.
- Pretending that proximity to people from different backgrounds will bridge the gaps and that people will learn to appreciate the "otherness" of colleagues simply by working with them.
- Launching naïve or superficial programs (online training, Starbucks-like Race Together campaigns, etc.) believing that they have the power to make everyone a WE.
- Establishing formal, permanent positions or teams to deal with *Us versus Them* issues; naming a Director of Diversity & Inclusion (Salesforce, Apple, and Uber are just some well-known companies that have done so) and assuming that you've delegated away the problem.

While creating positions like a Director of Diversity & Inclusion (or Diversity, Equity & Inclusion) is a good first step, it shouldn't be the last one. The organizations that handle cross-cultural issues with great effectiveness usually do the following:

- Involve leaders as de factor directors of diversity. These senior executives are actively, visibly, and regularly engaged in promoting cross-cultural understanding. They not only model appropriate behaviors (e.g., creating diverse senior-level teams) but participate in training programs designed to foster awareness of and appreciation for differences.

- Notice if all the decisionmakers represent a dominant culture and make changes to increase the number of diverse voices at the table.
- Bring cultural data into the organizational conversation as General Mattis did in Iraq by insisting his troops learn words in another language and understood norms of behavior in a different place.
- Foster effective conversations about topics such as ageism, sexism, and racism. These conversations raise people's consciousness and help them think about their own behaviors and beliefs.
- Engage in self-reflection that challenges old and accepted paradigms of dominance through formal and informal channels.
- Encourage and exhibit emotional bravery. Be willing to have difficult conversations, and demonstrate an ability to listen rather than just to explain, deny, or defend.
- Set measurable goals for hiring, retention, and promotion of non–home team employees.
- Tie Diversity, Equity, and Inclusion goals to business goals.

AN ENGINE POWERING CROSS-CULTURAL UNDERSTANDING

I've witnessed numerous instances when, seemingly against all odds, groups from different cultures found ways to move from an *Us versus Them* stance to the unity of WE. Let me share one of these examples with you—an example that took place a while ago but is still relevant today.

Race car driver Bobby Rahal made a one-year agreement with Honda Performance Development to test Honda engines on the IndyCar racing circuit. Honda was a dominant engine manufacturer in Formula One racing, then a mostly European sport. IndyCar, on the other hand, was a very American sport anchored by its namesake track in Indianapolis, Indiana. It was the beginning of a long experiment to see if Honda, who had been so dominant in Formula One, could translate their engineering skill to a completely different type of racing. For Rahal, it was a chance to be an early adapter to a new engine supplier.

For one year, Bobby Rahal agreed to provide the chassis, a driver, and a team of ten mechanics. Honda agreed to provide the spec engines along with a team of ten engineers from Japan. The group would all work together in a garage in Hilliard, Ohio, where they would hook up the different spec engines, test these engines on racetracks across the country, and analyze the data in order to figure out what worked and what didn't.

Two months before the team from Japan arrived, I was hired as the translator for the Rahal team. I had spent time on assembly lines and around cars, but my first trip to the Rahal team garage was a surprise. The Honda engineers that I had worked with in Japan had been quiet, bookish, and more interested in calculating numbers than in speaking a foreign language. By contrast, the Rahal team garage was filled with large men, many with beards and tattoos, talking loudly and joking raucously while surrounded by power tools. I immediately saw that communication between the fast-talking, loud Rahal guys (whom I affectionately referred to as the Gear Heads) and the taciturn Japanese engineers was likely to be a problem.

The solution to communication, I explained to Bobby Rahal, was to teach the Gear Heads how to speak Japanese. And he agreed. The goal was not to become fluent. I already knew that the Japanese engineers would know much more English than I could ever teach the Gear Heads in two months. The goal was to have the Gear Heads introduce themselves in Japanese on the day the two teams met for the first time. If the Gear Heads made this effort, it might make the Japanese guys feel more comfortable using the English they had been required to study since junior high school.

Every day at lunch, for two months, the Gear Heads and I sat around a conference room practicing basic sounds and words. The Gear Heads were cooperative, but their skill level varied greatly. One of the youngest members of our group, Joe, was terrible at learning languages. He was a smart guy but unable to grasp the basics of Japanese. For Joe, the trouble was remembering key phrases. I noticed that he had a default phrase that he would blurt out when no other words came to him. Joe's phrase was, "*Ohayo gozaimasu,*" meaning "good morning."

Two months later, a phone call from the Columbus airport let us know that the Japanese team was on its way. It was about five in the evening and the arrival had been closely followed. All ten members of the Honda team would drive directly to the garage where our group would greet them.

Dennis, the leader of the Gear Heads, was a tall military veteran who still wore his hair in a close-cropped buzz cut. It would be Dennis's job to lead the introductions. We gathered in a half circle near the front door with Dennis at the center. Standing right next to him, I noticed sweat trickling down his face.

When the Japanese team arrived, they silently and hesitantly entered the room and formed a corresponding half circle. They looked nervous and tired. I knew that for many of them this was their first time outside of Japan.

Dennis stepped forward and in his large and booming voice said, "*Boku wa* Dennis *desu, dozo yoroshiku onegaishimasu.*" His pronunciation was terrible, but the words hit their mark. The Japanese engineers looked at Dennis in amazement. Then, before they could respond, the next Gear Head stepped up. "*Boku wa* Steve *desu, dozo yoroshiku onegaishimasu.*" And one by one the Gear Heads introduced themselves in horribly pronounced yet intelligible Japanese. The Honda guys visibly relaxed. Their frowns of anxiety and exhaustion transformed into delight as they listened to the familiar yet mangled Japanese sounds coming from the Gear Heads.

Finally it was Joe's turn. As expected, he was nervous. And instead of introducing himself, he blurted out *"Ohayo gozaimasu,"* to the twenty men assembled at nearly six o'clock at night. Everyone in the room burst out laughing. Joe, the entire Japanese team, Dennis, and I all laughed, and this laughter changed something. It bridged a wide and deep gap of language, geography, and ethnicity. It broke the tension we all had felt as we were kicking off this new and unfamiliar initiative.

On the surface, these two groups of men looked and sounded very different from one another. The brief and genuine moment of laughter was a profound departure from the inherent *Us and Them* nature of the meeting. For a moment, the two groups connected: when they all laughed at the same thing, it was a WE moment that transformed the group.

The Gear Heads' effort to learn a few words in another language made this moment possible and communicated an important message to their new teammates from Japan. The message was that it was okay not to be perfect speaking the other's language because we have the same goal, which is to build a super-fast race car. Like people in most *Us and Them* situations, the men in this group figured out that they had way more in common than they had differences. They all loved cars. They all wanted to succeed.

The team worked extremely well together in the garage, at testing, and even after hours. Even though our language lessons stopped because the Gear Heads had to spend their time working on the race car, I would overhear impromptu usage of Japanese by the Gear Heads in the shop. On weekends, there were picnics, volleyball games, and opportunities to sample products from one of Bobby Rahal's sponsors, Miller Beer. A strong connection developed between the American Gear Heads and the Japanese engineers. They communicated directly about problem-solving and built relationships across language and culture.

A year later, Honda officially entered IndyCar racing, winning their first race. Over the next ten years, they expanded their presence and accumulated successes. And then, on May 30, 2004, race car driver Bobby Rice, driving for Bobby Rahal's team, won the Indy 500 using a Honda engine.

This group represented multiple *Us versus Them* divisions, including nationality, geography, language, race, and ethnicity. They built trust by deliberately engaging in WE-building, which continued to impact the team. In 2020, Rahal's team again won the Indy 500 with a Honda engine and Japanese driver Takuma Sato behind the wheel.

Moving Forward

We are part of a diverse and deeply interconnected marketplace. In the course of a few months in late 2019 and early 2020, a global pandemic impacted the health of hundreds of millions of people, devastating financial markets on every continent and substantially altering daily life for billions of people around the world. Shortly thereafter, protests around the world broke out demanding racial justice and an end to oppression of Black people in America. Learning how to work across differences is more important now than ever before. Our goals may be as critical as discovering a vaccine or repairing racial divides or as inconsequential as meeting someone for the first time. No matter what problem we are trying to solve, a WE-mindset will benefit us all.

 TIPS FOR WE-BUILDING WHILE WORKING FROM HOME

Due to concerns of spreading the COVID-19 virus, working from home became a reality for many. As we will examine in later chapters, the first steps of WE-building involve data-gathering and self-reflection and therefore can be done in private:

1. Foster **Awareness**
2. Self-**Assess**
3. Take **Action**

The third step is taking action, which is most effective when interacting face-to-face with others. But even though face-to-face interactions are the most effective mechanism to build trust across difference, we can still close *Us versus Them* gaps while being physically distant. Research shows that e-contact can be a useful tool to promote social harmony.[25] Studies have shown that specially designed online programs can promote connection between groups with longstanding rivalry, such as Catholics and Protestants in Northern Ireland.

When it comes to Taking Action to understand a "them" cultural group, anyone can start with steps like researching online or reading an article, book, or blog post. Watching a documentary or listening to a podcast are additional WE-building actions that can be done on your own. Leaders and individuals can accumulate knowledge of a "them" group while working from home for extensive use later.

Virtual mentoring and buddy programs are other ways to promote connection across difference while working from home. These tools will position all employees to be well prepared to tap into a valuable and underutilized resource—the innovation, creativity, and energy that resides in the spaces between longstanding *Us versus Them* gaps.

2

THE SYNERGY OF CROSS-CULTURAL COMPATIBILITY

The Benefits of Bringing People Together

IN 1997, MY first job as a cross-cultural consultant took place on the eighty-second floor of Tower 2 of the World Trade Center, where a group of ten Japanese executives of The Chuo Trust & Banking Co., Ltd. sat around a conference table looking like they were about to undergo painful dental procedures. None of them wanted to be there. It was a mandatory cross-cultural training session that had been forced on them by the HR manager, Mr. Sato. Chuo Trust & Banking employed more than thirty Americans and there had been complaints about the company's dominant group—all Japanese and all male. "They do not know my name." "They never listen when I speak in meetings." "They never talk to me unless it's to point out a problem." These common complaints by the English-speaking staff revealed an *Us and Them* gap that had festered for years.

I nervously displayed more than a hundred plastic transparencies on a bright overhead projector, giving advice to men twenty years my senior. Almost everyone in the room had the same attitude: Why are we here wasting time when we should be working? Mr. Sato had explained to me that these men had been carefully chosen by the company to work in New York because they were talented and skillful. They were deeply invested in the success of the company and worked long hours. "So what if I don't know everyone's name?" I heard one participant say to Mr. Sato, "Cross-cultural efforts are nice, but it does not impact our business."

For the first few years working as a cross-cultural consultant, I felt the same way. These were profitable enterprises run by experienced, hardworking professionals with decades of international experience. I was glad to have the work, but a part of me wondered if there was a bottom-line benefit to the company. Paying attention to cultural data—understanding the underlying values, figuring out what was considered normal office behavior, and bridging *Us and Them* gaps—had been valuable to me working in Tokyo for Honda Motor Company when I was twenty-two years old and new to the working world. But did paying attention to cultural data matter to successful professionals? Was it critical for high-functioning leaders to spend a day away from the office discussing strategies for narrowing gaps? Or was this a luxury that would never have bottom-line results? The answer I was looking for would take a few years to arrive, but when it did, it was loud, clear, and expensive.

THE COST OF DOING NOTHING

Headlines in the *Wall Street Journal* and the *New York Times* announced claims of bias at companies like Coca-Cola, Abercrombie & Fitch, and Nextel.[1] Foreign-based companies were called out for discrimination against American employees. Over the years, this ignominious list included General Electric, IBM, Nike, Ford Motor Co., Morgan Stanley, and Lowe's. Each was charged with discrimination based on age, disability, or other factors that are protected by law. While I personally do not know what actually happened at those companies, the real cost of not paying attention to *Us and Them* gaps was printed in black and white in the most important newspapers in the world.

Lawyers were engaged, employees gossiped, officials had meetings, and executives made hard decisions. Professionals who could have been working to generate revenue for the company were occupied with lawsuits. Costs grew in the form of low morale, poor corporate image, and monthly legal payments. Finally, after years of litigation, settlements were reached, documents were signed, and checks written. Coca-Cola paid $192.5 million.[2] Abercrombie & Fitch has paid millions in more than three separate settlements.[3] Nextel settled for $176 million and Morgan Stanley $46 million.[4] And even though I had no access to the conversations that went on inside those companies, one thing I know for sure is that *Us versus Them* culture gaps contributed to huge business costs that have impacted the bottom line for many years.

ABILITY TO SEE A PREDICTABLE PATTERN

At the heart of each of these lawsuits was an unresolved *Us versus Them* dynamic—white versus Black, men versus women, young versus old. The "home team" in each of these companies did not successfully bridge the gaps through hiring, compensation, promotion, and inclusion.

One of the most important benefits of creating a WE culture is an enhanced ability to see a predictable pattern before it becomes a legal—and therefore also a business—problem. Lawsuits are a costly consequence of *Us versus Them* dynamics both in terms of damage to the internal community and to the financial well-being of the organization. Lawsuits are evidence that companies have invisible culture gap problems that those in power cannot or will not see.

A predictable pattern often occurs if the *Us versus Them* dynamic is not addressed. It starts with an *Us and Them* moment, where one person feels like the outsider. Here are real examples from the workplace:

- An English-speaking white man is in a meeting with five Japanese men discussing a business problem in English. Suddenly, all of the Japanese men start speaking in Japanese without any explanation.
- A female executive is sitting around a conference table with other executives, all men, when the CEO says to everyone, "We've got to stop jacking around."
- A Black man joins a department of ten people, all of whom are white. Two of the people in the department never introduce themselves and never greet him in the morning though they consistently offer friendly greetings to white colleagues.
- In a workshop, the facilitator describes factors of identity by showing a slide listing gender, race, national origin, and age but does not mention sexual orientation. A gay employee feels left out.
- During a casual conversation among four colleagues, one member mentions his Ivy League alma mater and two other members share that they also went to Ivy League colleges. The three Ivy League graduates talk about their shared experience and the non–Ivy League colleague sits in silence.
- In a lunchroom, five colleagues are eating lunch. One of the employees is a recent college graduate (Generation Z) while all others are older (Generation X). The older colleagues are talking about their kids and schools in the community while the recent college grad takes out her phone and takes a photo of her sushi bento box lunch. One of the older employees jokes around and says to her, "You kids can't eat a meal without taking a photo first!" Everyone laughs.

Some of these incidents may seem minor: they often pass unnoticed in organizations. I'm not suggesting that companies should treat them as if they were horrific acts of discrimination. Rather, I'm advocating the higher level of awareness that exists in WE cultures. These moments are yellow flags that a pattern may exist or be starting. If they are heeded, problems can be solved with little or no organizational damage.

In WE cultures, leaders spot these moments, recognizing that they can cause hurt feelings and irritation. For some people and in some situations, this moment is forgotten and does not lead to any bigger problems. But in other cases, the small rift caused by that *Us and Them* moment produces higher sensitivity. Then the next innocuous comment, careless gesture, or joke is misunderstood and feels like an attack, which makes the gap deeper and wider for the person who is a *them*. Over time, real and perceived injustices fester. Sometimes, real injustices accumulate until one day the person who feels like a *them* decides to do something about it.

WHAT HAPPENED AT COCA-COLA

In 1988, Linda Ingram was hired at Coca-Cola as an information analyst. She was the only African American in her department.[5] Eleven years later, she was a plaintiff in the class action lawsuit against Coca-Cola for systemic racial discrimination.[6] Ingram's *Us versus Them* moment happened in 1996 after a white supervisor allegedly criticized her work performance and told her, "This is why you people don't get anywhere." After years of feeling like a *them*, and inspired by the actions of Bari-Ellen Roberts, the lead plaintiff in a successful lawsuit against Texaco that resulted in a $176 million settlement, Ingram contacted civil rights lawyer Cyrus Mehri.[7] Supported by three other codefendants, abundant human relations documentation substantiating their claims, and the timely resignation of Carl Ware, the only African American senior vice president in the company's 113-year history, the lawsuit was settled for $192.5 million.[8] In addition to financial payouts, the company agreed to form a seven-member task force that fundamentally altered the direction and culture of the company.[9]

TWENTY-FIRST CENTURY SECRET WEAPON

The benefits of creating WE cultures in twenty-first-century organizations are like the benefits of exercising or healthy eating: many of us understand these are good practices, but prioritizing them takes time and effort we would rather allocate to other endeavors. Until something goes wrong. Predictably, it's not until we encounter pain that we grasp the necessity to adjust our own behavior.

Enormous demographic changes in the American workforce have taken place over the past thirty years, and for companies that did not adjust there has been a cost. Hedge funds that could not successfully integrate women into the workplace have paid millions in fines and settlements. Retailers like Gucci, Prada, Adidas, and H&M have faced high-profile social media campaigns to boycott their companies following the release of insensitive products.[10] Wells Fargo, Fox News, and Walmart are names of other top-tier companies that failed to successfully include people from the non-dominant group and paid a hefty price.[11]

The irony is that there are encounters every day that can either result in an *Us versus Them* moment or a WE-moment depending on how the encounter is handled. These are golden opportunities for a leader or any employee to take positive action to build connection. If we look at the Cross-Cultural Continuum from Chapter 1, we can see how these daily interactions like greeting a fellow employee, leading a meeting, or engaging in small talk provide golden opportunities for anyone to take deliberate WE-building action.

CROSS-CULTURAL CONTINUUM

NEGATIVE CULTURAL IMPACT ⬅	⊖ ⊕	POSITIVE CULTURAL IMPACT ➡

GAME-CHANGING	CONSEQUENTIAL	INCONSEQUENTIAL	INCONSEQUENTIAL	CONSEQUENTIAL	GAME-CHANGING
Significant, long-term negative outcome.	Measurable negative outcome.	Not meaningful enough to cause measurable negative outcome.	Not meaningful enough to cause measurable positive outcome.	Measurable positive outcome.	Significant, long-term positive outcome.
Damage caused is difficult or impossible to repair. Some permanent damage is done.	*Time required rebuilding goodwill and trust. Money spent on solutions. Formal apology necessary.*	*Resources are not impacted. Register a moment of confusion.*	*Resources are not impacted. Register a moment of connection or clarity.*	*Achieve improved communication and relationships. Trust and goodwill established.*	*Achieve excellent communication and teamwork in culturally diverse group.*

Most of our daily interactions hover around the inconsequential categories and therefore our behavior does not have a huge impact. But well-meaning people can quickly and unintentionally swerve into consequential or game-changing categories by joking, complaining, or gossiping, and this leads to trouble.

Let's look at three common situations:

MORNING GREETING

NEGATIVE			POSITIVE		
Game-changing	Consequential	Inconsequential	Inconsequential	Consequential	Game-changing
Repeated joking, misuse of name, or insensitive nicknames day after day. Actively avoiding others.	Attempt to be humorous by greeting a person using insensitive nickname. Or using wrong name, or mispronouncing name. *Good morning, Jackie Chan!* (to Asian person)	Neutral expression; Ignore others. *No greeting*	Smile; General greeting. *Good morning.*	Smile; Specific greeting. *Good morning, Samira.*	Smile; More specific greeting based on knowledge of person. *Good morning Samira. How was your commute today?* Or, *How was your son's basketball game yesterday?*

LEADING A MEETING

NEGATIVE			POSITIVE		
Game-changing	Consequential	Inconsequential	Inconsequential	Consequential	Game-changing
Only listen to dominant voices. Ignore ideas from minority voices but recognize those same ideas when shared by dominant voices. Talk over minority voices.	Make space for dominant voices only. Joke around about culturally sensitive topics including race, ethnicity, age, sex/gender identity, sexual orientation, or other factors. *Let's let the old guy tell us what he thinks.*	Carry on without any attention to difference and ignore non-dominant voices.	Carry on without any attention to difference but notice non-dominant voices.	Affirm value of different perspectives. Make space for non-dominant voices, if necessary. Model good listening and do not make any culturally insensitive jokes or comments.	Actively promote listening. Shut down any talk over behavior and don't tolerate joking about sensitive topics. Magnify minority voices if others are not listening.

SMALL TALK

NEGATIVE			POSITIVE		
Game-changing	Consequential	Inconsequential	Inconsequential	Consequential	Game-changing
Gossip or complain about other employees because of factors of identity. *Does anyone in the Accounting Department even speak English? All they do is chatter all day long in Chinese.*	Talk about stereotypical topics related to factors of identity. For example, *Do you like burritos?* to a Latinx person. *Do you follow LeBron James?* to a Black person.	Talk about inconsequential topics.	Talk about inconsequential topics.	Deliberately talk about factors that are shared experiences. *How was your commute today?* Deliberately seek commonalities through conversation, *Did you watch the game yesterday?*	Talk about common factors. Share appropriate information about yourself or ask questions to get to know the other person. Listen. *I'm a Cardinals fan. Do you follow baseball?*

The negative consequential and game-changing behavior above is often referred to as *othering*. This behavior includes everything from unintended harm caused by joking to outright discriminatory acts. WE-building is the antidote to othering. It is the proactive, deliberate effort to seek commonality and create connection. WE-building can range from the simple effort to say someone's name correctly to the radical effort to educate oneself and do the foundational work necessary to combat persistent injustice. The results of WE-building can have an immediate and positive impact on every measure of business success.

Let's take a look at the four biggest business benefits of creating a WE culture.

1. Increased profitability
2. Increased innovation
3. Improved communication
4. Early warning system

INCREASED PROFITABILITY

WE corporate cultures build cohesion among diverse people, while fragmented teams do not. Cohesion leads to better results. Increased profitability is one of the most important outcomes when people pull together toward a common goal rather than operate in relative isolation. In contrast, *Us and Them* corporate cultures either carelessly resort to longstanding divisions or even amplify differences that prevent cooperation toward any shared goal, even one as obvious as remaining competitive.

Early in my career, when I worked primarily with Japanese companies located in the United States, I saw many examples where hard-working and well meaning Japanese leaders of U.S. companies failed to build a WE culture and it harmed profitability. In one typical case, a new Japanese president was transferred into an American auto parts manufacturing subsidiary and nearly destroyed the fragile relationship between the

Americans and Japanese in the company. The Japanese president started to call for meetings about important production initiatives only with Japanese staff, even though some of the Japanese staff were very junior. The high-ranking American employees were left out of these meetings without any explanation. So, the American staff started to hold separate meetings to discuss the same issues.

When Japanese colleagues received new direction from the Tokyo headquarters, they sometimes forgot or they did not take the time to share the data with American colleagues even though American colleagues wanted to be included. Instead, the information would come out in a discussion almost as an afterthought. This further irritated American colleagues and made them feel unimportant. So when new information came to the American employees from customers and contacts in the local industry, they did not share this information with their Japanese colleagues. The lack of sharing from both directions undermined trust in the office. It also put the company at a disadvantage in the marketplace because customer feedback was not incorporated quickly, and new directions from the parent company were not communicated throughout the office.

Eventually, the *Us and Them* dynamic grew so deep that it disrupted the company's ability to meet an important delivery deadline with their largest customer in Canada. Fearing that they would lose the Canadian business, the subsidiary agreed to air-freight the auto parts to Canada, cutting their profits in half.

This same kind of *Us versus Them* dynamic impacts thousands of American companies. When the sales department acts as though they are more important than the marketing department, the *Us and Them* dynamic causes division and lack of cooperation. When members of the executive team swagger around the office acting like they alone are responsible for profitability, non-executive team members feel like *thems* and divisions grow. But WE corporate cultures affirm the importance of both sales and marketing, both executive and non-executive roles in an organization in order to promote overall goals. WE organizations and WE leaders proactively create an environment where diverse points of view stimulate alternative and innovative conversations—which translates directly into revenue. This is what happened at a small and successful wholesale seafood business that was acquired in 2014 by a Japanese conglomerate.

Concrete Benefits of WE-building

The acquisition by the Japanese conglomerate caused a shift in the company culture, especially after four Japanese executives set up offices in the U.S. location. Ken Smith, the company's Vice President of Sales, and many local American staff experienced a distinct separation between the four Japanese employees sent from their Tokyo headquarters and the rest of the workforce. The four Japanese men sat next to each other in one corner of the office, spoke Japanese most of the time, and rarely interacted with the local staff. The local American staff seemed equally uninterested in the Japanese staff and worked with one another almost exclusively, as they had prior to the buyout.

Ken Smith, however, had participated in my WE-building workshop and was trained to be on the lookout for *Us versus Them* dynamics. Rather than fall into predictable *Us and Them* behaviors, Ken decided to take a WE approach with his Japanese colleagues. Instead of leaving them alone, he made an effort to get to know each of the four men. He learned to say "good morning" in Japanese, learned to say their names correctly, and invited them out to lunch on occasion. He suggested a change in the seating arrangement and separated the four Japanese colleagues so that they were dispersed throughout the office. Ken's efforts paid off in a big way on a business trip to Japan.

Prior to the acquisition, Ken had tried to create a new product line based on a relatively new type of seafood, Argentinian red shrimp. The shrimp was sold by select sellers who preferred big orders. Ken was interested in buying only large-size shrimp because that is what he could sell to American supermarkets. Because of Ken's limited interest in buying only one size of shrimp, he had not been able to make a competitive purchase.

During Ken's business trip to Japan, his colleague Hiro took him to a food show in Tokyo. At the show, Ken saw the product he had been unable to buy. Ken learned from Hiro that the Japanese parent company had access to Argentinean red shrimp but that consumers in Japan preferred the smaller, head-on variety for sushi. Ken explained to Hiro that U.S. customers preferred the larger, head-off, easy-peel size. Together they leveraged a large order for both big and small shrimp for a very good price. They purchased four hundred thousand pounds of product, which they successfully sold in their respective markets. The following year they increased the order and have continued to increase in subsequent years, contributing to millions of dollars in additional revenue for both the parent company and the subsidiary.

Ken and Hiro do not speak the same native language, and they do not share similar backgrounds—which is precisely the reason they were successful establishing an entirely new product line once they got onto the same team and acted like teammates. Ken understood the product and how it would fit the American market, and Hiro had access to the product and understood the Japanese market.

The relationship that Ken actively sought out with Hiro developed over time. It started with simple gestures by Ken to bridge the *Us and Them* gap. Ken did not know where his gesture might lead. As their face-to-face interactions continued, their mutual trust grew. When the trust reached a certain level, Ken felt comfortable to engage in a conversation about his own failure in this market, which led to a solution. This is WE-building.

Small Gestures

I met Angelo, the manager of the Engineering Subsidiary Department of a Korean automobile manufacturer in the

Philippines, who told me about a similar experience. In 2017, he and his company secured a lucrative contract with the Philippine government to sell a large volume of vehicles. In order to comply with the specification, the vehicles needed some modifications, which Angelo and his team in the Philippines managed for the first production run. But to minimize cost and to increase productivity, the Philippine subsidiary made a request to their Korean headquarters to modify the rest of the vehicles before they were sent to the Philippines. Angelo and his team went to Korea in November 2018 to discuss this request in more detail.

The engineers in Korea were not enthusiastic about the requests. It seemed to Angelo that this was a result of classic *Us and Them* tendencies revealed by countless global corporations—the perceived superiority of headquarters versus a subsidiary. They seemed to be slightly offended that the subsidiary was suggesting that the headquarters should be the ones to adjust. Angelo felt that there might have been some miscommunication due to language differences. He didn't want to return to the Philippines without a solution, but rather than give up or get angry, he turned to cultural data.

"I researched their culture and studied how to request things in their language more politely," he told me. "I also learned some of their words and used them as part of my email message." Angelo looked for and talked about common factors between members of his team and his counterparts in Korea, such as who loved coffee, who ran 5Ks, and who liked Indian food.

When Angelo returned a month after his first visit, he noticed a slight softening of the attitude from the Korean team. This gave him an opening to reintroduce the idea of modifying the vehicles in Korea rather than in the Philippines. The Korean team was much more flexible and agreed to almost all of what Angelo requested. As a result, the contract for the Philippine government increased from seven hundred vehicles to one thousand and is expected to grow. The following year, the parent company gave an award to Angelo's company for their effort and success. Angelo told me that he is certain that learning about Korean culture and looking for the shared factors between the two different ethnic groups within the same company helped to establish a connection that contributed to good communication and the success of the project.

Diverse teams, when operating in a WE corporate culture, get better, more profitable results. Through specific WE-building efforts, companies can leverage one of the most fundamental goals of any enterprise: profitability. In the case of Ken and Hiro, building trust and sharing information led to establishing a new product line. In Angelo's case, he was successful at influencing the dominant Korean headquarters' culture to adjust to the subsidiary's request, which resulted in increased orders and higher profitability for all.

INCREASED INNOVATION

Diverse people bring fresh perspectives to common problems. This diversity may be related to factors of identity such as their race or national origin or sexual orientation. The combination of diverse experiences, ideas, and opinions, when mixed in a positive, productive manner, produces innovative solutions to tough problems. Including a wide range of voices to generate new ideas and create new products is a valuable mechanism for any organization—but especially for those in highly competitive markets or during a crisis.

During the COVID-19 pandemic, innovation across difference was accelerated and contributed to better testing and treatments. Scientists, engineers, and inventors of all kinds shared open source designs for DIY masks, face shields and nasal swabs as well as graph data. Other common global problems such as poverty, climate change, and hunger will be more effectively solved with innovations that result from a WE mindset.

For example, the Norway-based Coalition for Epidemic Preparedness Innovations (CEPI) funded an international consortium of virologists at the University of Pittsburgh, the Pasteur Institute in Paris, and Themis in Vienna to work on developing a vaccine for COVID-19.[12] Online archives medRxiv and bioRxiv shared academic research well before the data was published in medical journals.[13] Chinese researchers who had been dealing with the problem longer than any others provided significant coronavirus research to the archive.

American history has many examples of leveraging cultural differences for game-changing success. One of these stories was not known to most Americans until after 1963, when the U.S. government unsealed classified documents that told the story of the Navajo code talkers during WWII.[14] Navajo men were recruited by the Marines for their unique language skills. Navajo was an unwritten language at the time and has complex grammar, so very few non-Navajo people understood it.[15] These soldiers created an original code based on the Navajo language. This code was used during the war to communicate throughout the Pacific theater. It was an effective tool for communicating across enemy lines. The special Navajo team started with twenty-nine soldiers and eventually grew to two hundred. The code talkers played a vital role in various battles, including Guadalcanal and Iwo Jima. Their code was never broken.

In the international aid world, many organizations operate on an *Us and Them* basis, where the culturally dominant *us* is white, Western, and wealthy. Due to the high cost of overhead and high levels of corruption, many aid organizations are not effective in their giving. There are conflicting views on how effective foreign aid is, especially aid that actually reaches local leaders.[16]

Unfortunately, there are plenty of examples of efforts by well-meaning organizations to address real areas of need with culturally careless solutions, such as sending computers to children in places without electricity or a program to develop crop management in an area where conditions were not good for farming.[17] World Connect is a rare nonprofit organization that operates on a WE approach by partnering closely with local people around the world to support charitable projects. Rather than exporting cookie-cutter solutions, developed from afar by a different cultural group, World Connect relies on projects generated at the grassroots level to create innovative solutions. They limit overhead by limiting the number of non-local staff onsite and instead develop relationships with local leaders who initiate and manage projects. World Connect has established relationships with the Peace Corps, CorpsAfrica, and other volunteers who partner with people in local areas and provide a link between the local community and World Connect which is based in New York. Every project application is generated by local people in more than thirty countries.

For example, in Dassilame Soce, Senegal, the community wanted to improve sanitation because uncovered wells and inadequate latrine facilities caused high levels of e-coli contamination in the water.[18] Other aid organizations had failed when faced with similar situations because they imported equipment that could not be easily replaced or repaired. But leaders in Dassilame Soce used a local blacksmith to make new well covers and local people built their own latrine pits with supplies funded by World Connect. Over a three-year period, the community built over two dozen public and private latrines, which resulted in improved hygiene and decreased disease.

In an interview I conducted with Executive Director Pamela Nathenson, she reported that corruption is less of a problem with World Connect projects because local people are creating business, educational, and improved health opportunities for their own families and neighbors.[19] Relying on local voices also enables World Connect projects to be sustainable over long periods of time because those who create the solutions also benefit directly from them, unlike other projects that are simply exported from overseas.

"Humility is necessary," Nathenson explained. She and her colleagues are constantly aware of how they are perceived when they communicate and interact with fund recipients, especially when they make visits to project locations. "We are even careful about what kind of car we rent," she explained. "Showing up in a big white truck makes us look like big aid organizations." Her goal is to build connections and avoid the inherent *Us and Them* dynamics in all of her choices. "I always pick a tan sedan."

IMPROVED COMMUNICATION

Mike Ritter, an employee at a New York financial institution, was put in charge of managing an outsourced technical team in India. Estimates show that 94 percent of Fortune 500 companies outsource at least one major business function.[20] Mike's bosses in New York had decided to lower costs, and selected the company in India for its technical expertise. Mike communicated various requests regularly via email with his counterpart, Arjun, who was located in Bangalore.

At first, Mike was very happy with the performance of the team in India. Communication was smooth, and Arjun readily agreed to every request that Mike's bosses made. But when the first deadline arrived, Arjun did not send data to Mike as he had agreed. When Mike asked for an explanation, Arjun told him there had been some temporary problems and that he would send the data immediately. Two days passed with no data. Mike's bosses were impatient. Finally, Arjun sent the data to Mike but it was incomplete and did not meet the specifications they had agreed to at the beginning of the project.

Like thousands of other American firms that outsource to companies in different countries, Mike was learning that differences in expectations can have a big impact on bottom-line results. In 2018, Deloitte Consulting research showed that 70 percent of American companies that outsourced abroad had a negative outcome, including premature termination of the relationship.[21] Many companies were found to have brought the outsourced function back in-house due to time lost, frustration, and cost increases.[22] Other studies revealed that lack of up-front planning, failure to communicate clear expectations, and failure to share information were common problems in outsourcing arrangements.[23]

One of Mike's bosses immediately regretted the outsourcing decision and began lobbying for termination. But Mike suspected that cultural expectations had gotten in the way of success. He got on a plane and made a visit to Arjun and the team in Bangalore. They discussed the project and got to know each other better.

During the three days that Mike and Arjun spent together, Mike made an observation that he had not noticed prior to the trip. Arjun never said *no* to him. It didn't matter if they were discussing the scope of the project or where to have lunch or what time they would meet, whatever Mike suggested, Arjun would agree without complaint. However, Arjun didn't always follow through with what he had agreed to do.

This was a game-changing realization for Mike who, like many American professionals, believed that saying *no* was an essential business skill. Mike had made an incorrect assumption that Arjun would say no or would disagree if he needed to. But during those three days together, Arjun was agreeable in a way that Mike had never before witnessed in the professional world and certainly never in New York, where people directly refused assignments and challenged their bosses on a daily basis.

This insight inspired Mike to take action. He started to research cultural differences between India and the United States and learned that the typical yes or no binary, so common in the United States, was uncommon in places like India and Japan. Other cultures feel that saying no to a superior is disrespectful and would be detrimental to the relationship. Mike learned to listen more closely to "hear between the lines" when he spoke with Arjun. If Arjun said, "I'll let you know," instead of "yes," then Mike understood that there were some unresolved issues. If Arjun paused or hesitated before agreeing, Mike knew there was a reason for his delay and took this to mean the answer was not a definite yes.

Each time this happened, Mike would ask questions to learn additional information so he could offer support to Arjun. At the same time, Mike managed the expectations of his New York bosses, who had never been to India and had no awareness of the cultural differences. Soon, Mike was able to achieve clear communication with Arjun. Instead of assuming that Arjun's predictable, initial agreement was the final word on a specific issue, Mike listened more closely and worked harder to gain clarity. They spoke more frequently, and within a few weeks, deadlines were being met and the project got back on track.

Not Too Big to Fail

Miscommunication often occurs because of different languages or because of different meanings in the same language. But miscommunication also occurs because our cultural habits and norms are easily misunderstood. One of the most well-documented corporate failures of an American company is the case of Walmart's spectacular nine-year failure in Germany starting in 1997 and ending in 2006.[24] Every analysis of this case points to the lack of attention to cultural issues as a key factor for the failure.[25] Rather than adjust to the German way of doing things, Walmart simply imported its formula directly from the United States, assuming what worked so well at home would necessarily work well abroad.

The first CEO of Walmart's German Operations was Rob Tiarks, an American who had been extremely successful leading two hundred stores in the United States. Tiarks did not speak German and decided to make English the official language in the German Walmart headquarters. Other American cultural values and practices were directly imported without deference to German cultural norms. For example, Walmart insisted that clerks and greeters smile at shoppers as they walked in the door.

This was off-putting to German shoppers, who generally do not smile at total strangers. Germans also have a cultural tendency to prefer shopping independently and without interaction with store clerks, so encountering enthusiastic greeters who asked them "how can we help you?" the moment they walked in the door was another unwelcoming factor. Chanting the company slogan at the start of every work shift reminded German employees of their authoritarian past. Walmart's imposition of practices that were tailored to appeal to American consumers on a German population that was repelled by them contributed to few shoppers and unsustainably low sales. After nine years, Walmart abandoned its venture at an estimated loss of $1 billion.

In WE cultures, leaders and employees feel comfortable communicating more often and with greater candor. They are alert to misinterpretations and take steps to solve miscommunications when problems are still small and manageable. If Mike had not gone to India and recognized Arjun's tendency to prioritize agreement over achievement, it's likely that the relationship would have suffered and possible that the contract could have been terminated. If Rob Tiarks had bothered to learn even a little German, perhaps he would have discovered that directly importing behavior like daily chanting and smiling was not a winning strategy. Addressing underlying differences between people from different backgrounds is a hallmark of WE cultures and WE people.

EARLY WARNING SYSTEM

Organizations need early warning systems because the dominant group tends to view situations from their myopic perspective; they don't see problems until they are so big that they can't be ignored or solved easily. Homogeneity breeds arrogance. Like the executives at Chuo Trust & Banking at the beginning of this chapter, their largely homogeneous group didn't realize that they had to adjust their business practices to enhance the value of others outside of their group.

When leaders possess a WE mentality, they are much more sensitive to the needs of all the groups within their organization. An alarm goes off in their heads when problems start to arise, not after they become impossible to ignore. When key people learn to spot potential *Us and Them* situations, they can act quickly and effectively.

The most obvious examples of this are leaders who do not fit into the dominant culture of their organizations because they, by virtue of their own identity and life experience as a *them*, are more sensitive to *Us versus Them* dynamics. When Honda Motor Company set up its first factory outside Japan in Marysville, Ohio, they hired many American men who had experience in manufacturing. But they also hired Susan Insley, an American lawyer. Insley brought a new perspective to a corporate culture where much of the power resided with Japanese men. Insley established herself as a valuable asset in her role as a lawyer and as someone outside the male norm. She actively supported women and helped establish a culture of inclusion, and eventually became the highest-ranking woman in the American auto industry at the time as Senior Vice President of Honda of America Manufacturing, Inc.

Susan Insley was a prominent, successful woman in a heavily male-dominated industry and company. She was one of the reasons I joined the company right out of college. I didn't know anything about automobiles or manufacturing, but when I saw Susan as a leading voice in the company, it made me feel like I, too, could belong. When Susan spoke, others listened. She was smart and hardworking. And she was female like me.

I saw how Susan and other senior women brought attention to issues others may have missed. Their example inspired me to address a problem I noticed on my first day of work in Japan. It would take years to achieve change, but my efforts would impact the company culture at Honda Motor Company decades before other Japanese companies followed suit.

On my very first day of work in Tokyo I wore a cream-colored Liz Claiborne suit and carried a matching beige briefcase as I walked into Honda Motor Company's headquarters for the first time. I had cut off my beaded bracelets from college and straightened my hair in an effort to look the part of international businesswoman. As the only American female in a company of three thousand Japanese employees, I felt conspicuous as I walked around the building with my new boss, Mr. Hino. He gave me an ID badge and showed me to the cafeteria. Then he handed me off to two women who took me into the women's locker room. The two women, like all the other women I had seen that morning, wore a blue polyester vest and skirt with a white-collared blouse. The women sized me up and handed me two uniforms. "This is what we wear," the older woman said. The uniform was the opposite of the image I wanted to project—it was unprofessional and dumpy. But I was the visitor, so I felt that it was my job to adjust to the rules even if I didn't like them.

I worked alongside ten Japanese women, all of whom were young and unmarried like me. They spoke polite Japanese in high-pitched voices and welcomed me as best they could, even though no non-Japanese woman had ever before worked in their group. We answered phones and arranged the daily schedule for the company's top executives. We served tea and cleaned ashtrays during important meetings. I struggled to learn the many written and unwritten rules of the office. Wearing the ugly uniform was just one of the many adjustments I made to fit in.

At lunchtime we ate according to a rotating system so that half the group would always be in the office in case executives needed support. I would go out for lunch with one group every day. I shared tea breaks and slowly got to know my new colleagues. In late October, after working in the office for nearly two months, I decided to host a Halloween party for my colleagues in my small apartment. The women brought costume masks, and we ate snacks and drank wine. That night I got to know two of the older women, Yumi and Miki, much better. The three of us started to go to lunch together on a regular basis. This led to a closer relationship. Sometimes on the weekends we would meet up for a meal at our favorite Vietnamese restaurant.

Yumi, Miki, and I talked about our families, about travel, and about work. Miki had a quick wit and a delightfully contagious laugh. We joked about the executive who smoked nonstop or the one who pulled his pants up too high. Yumi was generous and frequently took time to explain difficult Japanese phrases. As with any friendship, I felt more and more comfortable as time passed. We spoke more openly about sensitive topics—dating, our futures, things that bothered us.

It was during one of these conversations that I learned that Miki and Yumi didn't like wearing the women's uniform. It was a surprise. Over two hundred women in the company wore the blue polyester uniform every day, but I had never heard a single word against it. Miki and Yumi admitted to me that most women didn't like wearing the outdated, ugly uniform but felt there was nothing they could do about it. It was a shock to hear this. For months, I had assumed that I was the only person in the entire company who hated the uniform. It was a game-changing piece of information.

Many months later, the company sponsored a Quality Circle initiative to encourage employees to generate ideas for improving the company—to save money, save time, or improve safety. I decided this was the perfect opportunity to do something about the uniform that I now knew women didn't like. So I started a group to abolish the women's uniform policy. We researched the cost, the history, collected an opinion survey, and made an official proposal. It took more than a year, but our group was successful in persuading the company to change the corporate policy. As a result, women in the company stopped wearing the uniform, which removed a subtle barrier to equality and advancement and fostered a more professional environment for female employees. It also saved the company money in terms of the cost of the uniforms and locker room space. I did not predict it at the time, but that rule change nearly thirty years ago has had a positive impact on the corporate culture and on the lives of thousands of professional women.

Incentivizing WE-building

When organizations allow their employees to suggest and initiate new ideas, the results can change the company culture for the better. Quality Circle initiatives are based on the assumption that employees who actually do a job have distinct insights into the ways that job can be improved. These circle activities are a systematic way to involve all employees in their mission to improve quality, safety, and cost. Honda continues to encourage employees to suggest improvements, and every year the company recognizes the best ideas with awards, like one for putting wheels on parts bins that resulted in a 20 percent increase in assembly speed—translating into millions of dollars of savings.

Employee Resource Groups (ERGs) and Affinity Groups are a modern equivalent, where employees who represent a shared identity factor can support each other and can advise their companies due to their distinct insights into the business community. Thousands of such groups have been successful over the past decade by fortifying individuals and their organizations through identifying new customers, retaining diverse talent, and improving the reputation of an organization.

The ERG for Black employees at Snap Inc., parent company of the popular messaging app Snapchat, hosted a town hall following Black Lives Matter Protests where members of the group spoke about their experiences being Black at work and in life. Over a thousand employees joined the livestream not as participants but as listeners. In a webinar describing the event, Vice President of Diversity, Equity & Inclusion Oona King said, "Our Black ERG has profoundly changed the way our C-suite thinks about this."[26] Hearing first-person stories transformed the theoretical into the personal and gave urgency to issues of racial oppression in a way that a spreadsheet never could.

In a New York financial institution, the foundation arm was tasked with donating $250,000 every year to expand access to financial services to low and moderate income groups. Rather than continue giving to the same organizations it had in the past, the foundation partnered with five Employee Resource Groups within the company and created an initiative to increase Millennial engagement.[27] These underrepresented voices generated a new list of underserved nonprofit groups to receive charitable donations. This initiative helped invigorate young people within the company by giving them a voice in how charitable donation decisions were made. It also helped the company promote its brand among a younger generation, which will influence future recruitment.

CREATING ENLIGHTENED TWENTY-FIRST-CENTURY ORGANIZATIONS

Benefits are almost guaranteed once a company demonstrates real commitment to creating a WE culture. Policies and programs that encourage connection between different departments and different people will pay off as employees see that speaking up early about dynamics is rewarded. When companies encourage a bottom-up approach toward reducing *Us and Them* gaps, they empower their employees to engage in more genuine and productive ways and see the benefits of their efforts magnified.

How to Know if Your Company Is Benefiting

1. What is the level of awareness among top leaders in your organization that promoting WE goals is directly linked to profitability?

   High   Medium   Low

2. How skillful is a typical manager in your organization at leveraging diverse voices and viewpoints toward generating new revenue streams?

    Very well equipped   Average   Not well equipped

3. How much time and effort does a typical manager use to promote innovation by actively including historically non-dominant people?

    Always   Sometimes   Almost never   Never

4. How often in the past six months has there been a formal or informal evaluation of communication between different key departments?

    More than two   One   None

5. How often in the past six months has there been a formal evaluation of trust and functionality between different key departments?

    More than two   One   None

6. How skilled is a typical manager at facilitating interdepartmental connection between key departments, including communication, relationship-building, and teamwork?

    Very comfortable   Somewhat comfortable
    Not comfortable   Deeply uncomfortable

7. How many early warning mechanisms does your organization have in place to actively notice yellow flags representing *Us and Them* tension (for example, people from the non-dominant culture in positions of authority, D&I or DEI Director tasked with identifying issues, ERG leadership focused on assessment, opportunities for bottom-up initiatives)?

    More than two   Two   One   None

8. How frequently are common WE goals discussed at a company-wide level?

> Ongoing basis   Sometimes   Rarely
> Only when there is a problem   Never

9. How frequently do leaders in the company officially promote WE-building in the organization?

> Ongoing basis   Sometimes   Rarely
> Only when there is a problem   Never

10. How frequently are benefits of a WE culture discussed informally in the organization?

> Ongoing basis   Sometimes   Rarely
> Only when there is a problem   Never

The goal of these questions is not to achieve a perfect score. Rather, the goal is to measure awareness of WE-building in the workplace. If the assessment reveals many *low*, *none*, or *never* answers, it's time to take a close look at your priorities. Any organization will get better results when employees from diverse backgrounds and from different parts of the organization cooperate in a cohesive way. Benefits will quickly accrue when every manager and leader integrates WE-building throughout the organization.

3

CONVENTIONAL WISDOM VERSUS PRACTICAL KNOWLEDGE

The Need to Close Deep Gaps (Rather Than Create Superficial Bridges)

WHEN SAMUEL MWANGI joined the branch office of a large Brazilian oil & gas company in Nairobi, Kenya, in 2007, there were only two Brazilian colleagues in the office. Samuel and his five Kenyan colleagues spoke Swahili and English, which was the common language. As business grew, more Brazilian nationals moved to the Nairobi office. As the number of Brazilian employees grew, so did use of Portuguese. As the Brazilians used more Portuguese among themselves, the Kenyan employees started to use more Swahili. Samuel noticed over the years that use of English as a common language diminished, which reflected an increasing *Us and Them* dynamic in the office.

On occasion, Samuel was invited to join with his Brazilian colleagues for dinner, but sometimes they spent more than 70 percent of the meal speaking in Portuguese. Samuel guessed that his colleagues had invited him to build their relationship and improve communication. But as he sat listening to a language he didn't understand for such a long time, he had the feeling that he would have been better off staying home.

Samuel's colleagues relied on a classic tactic to close gaps—socializing. But it backfired because of poor execution. This is the enduring problem so many leaders face around the world when trying to deal with cross-cultural issues—how to ensure that their efforts are effective.

Awareness of closing *Us and Them* gaps is higher today than any other time in U.S. history. There is no question that American companies have put resources into recruitment, hiring, and promotion of people from non-dominant groups, especially in the past ten years. However, it is important to look beyond statistics and ask who is making the decisions, how is power and wealth distributed, and what ongoing effort is made to create a genuinely inclusive and diverse organization?

Yet, despite all the increased attention to the issue, according to EEOC reports, employment discrimination claims and lawsuits are up.[1] In 2018, the EEOC filed 50 percent more sexual harassment lawsuits than in the prior year.[2] More than $70 million was recovered for victims compared to $47.5 million in 2017. The number of charges filed increased in every category, including sex, disability, race, age, national origin, color, and religion. The truth is that many types of bridge-building efforts are not effective at closing real gaps. Not all efforts are created and implemented equally. For busy business leaders, trying to stay ahead of the game can feel like an impossible task.

Leaders may think:

- I comply with our diversity policy.
- I hire a diverse staff.
- I participate in training initiatives.
- I support our Diversity & Inclusion Director.
- I encourage Employee Resource Groups.
- I promote Supplier Diversity and Mentorships and Pipeline programs.
- I join social activities.

"What more do I have to do?" they may ask. It is a reasonable question.

The answer resides in two factors. First, what is the efficacy of each approach? And second, are leaders themselves fully engaged in doing the foundational work necessary to narrow gaps? Some diversity initiatives are like a well marketed short-term diet. The programs look and sound good. They come with flashy slogans offering low prices or a celebrity spokesperson offering cheerful guarantees. But just like shortcut diets, the initiatives don't work, because what it takes to make real progress is consistent and incremental behavioral change. There are no shortcuts for that.

Promoting diversity and inclusion initiatives is generally better than no initiatives at all. Google, for example, sponsors fifteen different Employee Resource Groups with associations based on race (Black Googler Network, Asian Googler Network), ethnicity (Filipino Googler Network, Iranian Googler Network), sexual orientation (Gayglers), gender expression (Trans at Google), age (Greyglers), and more, like Google Veterans Network. But these groups can backfire if their mission to educate others and build awareness in the organization is not integrated into the way a company operates. If you've got an all-white male leadership team who view ERGs as a way to outsource the "diversity problem" rather than hear and respond to the voices of underrepresented groups, you might find that you have a bigger problem on your hands. A client who left a large New York bank told me that the ERGs were completely separate and not integrated into the overall mission of the company. Instead of providing support and acting as a resource for the organization, they became breeding grounds for complaints and gossip and contributed to a toxic environment at the company.

The exact same initiative may succeed in one company while it fails in another company based on the degree of thought that went into its execution as well as the individual commitment each person, especially each leader, makes to the program. Effective initiatives are rare because many people underestimate the bias that employees from marginalized groups experience.[3]

For example, hosting a company-wide social event sounds like a guaranteed way to build relationships, strengthen community, and improve communication. But if individuals show up to eat birthday cake or drink cocktails at happy hour and only socialize with folks they already know, then the event, like Samuel's dinner out with his Brazilian colleagues, may as well not have happened.

One way to assess the potential efficacy of any gap-bridging undertaking is to examine the characteristics of effective and less effective initiatives.

Characteristics of Less Effective Initiatives	Characteristics of More Effective Initiatives
Passive	Active
One-way	Two-way
Risk-free	Requires some risk-taking
Comfortable	Potentially uncomfortable
No outside effort required	Outside effort ongoing and required
Unchallenging	Challenging
Us and them identity remain intact	Actively redraws the lines of belonging
Checking a compliance box	Starting point for deeper understanding
Beginning, middle, and end	Beginning a process of change
Colorblind, culture-blind	Accepts existence of inherent differences
Superficial	Deep and factual data
Vulnerability not required	Vulnerability required
Humility not required	Humility required

Let's look at the six most common approaches organizations use to manage cross-cultural issues and examine their efficacy.

Diversity Policies

These are written statements that provide guidance on being fair and inclusive within an organization with respect to hiring, employment, and community engagement. These policies should be comprehensive and should tie into other corporate policies such as codes of conduct and employment contracts. The goal of these policies is to consistently foster a work environment where all employees feel valued, accepted, and included. While heightened awareness of Black History month or Juneteenth are positive gestures, substantive change will only occur by addressing structural issues through improved policies.

Director of Diversity and Inclusion (or Diversity, Equity, and Inclusion)

This is a professional role that was almost unheard of twenty years ago but is now popular in virtually every major corporation. Following Black Lives Matter protests, job openings in the D&I space more than doubled.[4] People in these roles are responsible for launching diversity, equity, and inclusion initiatives within the organization as well as monitoring and enforcing corporate standards. Unfortunately, some of these roles are positioned under the HR umbrella rather than as a separate function with real authority. A key factor for effectiveness is the degree to which these professionals have control over a budget and access to senior decisionmakers in the company.

Training and Development Courses

Training and development has been around for a long time in corporate America. The topic of diversity and inclusion training is relatively new and has grown in importance over the past ten years. The content of training can vary widely from brief online offerings to intensive days-long seminars. Everyone in a company should have the same training, not just managers, in order to provide common tools and language for solving problems and creating solutions. Training that involves face-to-face interaction and some type of ongoing commitment and accountability is essential.

Employee Resource Groups

ERGs are voluntary groups of employees who share an identity factor such as race or sexual orientation, or have a common life experience such as being a military veteran. These groups provide support, enhance career development, promote personal development, and facilitate outreach to the larger corporate community. The social aspect of such groups is useful, but the most productive groups are ones that advance the corporate mission by generating strategic initiatives. ERGs that are completely outsourced window dressing, with no involvement from leadership, can easily devolve into forums for gossip and complaints and little else.

Targeted Programming
(Supplier, Mentoring, Onboarding, Pipeline)

These are programs that proactively identify and encourage historically underutilized people and groups to broaden the range of collaboration. Supplier programs, Diversity Mentoring, Onboarding, and Diversity Pipeline programs all work toward increasing the role of historically underutilized people. Unfortunately, many such programs are doomed to fail because the people charged with managing and monitoring them either have no real power and budget, or have little connection themselves to the historically underutilized groups.

Social Activities

This is a classic way for any group of humans to interact in a relaxed atmosphere and get to know one another. These events range from DIY, low-cost potluck lunches to all-expenses-paid retreats abroad. As stated above, the range of effectiveness can be impacted greatly by the amount of thought put into the event as well as the degree of personal commitment of each participant, especially leaders and those who identify with the home team in an organization.

WE-BUILDING

As the six approaches described above indicate, it's not *what you do* so much as *how you do it* that determines effectiveness. Generally, when organizations embrace any of the approaches in a superficial way—they hire a Director of Diversity & Inclusion and believe they've solved their problems or launch generic diversity training programs—the results are poor. When companies implement effective approaches, it's often because they've integrated WE-building concepts into the construction.

WE-building is any action or initiative that successfully narrows a gap between *us* and *them* through individual behavioral change. When individuals work through the three WE-building steps—Awareness, Assessment, and Action—they will confront the real barriers toward creating an inclusive workplace. For any given person, gaining awareness of these barriers and then measuring one's own personal level of engagement with *them* groups will provide a road map for action. Transformation of an organization occurs when individuals inside those organizations engage in the foundational work necessary to narrow divisive gaps.

Fortunately, business leaders can easily measure the efficacy of any effort to narrow gaps by asking two simple questions.

1. Does the initiative help people build trust?
2. Does the initiative actively redraw the lines so that a greater, more diverse number of people feel that they belong?

Sometimes, programs are launched without deeply considering potential outcomes. Passive or singular experiences such as completing an online survey may provide useful data, but they will not motivate a change in behavior by themselves. Meaningful change will happen only when individuals are motivated to make new choices and systems are in place to support those individuals and hold them accountable.

Asking the above two questions before approving any expenditure toward a corporate initiative can help planners make small adjustments that will transform an event from a superficial activity into one that can make a difference. Unfortunately, many companies are satisfied with a superficial plan when they could achieve a meaningful plan with just a small change. As a result, they miss opportunities for meaningful exchanges that were almost within reach.

One way to identify this small change is to make sure you have a diverse decisionmaking and planning team. Far too often I have seen programs launched by a homogeneous, home team group who may be well meaning but simply do not have the viewpoint to create a truly inclusive program. Creating meaningful initiatives will be discussed further in chapter 6.

For example, a company may commit its employees to a day of mandatory training but fail to include socializing, where participants are organized into mixed lunch groups or encouraged to interact with people they do not know through coordinated or casual mechanisms. These are valuable opportunities to reinforce the lessons of the training and to provide participants with an immediate opportunity to practice what they've just learned while strengthening connections with their colleagues.

Developing Intercultural Relationships

Fortunately, some companies understand that a combination of training, socializing, and follow-up accountability are important for both developing trust and redrawing the lines of belonging. This is what happened at an international shipping conglomerate that was seeking ways to improve communication throughout its culturally diverse organization. The company had recently hired a new HR employee named Lisa with a background in Industrial Organizational Psychology. Lisa and I developed a one-and-a-half-day program to help people in the company build connections across national identity differences in the United States, Mexico, Brazil, Canada, England, and Germany. We incorporated skill-building instruction as well as dedicated social time, including a group lunch and a casual happy hour following the training. Lisa had a keen appreciation of both formal and informal time when individual employees could exchange concerns and ideas and develop their relationships.

Lisa and I traveled to more than a dozen offices, including the one where two employees, LaVonda and Masa, worked. These two employees, one American and the other Japanese, had worked together in the same Houston office for years without saying more than "hello" to each other. They were two people representing distinct cultures in an organization where the gap between English-speakers and Japanese-speakers was wide. Even though Americans and Japanese had been working together in this office for more than twenty years, there was little connection and trust between the two groups.

LaVonda, a thirtysomething African American woman who was born and raised in Texas, had worked in the company for three years. During that time, she had engaged in limited interaction with the dozen or so Japanese staff in the office, who were generally quiet and kept to themselves. LaVonda was a natural people-person. She gave warm greetings to anyone in the office but felt some of the Japanese staff seemed cold and noticed they sometimes did not reciprocate her friendly hellos.

Masa, a thirtysomething Japanese man, had grown up in Japan, a place that is nearly 98 percent homogeneous. His entire life was spent interacting with other Japanese people who looked and sounded like him. He studied English in school but rarely used it. Before arriving in Houston six months earlier for his first assignment outside Tokyo, Masa had never before met an African American person. He was afraid of doing or saying something offensive so, like many of his Japanese colleagues, he kept to himself and interacted mostly with other Japanese people.

Fear and uncertainty caused Masa and most of his Japanese colleagues to avoid meaningful interaction with their American colleagues. Most of the Japanese staff never interacted much more than saying a brief hello to English-speaking colleagues if they passed in the halls. Proximity to one another had not led to meaningful integration. If anything, the gaps that existed because of the differences in U.S. and Japanese culture had led to even more distinct *Us and Them* behaviors: Japanese and Americans held separate meetings, ate lunch separately, and almost never socialized together.

These two people spoke different languages, ate different food, and had different life experiences. But the biggest gap between them—the one each of them believed about the other—was a gap that did not actually exist. It was a *perceived* gap based on misinformation and assumptions.

This dynamic was disrupted by the opportunity Lisa and I had designed and by the willingness of Masa to take a big risk. During the workshop, LaVonda and Masa participated in various group activities and learned about bridging the *Us and Them* dynamic. There was frequent face-to-face interaction throughout the session. After the workshop, the employees walked to a local sports bar for the happy hour. Masa and LaVonda ended up sitting at the same table enjoying some refreshments. Masa later told me he was emboldened by a day of teamwork and also encouraged by LaVonda's extraordinary warmth. Masa turned to LaVonda and said, "May I ask you a question?"

"Sure," LaVonda replied in her friendly manner. "Ask me anything."

There was an awkward pause, as though Masa was possibly reconsidering what he was about to do. "Don't you Americans look down on us Japanese because we lost the war?" Masa asked in careful, slow English.

"What!? No!" LaVonda said, clearly surprised. Then she said, "I thought you Japanese looked down on us Americans because you are the bosses of this office."

Masa replied, "Not at all!"

Over the next few minutes, each of them explained how they had arrived at two separate and incorrect conclusions. Masa told LaVonda some of the postwar stories he had picked up from movies in Japan that suggested that Japanese were inferior. LaVonda explained that when Japanese colleagues had neglected to greet her at work or refrained from simple small talk she had assumed they felt superior.

"I think they are afraid to speak in English, like I was," Masa confessed.

It was a game-changing conversation for both of them. At the end of the gathering, they agreed to have lunch together soon. Several weeks passed before that lunch took place, but when it did, it was a huge success. LaVonda and Masa each brought along a friend. The group of two Americans and two Japanese went out for Chinese food. This simple act, people from different backgrounds choosing to go out to lunch together, had rarely happened. Every few months, they would plan another lunch and their tradition grew in popularity. Sometimes they would have two carsful of people joining the outing.

"It was so fun," LaVonda told me years later. "We would talk about all kinds of things." People from these two divided groups learned each other's names, laughed about their common office experiences, and shared tips on managing Houston's awful traffic and where they could find the best Italian food in town.

When LaVonda had a baby, Masa and his wife got her a gift. A year later, Masa and his wife had a child, so then parenting became another shared bond between the two. This example shows how trusted colleague relationships start with a simple act like starting a conversation with someone new at a company-sponsored event. These small gestures can lead to meaningful connection over time, and even friendship. Research repeatedly shows that having trusted relationships and friendships in the workplace leads to higher levels of engagement and productivity.

"That conversation changed my life," LaVonda shared years after she and Masa had opened up to one another and discovered that they had way more in common than they thought.

Over time, LaVonda and Masa changed the way they thought of themselves in relation to each other. They were not representing binary American versus Japanese groups. Instead, through conversation, shared meals, and increased face-to-face interaction, they redrew the lines of belonging around their identities as parents of young children, as people living in Houston, and as trusted colleagues working in the same company. Their identities as people of different ethnicities and national origins and gender did not change. But instead of defaulting to superficial, stereotypical binary *us* and *them* dynamics, they successfully drew new lines of belonging.

Trust is built up over time through face-to-face interactions.

FOUR STAGES OF BUILDING TRUST

Some companies have numerous programs to foster cross-cultural understanding—seminars, workshops, training modules, and so on—but they are missing a critical component that makes WE a reality: trust. It's one thing for people to understand intellectually why they should appreciate other people's differences. It's something else entirely to move past this understanding and be open and honest with them as Masa was with LaVonda. When widespread trust exists across differences, it's a sign that organizational programs are working.

The Trust-Building Scale is a continuum that measures the depth of any relationship in the workplace. It starts with *stranger* status, moves to *acquaintance*, then *colleague*, and can eventually progress to *trusted colleague* status (see Figure 2).

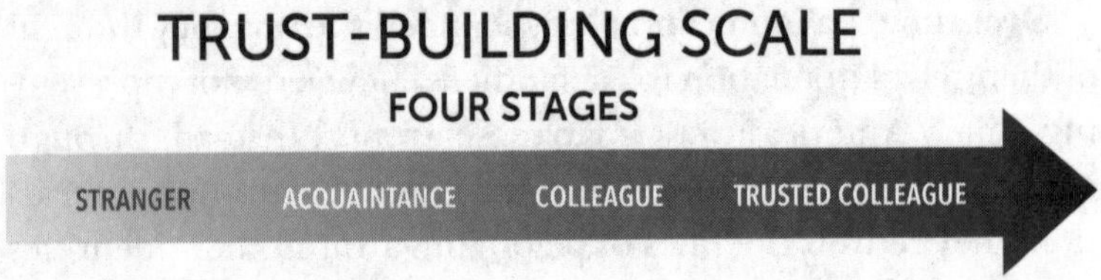

TRUST-BUILDING SCALE
FOUR STAGES

STRANGER   ACQUAINTANCE   COLLEAGUE   TRUSTED COLLEAGUE

FIGURE 2

At the *stranger* stage, the phrase "I don't know you" describes the level of familiarity. The next stage, *acquaintance*, is defined by "I know basic information about you." This includes knowing someone's name, their area of work, and other basic factors, including things you can often discern by looking at another person, like age, gender, and race. It is important to remember that what you see about another person's identity may not match how that person identifies themselves and that visual data alone is not an adequate way to accurately assess another person's identity. The *colleague* stage is characterized by the phrase "I know meaningful information about you." This includes topics such as work history, skills, hobbies, and background. The final stage, and the goal for establishing strong professional relationships, is the *trusted colleague* stage. This stage is achieved over time through open and honest communication. Trust is developed by consistently setting clear expectations and meeting those expectations. A trusted colleague relationship will develop through shared experiences, self disclosure and an understanding of one another, despite inherent differences. In this stage, differences in factors of identity that are visible such as gender, ethnicity, or race become subordinate to the shared experiences and trust that has been established (see Figure 3).

FOUR STAGES OF TRUST-BUILDING

STRANGER	ACQUAINTANCE	COLLEAGUE	TRUSTED COLLEAGUE
I don't know you.	I know basic information about you.	I know meaningful information about you.	I understand you and trust you based on shared experiences.
No interaction	*Name, occupation, primary factors*	*Secondary factors including hobbies, skills, and background*	*Personal information, established connection despite disagreements or differences in identity*

FIGURE 3

Moving from acquaintance to colleague is often an easy progression if someone is willing to take the risk to deliberately suggest some type of WE-building activity. A Japanese executive, Mr. Kato, who worked for many years as president of a manufacturing company in North Carolina, told me that at first he had trouble moving beyond the acquaintance stage with local employees. Then he decided to have a weekly meeting with each of his five top American leaders. At first, they spoke only about work matters, but over time, their conversations grew to include topics like sports and family.

One of the five leaders was a lawyer, Bill Jones. Mr. Kato and Bill built up their relationship to the colleague stage, which Mr. Kato felt was sufficient. But then a difficult situation pushed them into the trusted colleague phase. A senior plant manager had to be fired unexpectedly. Mr. Kato had never before fired anyone since it is very unusual to terminate employees in Japan. He had no idea how to handle the situation. He and Bill spoke at length and developed a plan. When Mr. Kato fired the senior plant manager, Bill Jones was at his side providing moral and legal support. It was one of the most difficult things Mr. Kato had ever done. After that, Mr. Kato told me, he felt like he could trust Bill Jones with anything.

Proximity to people different from ourselves is not enough to build trust.

LEADERS MAKE THE DIFFERENCE

Leaders who demonstrate a commitment to working cooperatively with people or groups or departments that traditionally have been viewed as competitors or even enemies are actively redrawing the lines to include a larger, more diverse group of people. Effective leaders will actively promote new alliances within their organizations.

Rick Nelson, manager of a twenty-four-hour IT service center in a large Canadian city, was trained to foster a WE culture in his organization. This was especially important since only four out of seventeen employees in his office were born and reared in Canada. The others had emigrated from countries including China, Vietnam, Mexico, and Venezuela. Rick's company had a tradition of hosting a Christmas party every year. Knowing that more than half of his staff did not celebrate Christmas, Rick decided to limit the emphasis on Christmas and renamed the event a Holiday Potluck. He invited each employee to bring a favorite dish to share, making sure to use neutral language that avoided stereotypes. The employees were excited about the event and put extra effort into the food they brought. Unlike years past, everyone volunteered to join.

During the potluck, Rick encouraged each person to share examples of their family traditions. Not everyone celebrated Christmas, but everyone did have time off. Some people shared stories that related to the Christmas holiday like opening gifts, going to church, and preparing special meals, while others talked about treating family members to dinner or a special activity. It was a great success as a social event.

The next day, Rick was surprised when one of his Chinese-Canadian employees, Kevin Chen, approached him and volunteered to work on Christmas Eve. Since their service center would be open that night, they needed at least one person at the help desk. In the past, this undesirable time slot had been assigned based on seniority so the lowest-ranking member was assigned to the job. Kevin told Rick that after hearing about the special Christmas traditions that some of his colleagues had, he didn't mind taking that time slot.

Recognizing different cultural traditions strengthened bonds and morale on Rick's team. Calling the event a Holiday Potluck is an example of both celebrating the dominant Christmas holiday *and* including those who did not grow up with those traditions. Rick's actions were magnified by Kevin's offer to volunteer for the Christmas Eve shift, which led to more goodwill and deeper connections among a diverse workforce.

So, how do leaders in an organization get employees to interact with new people? The answer is that leaders themselves must model this behavior. If you are a leader, especially if you are one who identifies with the "home team" in your organization, you must make a visible effort to actively bridge gaps at social functions. You must consider who you eat lunch with, where you sit in meetings, who you invite to meetings, and so on. Without the full buy-in from organizational leaders, efforts to build a WE culture will be limited and possibly meaningless.

Everyone in an organization can contribute toward creating a WE culture.

WHO BELONGS?

Many social activities sponsored by companies to build connection among employees have the capacity for WE-building, but too often the participants don't use the opportunity to interact with new or unfamiliar people. Instead, they gather and talk with people they already know and with whom they feel comfortable. In part, this is human nature, but it does nothing to bridge gaps and move people into more trusting relationships. Proximity alone will not create efficacy. An "inclusion" box may be checked off and reported up the chain of command, causing lawyers and leaders to feel secure that liability has been minimized. But the *Us and Them* dynamics do not change.

Research shows that our capacity to identify people as either part of our in-group or out-group is quite fluid.[5] Since we humans seem to have an instinct to feel comfortable around people who are like us, it may be surprising that we are also highly suggestible when it comes to defining WE.

In one famous experiment at St. Andrew's University, researchers discovered that influencing a person's idea of WE through conversation alone could change one's behavior.[6] Researchers used European football fandom as a way to measure identity of in-group and out-group behavior. First, fans of the Manchester United football team were encouraged to highlight their loyalty and love of "The Red Devils" through completion of a written questionnaire and answering verbal questions. This exercise amplified their identity as Manchester United fans, so that when these people then saw an injured stranger in an "accident" prearranged by the researchers immediately after their interviews, they were more likely to help the stranger if that person was wearing a Manchester United jersey. And these fans were *less* likely to help the injured stranger if the stranger was wearing the jersey of the rival Liverpool team.

But when the Manchester United fans were encouraged through conversation to highlight their loyalty and love of the game of football, not a specific team, their identity as football fans (a much broader category) prompted different behavior. When these fans encountered an injured stranger, they were more likely to help a person wearing a football jersey representing any team—including the rival Liverpool.

Asking "what do we share" is key to bridge building across culture gaps.

REDRAWING THE LINES AROUND WE

WE-building is active, not passive. WE-building occurs because leaders have given thought to how a particular activity or initiative can be leveraged to redraw the lines around belonging. To be successful, WE-building must do at least one of the following:

1. Proactively create opportunities for individuals to *discover existing common factors.* For example, sponsor a social event and strategically facilitate conversation and individual sharing so that two different employees

might discover they both play the same sport, like ping-pong.

2. Proactively create experiences that *become shared factors* among a group of individuals. For example, setting up a ping-pong table and encouraging participation in the game through lessons, lunchtime games, or tournaments.

FOSTERING OPPORTUNITIES

Capitalizing on shared experiences has been a reliable strategy for bridging divides over the years. Sports diplomacy is a great example of how a shared factor can connect people from different backgrounds. For example, in 1971, a young American named Glen Cowan was in Nagoya, Japan, playing with the U.S. team in the Table Tennis Championship. Needing a ride back to his dorm, Cowan got on the Chinese team's bus and was warmly approached by one of their best players, Zhuang Zedong. This chance encounter led to an unexpected invitation for the U.S. team to fly to China before returning home to the United States. After more than twenty years without any diplomatic or economic interaction, this visit was the start of a new relationship between the two countries. Later referred to as "ping-pong diplomacy," this shared experience paved the way for U.S. president Nixon to visit China in 1972.

Finding ways to emphasize commonalities within the same company should be easy, but so often instead of cooperation and communication, American corporations fall into predictable *Us and Them* silos, whether they are sales versus marketing or engineering versus production or even New York versus Los Angeles. Instead of emphasizing the common goals, different departments battle for importance and power that can weaken the entire enterprise.

Leaders can make a difference by limiting unnecessary competition and fostering connection by focusing on common success or common struggles. In one financial institution, people from the front office and back office who never before met found commonalities because they worked on the same huge international deal. In a manufacturing corporation, production people and marketing folks bonded over a highly successful product that raised revenue for the entire company.

Leadership made a difference during the COVID-19 pandemic. One national leader who fostered connection by focusing on common struggles was Prime Minister Jacinda Ardern in New Zealand. Early in the epidemic, when the country had only 52 cases, Ardern made an 8-minute public televised announcement laying out a four level COVID-19 alert plan. Four days later, when the number of cases increased to 205, the entire country went into the highest alert level and national lockdown. After seven weeks of restrictions, the government announced that the country had no active cases of COVID-19 and life returned to normal without social distancing and other restrictions. Some suggest that despite the isolation and negative economic impact felt by many, the people of New Zealand are more united as a result of their approach. From the beginning Ardern framed the challenge with a WE-mindset by emphasizing the common goal. She said, "Please be strong, be kind and united against COVID-19."[7]

REDRAWING THE LINES

Let's refer back to the *Us versus Them* moments from Chapter 2 but look at them in a new way. Using a different lens, we can see an opportunity in each situation where a *them* moment can be transformed in order to promote connection among people from different backgrounds. Let's see how the *us* and *them* groups could have been redrawn into a single, more inclusive, group at the moment someone recognizes the cultural gap that's been created:

1. An English-speaking white man is in a meeting with five Japanese men discussing a business problem in English.

Suddenly all of the Japanese men start speaking in Japanese without any explanation.

Redraw: Say to the English-speaking man, "We are going to speak in Japanese for a few minutes to make sure we have a clear understanding of the problem. Then I'll tell you what we discussed and we can work together to solve the problem."

2. A female executive is sitting around a conference table with other executives, all men, when the CEO says to everyone, "We've got to stop jacking around."

   Redraw: Immediately acknowledge and apologize for the inappropriate language. Affirm that this type of crude language is not welcome.

3. A Black man joins a department of ten people, all of whom are white. Two of the people in the department never introduce themselves and never greet him in the morning.

   Redraw: As a person in the dominant culture, always be aware that a new person, especially one who is not in the dominant racial group, has joined. Welcome him warmly with introductions and daily greetings at a minimum. Pay attention to the behavior of others. If basic daily greetings are not extended to the one Black employee, then engage in a conversation with the two white members to encourage more collegial behavior.

4. In a workshop, the facilitator describes primary factors of identity by showing a screen listing gender, race, national origin, and age but does not mention sexual orientation and a gay employee feels left out.

Redraw: Acknowledge the mistake and affirm that the materials will be updated to include sexual orientation.

5. During a casual conversation among four colleagues, one member mentions his Ivy League alma mater and two other members share that they also went to Ivy League colleges. The three Ivy League graduates talk about their shared experience and the non–Ivy League colleague sits in silence.

    Redraw: Deemphasize the Ivy League focus of conversation and emphasize the college experience.

6. Five colleagues are eating in a lunchroom. One of the employees is younger and all others have more than ten years of experience. The older employees are talking about their kids and schools in the community. When the younger employee takes out her phone to take a photo of her sushi bento box, one of the senior people jokes around by saying to her, "You kids can't eat without taking a photo first!" Everyone laughs.

    Redraw: If a joke has been made that seems like it is excluding the younger employee, it may be worth apologizing first. Then, stop joking about a generational difference especially when there is only one person from that generation represented and instead find a common topic that everyone can participate in discussing.

FOSTER EXPERIENCES

The academic field of intergroup connection provides insight into effective ways to build trust between people from different backgrounds. One of the first to study this field was American psychologist Gordon Allport. He was a pioneer in the study of intergroup connection and created a theory of what constituted an effective approach to building intergroup relationships.[8] His studies revealed four important metrics for any two groups to successfully reduce prejudice and increase connection. First, the two groups must have equal status. Second, the groups must have a common goal. Third, the group members must work together to achieve the common goal. And fourth, successful contact between the groups must be supported by the surrounding community. Subsequent study of Allport's work revealed that not all metrics needed to be met in order to reduce prejudice, but that meeting his conditions would enhance positive outcomes.[9]

One example of this is a 2017 study by Stanford University PhD researcher Salma Mousa who created a soccer league in Iraq following the fall of ISIS in order to study traditional barriers between Iraqi Christians and Muslims.[10] Participants were placed on either mixed Christian and Muslim teams or all-Christian teams. After a four-month season, Mousa found that players on the mixed-group teams were more likely to join social events and more likely to voluntarily sign up to play with Muslims again.

A client in Germany had unusually high participation when they sponsored a volunteer garbage pickup day in their community. More than half of the company employees, representing more than ten different native countries, joined together on a beautiful fall day along with many of their family members. The company provided a nice breakfast at the office and then everyone went out to clean up together. This type of shared experience is good for the company, the employees, and the community in which they all live and work.

_____

When people do not share visible identity factors, then creating shared experience is crucial.

_____

TEAMMACHINE

One of the most effective tools I've seen used to narrow gaps quickly and meaningfully includes wood blocks, balloons, and some string. It is called the TeamMachine and was created by professor Pete Diehl in the 1970s.[11] The TeamMachine is a group exercise to simulate the silo experience, where different departments think only of themselves and may not share information, tools, or resources with other departments within the same organization. As a business consultant, Professor Diehl had noticed that departmental identities would often get in the way of an organization's overall success. Classic divisions such as sales versus marketing, manufacturing versus engineering, or corporate versus a branch office caused competitive behavior that undermined group success.

Professor Diehl's goal was to create a simulation to demonstrate how interdepartmental cooperation was essential for overall organizational success. He wanted highly individual, self-reliant, and skilled employees within the same organization to recognize that they needed one another to be successful as an organization. In his experience, he observed that most employees were keen on paying attention to their individual and departmental goals but often looked at other jobs and roles as separate, unconnected and less important entities.

The goal of the TeamMachine is to use simple wood blocks, string, and balsa wood to create a machine that will connect and function as a single unit. Participants are divided into random departmental groups and each is assigned a different section of the whole machine. Each group must build its part of the machine within a fixed time period. Then, all the departments must correctly connect their separate parts in order to build the whole TeamMachine. The key to success is for individuals to cooperate within their own group and for the groups to communicate and work together toward the final goal. The building directions are simple. But, as any manager can tell you, the reality of getting a group of grown-ups to collaborate is not particularly easy, especially when that group includes diversity in skills, personalities, attitudes, expectations, and cultural backgrounds.

The TeamMachine was originally designed as a tool to address departmental divisions. *Us and Them* gaps have expanded since the time the TeamMachine was created due to increasing diversity in race, religion, ethnicity, and other identity factors. More than ever, leaders today must use tools like the TeamMachine and create opportunities to form bonds across departmental and identity differences.

Over the years, I have facilitated the TeamMachine with thousands of professionals from bankers to health-care workers, teachers, and executives on four continents. From Brazilian businesspeople to Chinese engineers to analysts in New York, the ability to cooperate toward a common goal while prioritizing one's own work is a universal challenge. No matter what the industry, no matter what the country, humans struggle with *Us and Them* every day. The TeamMachine challenges this dynamic. Sometimes the groups are successful making the machine work and sometimes they are not, but the simulation has never once failed to engage the participants and inspire a WE-mindset.

The role of leaders, both formal and informal, can play a big part in framing shared experiences. As we saw in the St. Andrew's football experiment, perceptions about groups can be influenced by the way others talk and behave. Sometimes even a small nudge from one person to another, affirming the group goal and purpose, is enough to make a difference. Whether the activity is a potluck or an expensive weekend retreat, emphasizing common goals, fostering shared experiences, and working together will enhance success.

Superficial campaigns are an inadequate effort to bridging gaps without doing the work that closing big gaps requires.

YOU CAN'T CLOSE GAPS WITH COMMERCIALS

So many organizations go about attempting to close gaps in the wrong way. Even the U.S. government did this when attempting to address a critical *Us versus Them* dynamic today—the relationship between the Muslim and non-Muslim world.

The United States launched a military and economic war against radical Islamic fundamentalist terrorists immediately following the 9/11 attacks. At the same time, the Bush administration also attempted to narrow the U.S. versus Muslim gap with a well-meaning but ill-conceived and superficial campaign called Shared Values led by a former advertising executive, Charlotte Beers. Beers was appointed Undersecretary for Public Diplomacy in 2001.[12] She and her team spent $15 million producing a series of mini-documentaries called *Being Muslim in America*, meant to counter the negative misperceptions and hostile view of the United States among young Muslims throughout the rest of the world.

This effort attempted to treat a deep culture gap like a soft-drink promotion, with carefully curated images of attractive Muslims in the United States living a problem-free life. Rather than narrow the gap, the images and messages were so superficial they offended many Muslims, who viewed them as ignoring their deep cultural traditions in order to present a simplified version that appeared more American. Several countries like Egypt, Lebanon, and Jordan flatly refused to show the videos, viewing them as U.S. propaganda. The campaign was suspended after just one month and Beers resigned shortly thereafter.

This campaign, like many well-meaning corporate initiatives, was a failure because it did not move anyone along the Trust-Building Scale and did not redraw the lines around a broader community of WE. It was also likely developed by people with little firsthand knowledge of the Muslim faith and the real-world experience of Muslim youth in different parts of the world.

In 2004, President Bush recruited Farah Pandith to try a different approach.[13] Unlike Beers, Farah Pandith is Muslim, so she had a meaningful shared starting point as she began to develop a plan to counteract extremist recruitment efforts. During her ten years in government service, Pandith visited over a hundred countries and gathered valuable firsthand data, which informed strategies to combat extremist recruitment of vulnerable Muslim youth. She launched an umbrella organization called Generation Change to bring together young Muslim-American thought-leaders who work toward mobilizing against extremism as well as hundreds of grassroots programs that fight extremists. This coalition included young Muslim bloggers, hotlines for concerned parents, collective workplaces, and artists who made videos and music to promote connection, not hate.

In her 2019 book, *How We Win*, Pandith advocated for the use of strong military, law enforcement, and economic strategies in conjunction with meaningful programs that counteract extremist recruitment of young Muslims around the world. But she correctly pointed out a fundamental flaw in the U.S. government's approach over the years. This underlying defect can be seen also in corporate America. Pandith writes, "How could we muster a sustained and consistent effort when the officials responsible for designing and implementing programs lacked basic knowledge about Muslims and Islam?"[14]

This same challenge can be made in corporate America. So many corporations have done the work to hire and promote people from diverse backgrounds, but the people in charge remain overwhelmingly representative of a single dominant social group and tend to live homogeneous lives, remaining essentially isolated and uninformed about other social groups. There is a two-prong solution to this imbalance. First, more non-dominant people need to be in leadership positions. Second, current leaders who belong to the dominant social group must develop meaningful connections with people outside that dominant group. (This will be discussed in detail in Chapter 8.)

Over time, more non-dominant employees will grow into positions of authority; but until then, current leaders must take steps to increase their own understanding of *them* groups by examining their own level of understanding and direct engagement. Like many well-intentioned people, I suspect that Charlotte Beers did her best to help the U.S. government counter a growing threat of extremists looking to recruit young Muslims around the world. But people like Farah Pandith are better positioned, both through life experience and also an understanding that utilizing cultural data is essential. You don't have to share an identity to be able to build a WE connection. What you need is 1) the awareness that understanding a *them* culture is critical and 2) the willingness to do the work to develop deep understanding of that culture. We'll talk about how to do this in the following chapters.

Superficial campaigns are the strategic equivalent of a liquid diet, which might take pounds off quickly for a short time, but is not sustainable. Surface gestures can be a starting point, but cannot support the sustained effort required to gather worthwhile information that makes the difference between ineffective and effective approaches to bridging any *Us versus Them* gap. Campaigns can be useful for building awareness, but they can never substitute for a genuine connection that comes through face-to-face interaction.

Creating shared experiences and shared goals is an important strategy for building cross-group relationships.

TEAMMACHINE IN TOKYO

It was before 9:00 a.m. when I walked into a large conference room overlooking Tokyo on a beautiful autumn day in 2018. Thirty professionals, mostly men in dark suits, sat silently looking at their phones or paging through the thick binders that had been prepared for a weeklong management training session for future leaders in the company. The group represented twelve different countries and spoke nine different native languages. There were Black people and Asian people, Latinx and a few white folks.

Even though all the people there were connected to the same umbrella company, apprehension was everywhere. On the Trust-Building Scale, everyone fell to the far left, firmly in the *stranger* category. No one spoke. A heavy weight hung over the entire group—and this was only day one of a seven-day program of mandated togetherness.

Many of the activities that day were designed to reduce the feeling of intergroup anxiety that Gordon Allport and many others have studied.[15] In these uncertain situations, people ask themselves questions such as "How should I act?" "How might I be perceived?" and most importantly, "Will I be accepted?"

It was my job to kick off the program, first with a lecture on WE-building and then by facilitating the TeamMachine. The two common languages in the room were English and Japanese, so I presented my introductory materials bilingually, which seemed to put everyone a little more at ease. When I asked participants to interact in small group discussions, they followed my instructions, but the communication was stiff, formal, and cautious.

A company-sponsored lunch, which included a speech from the president of the company, followed the morning program. There was a deliberate effort to get people moving and talking by hosting the lunch without chairs. A young Japanese woman facilitated conversation by having specific people go to numbered tables with four other people. Then they were asked to talk among themselves to find something that all the people at their table shared. Some used translation apps or broken English to communicate. Each group reported out their commonality—everyone liked sports or had traveled to India or had children. It was the start of a process to break down the many barriers between the wide range of different people who had gathered for the week.

My many years of facilitating the TeamMachine in numerous different places helped me realize an important fact—most people are capable of working around linguistic, ethnic, religious, racial, and identity differences. They also, importantly, seem to *want* to do this. So, willingness and skill are not the biggest problem. The biggest barrier I have encountered is a lack of certainty about *how* to cross any barrier or gap.

A huge part of my job is simply providing an opportunity for connection and then nudging people into making that connection. Yes, humans are drawn to people who feel familiar for one reason or another. Many humans will hesitate to connect with someone they don't know well because they don't want to feel embarrassed, or worse yet, cause a problem or be rejected. But humans are also extremely adaptable, suggestible, and generally open to building new connections in the workplace, especially across cultural differences. But they need leaders who understand and model this path.

Every time I facilitate the TeamMachine, there is a moment about halfway through the exercise when I point out a fact that resonates with everyone. If one individual or one department in a larger organization behaves as a competitor with the others by not communicating, or by failing to cooperate or to share resources and information, this will weaken the entire team. The real competition, I say as I gesture toward a window or door, is out there. When individuals are overly concerned with their own goals, their own work, their own departmental or social group's success, they lose sight of the fact that they're all on the same team. When they don't keep this in mind, they often miss critical opportunities to have WE moments and WE conversations.

Leaders in today's diverse companies must understand this common need to build meaningful cross-group connections. They must inspire people to take actions that will build trusting relationships and create a sense of WE so that differences are not a problem to solve but rather a valuable resource to leverage toward success.

Leaders who model self-reflection will inspire others to do the same.

Intergroup anxiety was still high that afternoon in Tokyo when the thirty participants reluctantly gathered in their assigned groups and began the task of building a TeamMachine. Within minutes, they were fully engaged in the activity, gathering wood blocks and pieces of balsa wood and trying to design their parts of the machine. As time ticked by, the groups grew more focused. A feeling of anticipation and intensity grew. There was a lot of hand gesturing due to language differences. Several people frantically drew diagrams on scrap paper while others searched for images on their smartphones. Most members paid attention only to their part of the machine, although a few looked at other groups, aware that they would eventually have to work together to be successful.

A factory manager from Pakistan asked a colleague from the UK who worked in finance to get more balloons. A Japanese Director of Corporate Affairs carefully lined up wood blocks with a mining manager from Peru. A Brazilian director of a coffee business taped together pieces of balsa wood with the help of an American vice president of an aircraft company. People from different national, ethnic, religious, racial, and professional backgrounds were fully focused on the task at hand.

As the groups put their different parts of the machine together, there was confusion and uncertainty. I added pressure by calling out the number of minutes remaining until the deadline. Less than one and a half hours had passed, but the level of communication and cooperation had increased precipitously. Nervous laughter revealed a growing wish to be successful and the creeping awareness that they might not be.

With only five minutes to spare, the group gathered around the table where the newly constructed TeamMachine, looking a little like a simplified Rube Goldberg device, was waiting to be tested. A man from Kansas was selected to push over the first wood block like a domino to get the whole machine working. I was recording the event. Others in the room counted out loud, "Four, three, two, one!" When the man from Kansas hit the blocks, the row fell as expected, but did not trigger the next part of the machine. I heard a loud sigh from the group. "You still have time to rebuild," I said.

Several hands reached toward the table and reconfigured the line of blocks. I called out that there were two minutes remaining. Everyone seemed to be holding their breath. A Japanese colleague approached the man from Kansas and gestured firmly in the direction of the wood block, encouraging him to push firmly. The man from Kansas prepared to knock over the block of wood. The room got quiet for a moment.

"Four, three, two, one!" The man from Kansas knocked over the first block, which fell as it should then successfully triggered the next part of the machine, which led to the next and the next, triggering a dart that dropped and punctured a large balloon with a loud *pop!*

The crowd cheered. A triumphant feeling flooded the room. These colleagues from different locations in the world, these strangers who had been forced into conversation just a few hours earlier, gave each other high fives and pumped their fists in the air. It was a WE moment none of them would ever forget.

Closing deep gaps requires meaningful action and not just nice words. Actions by organizations and individuals will make the difference between a superficial, short-lived gesture and those that have a long-lasting and meaningful impact. Bridging gaps is a complex process. But most gaps can successfully be bridged with small gestures sustained over time, if the conditions are supportive. If leaders are strong role models and if individuals are provided with opportunities to look beyond superficial differences and build trusting relationships through shared experience, WE-building will occur.

ACTIONS

In the following chapters, we will examine organization-specific WE-building strategies. The following are general examples for any organization to incorporate.

Institutional WE-building Actions

- Social gatherings like group breakfast, lunch, or dinner where participants make a deliberate effort to speak in a common language and get to know new people.
- Employee Resource Groups (ERGs) with a strategic mission in addition to a social and support role.

- In-person training (Diversity and Inclusion, Anti-Bias, Harassment Prevention) that requires interaction, accountability, and ongoing learning.
- Team-building training that includes people from various departments and geographical locations engaging in authentic ways to build meaningful professional relationships.
- Job-rotation programs to build knowledge and experience with up- and downstream functions within the organization.
- Buddy or Partner Programs in which individuals volunteer to spend time together outside the office in order to build understanding and strengthen relationships.
- Mentoring Pairs or Mentoring Circles in which individuals volunteer to meet and discuss career and business objectives with one member in an advisory role.
- Boot Camp or Weekend Retreats where individuals engage in both casual and formal activities to build connection across boundaries for long-term development and deeper understanding.
- Exchange Programs in which individuals spend more than one month working and living in another location to build skills and relationships across geographical and national boundaries.

SECTION II

THE PROCESS

4

FOSTER GAP AWARENESS

IN THE SUMMER of 2015, I traveled to China with my family where we took a cable car up to the top of the Great Wall and hugged pandas at a research sanctuary in Chengdu. Each day started with a breakfast buffet in the hotel—something familiar to travelers around the world. But the breakfast buffets in China were different than any I had experienced before. They were lavish—with over a hundred different food items to choose from—everything from thousand-year eggs, spicy noodles, and fried cabbage to chocolate croissants, fresh pineapple, and pancakes. On the second morning, my oldest son discovered a waffle station among the many choices. This teenage boy was thrilled to find a familiar and delicious treat—fresh, warm waffles in Beijing! He eagerly prepared a full plate of waffles, added whipped cream, and, like American teenagers everywhere, proceeded to drown the plate with syrup. But when he took his first bite, he gagged! The syrup that he assumed would be sweet and maple was not. It was soy sauce.

So many American travelers have encountered similar sur-
prises—the girl thought she was eating chocolate in Japan but
it turned out to be sweet bean paste, the parents thought they
were giving their toddler apple juice in France but it was alcoholic cider. These experiences demonstrate a basic and universal truth about why WE-building is necessary—you cannot know
all the necessary data to bridge gaps based only on what you can
see. It's not enough.

The most fundamental skill required to narrow gaps is being
able to fully understand a *them* group by seeing invisible data.
This is WE-building's number-one superpower. It is a skill I wish
I had had early in my career. Everyone in your organization can
gain access to this superpower.

If you haven't yet seen the recent Academy Award–winning
documentary *American Factory*, I highly recommend viewing it as
a good way to see culture gaps playing out in a real company
setting. In the film, a Chinese manufacturer called Fuyao opens
a windshield factory in a failed GM plant in Dayton, Ohio. The
documentary reveals repeated episodes of culture clash between well-meaning, hardworking people, all of whom ostensibly share the same goal. The employees at Fuyao in Ohio have
trouble figuring out how to get along because few people had
learned how to access their WE-building superpower.

Without it, they bump up against one another over and over
until someone quits, is fired, or gives up. Unlike the temporary
unpleasantness of a mouthful of soy sauce–soaked waffles, the
stakes are consequential—employment, long separations from
family, and hundreds of millions of dollars in investments. The
two groups, American versus Chinese, have different views
about safety, overtime work, and union organizing. The film
captures many moments of culture shock by various groups. As
episodes of misunderstanding increase, goodwill starts to evap-
orate. The *Us versus Them* dynamic begins to permeate every
aspect of the endeavor, yet few are even aware that culture differences are at play. Instead, they ascribe negative motivations

and characteristics to the other group. The Chinese staff view the American workers as lazy and pampered because they expect to have weekends off. The Americans characterize the Chinese staff as overbearing because they are so focused on improving quality that they will problem-solve outside the nine-to-five time frame.

In one scene, an American worker complains about his Chinese colleagues, "It's like they don't even know what the rules here are."

This is exactly the problem at the heart of any *Us versus Them* dynamic. We don't know the rules about a *them* group, but we delude ourselves into thinking that we do. Instead of deliberately accumulating facts and firsthand experience, we rely on limited and sometimes inaccurate information. This inadequate data leads to negative characterizations. Instead of doing the work to more deeply understand another person or group or culture, we apply our own cultural norms to others and make assumptions based on what we can see and hear. It's like forecasting next year's sales expectations based on just six months of data. The partial data set may play out in the way we have presumed, but as my teenage son found out, making assumptions can sometimes leave a bad taste in your mouth.

The cultural norms any person accumulates over a lifetime are developed through the daily process of living side by side with other people in our social groups. We gather clues about how to behave by watching our parents, peers, and teachers. We observe how other people interact and notice what is acceptable or unacceptable. We learn in America, for example, that sticking up your middle finger toward another person is an insult while sticking up your thumb is positive. This is the universal process of socialization engaged in by people all over the world. Though the process is exactly the same, the end result—the concept of what is considered acceptable—is different based on the social group. So don't give someone a thumbs-up in Brazil if you want to show your approval, because they've learned to read this gesture to have the same meaning that the middle finger has to an American.

An obvious example of different outcomes is the way people greet each other in different countries. Japanese bow. Brazilians kiss. Americans shake hands. But in addition to these visible norms, there are invisible norms that have to do with the way we think, believe, and feel. These invisible factors are just as important as the visible ones, but they often go unnoticed. The invisible factors often shape the visible factors, so if we can understand or see the invisible data, it can make a big difference when it comes to understanding a *them* group.

Every culture has thousands of invisible rules, big and small. These invisible cultural norms are like the air we breathe: unless there is a problem, we don't notice it. Like air, cultural norms surround and support us every day in important ways. They are norms of behavior that are accepted as right and seem so obvious that they go unmentioned.

THE SUPERPOWER

The idea of seeing invisible data is based on the iceberg concept of culture developed by anthropologist Edward Hall in his 1976 book, *Beyond Culture*.[1] Essentially, Hall's thesis is that while there are many cultural differences on the surface, such as clothing styles and greeting protocols, there are many more invisible factors below the surface, including assumptions, values, and beliefs. Without a clear understanding of another person's invisible data, damage occurs, because people assume they are aligned when they are not (see Figure 4).

The way to see invisible values is to first assume that differences exist, then start collecting information through reading, asking questions, and logging time in first-person encounters. It is not necessary to *like* or *follow* other norms, but it is important to *understand* them. In many cases, it takes just a moment to pause and look deeper in order to understand information that

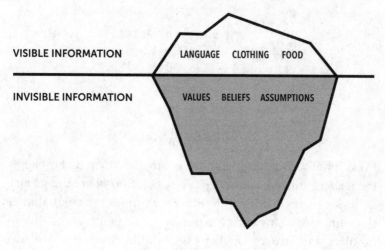

VISIBLE INFORMATION — LANGUAGE CLOTHING FOOD

INVISIBLE INFORMATION — VALUES BELIEFS ASSUMPTIONS

FIGURE 4

will explain otherwise confusing situations. But even in the twenty-first century, successful organizations with enormous resources often fail to do this.

In May 2014, Ohio-based Procter & Gamble debuted a new version of a laundry soap in Germany called Ariel 88.[2] The previous product, called Ariel 83, had been successful throughout Europe. Ariel 88 was a new name reflecting an increased amount of detergent that would clean five additional loads of laundry. But the debut did not go as planned. Within a week, every box of Ariel 88 was removed from shelves and Procter & Gamble issued a formal apology to their offended customers.

Their recall and apology had nothing to do with the quality of the laundry soap; it had everything to do with the invisible cultural meaning of the number 88. For many German shoppers, the number 88 is associated with Nazi propaganda. H is the eighth letter of the alphabet and 88 is used as a code for the abhorrent phrase "Heil Hitler." Procter & Gamble was either not aware that 88 had such a negative association in Germany or they were aware but didn't think it was a big deal. It was.

You cannot know another person's cultural
identity by looking at them.

ICEBERGING

Every employee, manager, and executive in America must apply
the iceberg concept of culture to any situation where the surface
behavior seems at odds with what they consider normal. Rather
than immediately judging a person or situation according to
familiar standards, as Esther's boss did in Chapter 1 (she was
the Haitian woman who had been taught to show respect for her
parents and others who were older by never looking them in the
eye), WE-builders pause for a moment and ask themselves if
they might be missing important data based on their lack of
firsthand experience. If they activate the WE-building superpower and look below the surface for information, the results
can be game-changing.

Culture gaps are predictable when people from different
backgrounds work together. Mistakes would occur less frequently if all differences were visible. My son would not have
made the same mistake if the bottle of brown liquid at the
breakfast buffet was clearly labeled *soy sauce*. But so much of our
lives are unlabeled and unmarked. This is why we need the
WE-building superpower. Once you are aware that culture gaps
exist and that the most important gaps are invisible, then it is
much easier to detect differences. I wish I had acquired this skill
before working in Japan.

When I started my first job after college, I had never heard of
the iceberg concept of culture. I knew that life would be different, but I felt deeply connected to Japan, having lived there for
a year in college and possessing basic Japanese language skills.

But my inability to see invisible data was the source of the biggest problem I encountered.

My job was to support a senior Japanese executive who was in charge of the North American operations. Like the other office ladies, my role was to serve tea at his meetings, answer his phone, and manage his schedule. Despite my efforts to learn, and without even realizing it, I damaged my relationship with the most senior office lady within the first week.

I was unaware of an invisible and powerful Japanese value: the importance of showing deference within a hierarchy. As an American, I had grown up learning to treat all people equally, no matter their age, race, religion, or job. My upbringing prevented me from seeing the rigid hierarchy among the ten women with whom I worked. What I saw was that everyone dressed alike (thanks to the corporate uniform policy) and had similar jobs. No one had a different title or an office with a door. We sat at exactly the same types of desks in an open space, so I mistakenly assumed this meant that we were all equal.

I attempted to build good relationships with all the office ladies and was polite and courteous to everyone. Unfortunately, and unknown to me, this was the wrong approach within that culture. Here's what I should have done: identify the most senior person and then prioritize this relationship above the others with small acts of deference. My day-to-day behaviors caused damage because I assumed a level of equality with the senior office lady. She, and everyone else in the office, believed that her many years of experience in the organization were valuable and should be acknowledged through a show of respect.

Damage to our relationship occurred every time she tried to teach me how to do my job. As a new person, I wanted to show that I was eager to learn. When she taught me a new process, I would invariably ask questions, or worse, I would just ask, "Why?" I thought I was showing interest and being thorough, in the manner my culture had taught me to behave. But this irritated her deeply. In response to my questions, she would grow impatient and mean. As the senior person in our group, when she took the time to teach someone junior like me, she was expecting no questions and just one response: "Thank you."

We didn't work well together. Our relationship didn't just make work uncomfortable and stressful, but it prevented us from working together innovatively, efficiently, and with agility. The iceberg concept of culture identifies the root of our problem. While I was doing all that I could on the surface to adjust—speaking in Japanese, wearing a uniform—under the surface I did not adjust at all. I was not even aware of the important differences residing below what I could see.

The truth is, it never occurred to me that invisible factors would impact daily life in the Japanese workplace. I never thought to look for invisible data or ask about it. But now I know better. Now I know that every person, family, department, company, and country has its own culture, has its own norms of behavior and patterns, some of which are visible and many of which are not. I know that I *don't know* important information and so I look for it. I ask questions. I pay attention to the way others behave before I act. I walk into new situations knowing that what I see, hear, and experience is just part of the data—the visible data. And rather than assume that I have all the information, I approach it as though I am joining dinner in someone's home where the hosts know which chair is assigned to each member of the family, and it's my job to find out which seat is available for me.

Invisible cultural data is everywhere.

Talented, hardworking people fail to look for invisible data all the time because cultural differences are undervalued. In the past, cultural differences seemed less relevant. But most of us know from our own experiences in daily life that diversity is increasing all around us. We are working with people who don't look or sound or pray like we do in greater numbers than ever before.

Without knowing your organization, I can predict that it has grown more diverse over the years, among your employees, your customers, or your B2B partners. Look around. What do you see and hear in your workplace? Are there people from different backgrounds? If so, you're going to need the following WE-building tools.

TOOLS FOR FOSTERING GAP AWARENESS

After twenty-five years of working with people from different backgrounds, I now see that the first step of WE-building—*fostering awareness*—is crucial to minimize the negative impact of difference. Fostering awareness means that we must see differences not as better or worse, good or bad, but simply different. If we look at cultures as equal, not as inferior or superior to other cultural groups, we can foster the awareness that so many people either can't see or don't want to see. Once we have awareness, we can move on to the next two steps, which will enable us to do the foundational work necessary to create an equal, multicultural coalition.

Awareness Building Tools

1. Encourage Cross-Cultural Conversation
2. Share iceberg stories
3. Introduce the Identity cloud exercise
4. Practice the iceberg self-introduction
5. Create awareness-building scenarios

1. Encourage Cross-Cultural Conversation

In companies with a diverse workforce or one opening foreign offices, try leading discussions to heighten awareness of gaps and highlight ways that this awareness will result in more effective teams.

Some of my clients incorporate Cross-Cultural Conversations into the onboarding process, while others set aside specific opportunities alongside other training or learning initiatives. These conversations should be led by a skilled facilitator who is comfortable talking about identity and can keep the conversation open, welcoming, and positive.

Ask the following questions:

- What is an example of a culture difference you saw or experienced firsthand?
- Did you expect this difference or was it a surprise?
- Did this cause any conflict?
- Did you have assumptions about the other culture before you encountered this difference?

Here are some tips to make this work:

- **Keep the conversation positive.** This conversation is not the place for complaints or direct criticism; rather it is an opportunity to share firsthand experiences as a vehicle for learning. It's important to monitor this. If someone shares a bad experience, it is possible to acknowledge that person's experience without suggesting that their experience is representative of the entire culture group.
- **Make sharing 100 percent voluntary.** No one should be expected to share. Many people are eager to share their own experiences and this can be a learning opportunity for everyone. Make it clear that sharing an example that

someone has read or learned about through trusted sources is also welcome.

● **Model the sharing you expect.** If others do not share easily, it is useful to share a personal example that is easy for others to relate to. Common observations include people in different countries driving on opposite sides of the road or time sensitivity examples where people in one culture have a rigid view of being "on time" while others are more flexible.

● **Express neutrality.** Clearly state that cultural differences are not viewed as good or bad, better or worse, but merely different. Sharing stories without judging them is a way to broaden awareness of culture in our daily lives.

● **Keep to facts and one's own experiences rather than repeating stereotyped assumptions.** There is always a danger of moving away from personal experience into stereotypes. Make sure this does not happen. Encourage people to speak from their own point of view and steer the conversation away from negative stereotypes.

I often start by asking for examples of geographical culture gaps because different norms are easier to see when we look outside national boundaries. Stories of encountering differences abroad illustrate the different ways people in different cultures handle similar situations. Even if you've never traveled abroad, most people can relate to these examples.

One of my favorite stories is from the actress Jenna Fischer who, after starring as the beloved receptionist Pam Beesly on NBC's *The Office* for nine years, went to London with her husband and two small children to shoot ten episodes of the TV show *You, Me and the Apocalypse*.[3] Fischer was by then a veteran actor and knew what to expect on set each day. But when she showed up to film the show in London, she immediately noticed a difference.

"They didn't have food on set," Fischer said. "It was so different from American sets where there is always craft services providing a constant supply of food, from fresh fruit to a grill guy who will take specific requests." Fischer adjusted by packing apples and peanuts for herself in her children's snack containers. Instead of unlimited craft service, her English coworkers stopped for tea. "Every day right around three, everyone would stop working and someone came around with a tray of tea cakes, biscuits, and hot tea. It was all so civilized."

2. Share Iceberg Stories

To make people aware of cultural differences, create an opportunity to gather and talk about differences. Use the iceberg concept to understand the stories. Encourage each person to look below the obvious, visible data to gain deeper understanding. Sharing real-life examples through deliberate conversations will help people build awareness of cultural differences. Ask people to share examples of culture gaps and look together for the underlying invisible data that explains the behavioral differences.

Share a story of your own or one you know will resonate with the members of the group. Anyone can gather data about a specific cultural group. Building a WE culture is achieved by understanding what is under the surface for the *them* group.

Going back to Esther's story, we can see that her behavior was misunderstood by the vice president because he failed to understand the invisible cultural data that motivated her behavior. If he had the superpower, he would have paused before deciding Esther was a liar and instead would have tried to understand her behavior.

Bridging gaps with others starts with an understanding of one's cultural identity.

---

3. Introduce the Identity Cloud Exercise

Discussing important identity traits in the workplace has been viewed as dangerous territory for many people due to legal concerns and the importance of ensuring fair and equal treatment of everyone in the workplace. Yet personal cultural identities are with us in everything we do whether we like it or not. Each human has an identity made up of many factors that include age, race, gender, sexual orientation, ethnicity, body type, family structure, nationality, religion, socio-economics, education, physical ability, neurodiversity, occupation, skills, life experience, and other characteristics. The way we grew up and with whom we grew up, no matter where or what those conditions, has an impact on our individual identities. Understanding your own identity is often a complex process. Some people spend years struggling with this while others don't seem to question it much at all. But regardless of the relationship or level of awareness a person has with his/her/their identity, gaining some awareness of our own identity is a necessary step toward understanding others.

There are fields of academic study devoted to understanding identity, including theories about core identities or psychological identities. Some academics talk about factors that are salient for a person, which means characteristics of a person that become more prominent in certain situations.[4] Others discuss identity states that change over time. Identity is a deep and important topic and directly impacts how individuals see themselves and relate to others.

Odds are, your team or direct reports are composed of diverse groups of people. They are not just diverse in obvious ways—age, ethnicity, and so on—but in less apparent ways as well. Helping people become aware of their identities is a step toward gap awareness. To facilitate awareness in your organization, introduce the image of the identity cloud (see Figure 5).

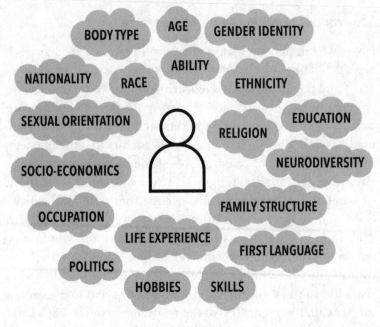

FIGURE 5

Explain that these nineteen categories are some, but not all, of the common factors by which people identify themselves. These are features of an identity that humans can use to describe themselves. Without requiring it, you can ask for volunteers to share what factors they consider most important to their identity. It is important that no one feels compelled to share this information. Keep in mind that some people may have aspects of their identity that they're not comfortable revealing to others in the group. Simply introducing the concept of the identity cloud is the point of the exercise.

A person's cultural identity is not a right or wrong measurement. It just is. A person may identify as female, male, transgender, or they might prefer no gender label at all. A person may identify as Black, white, Asian, Latinx, or another race and/or ethnicity. How we identify may or may not be reflected in our appearance, or the way we present to the world. Some aspects of our identity are fixed, like our age or birth order in a family, but many features are flexible and can change over time, like our occupation or life experience.

For most humans, generation, race, and gender identity are unchanging and highly influential factors. There are good arguments to add ethnicity, sexual orientation, and religion to this list. These six factors also inform many *Us versus Them* gaps. They are high-stakes factors that are easily misunderstood. As such, discussion around these identity factors can trigger anxiety and discomfort.

Because of this anxiety, many people learned that the safest way to manage differences is to act as though we don't see these factors. I, too, subscribed to that system, hoping that proximity to those who are different would naturally lead to improved interactions, closer relationships, and a true multicultural society where differences are embraced and our capacity for relationships across difference would grow. But that has not happened for many reasons, not least of which is an inherent flaw in the system. Existing power structures are resistant to change. Without acknowledgment of the six factors, corporate America, more often than not, defaults to a straight, white, male cultural norm.

Instead of defaulting to a dominant cultural identity (which we will discuss in detail in Chapter 8), leaders must foster awareness of multiple identity factors and also help people build alliances around factors like occupation, skills, and life experience. Instead of building alliances around immutable identity factors like age and race, leaders must promote connections around factors that are flexible and attainable for anyone. When they do this, the circle of belonging grows wider and there is more inclusion.

Discussing identity topics is not the same as discrimination against someone because of their identity. But these are sensitive topics with historical relevance that must be discussed in safe and appropriate ways by leaders and experts in every organization. Discussion should be welcome; discrimination must be rejected. Being able to see and to talk about these differences directly, honestly, and sensitively is part of the process of WE-building.

———

In order to successfully bridge culture gaps in the workplace, we must gather cultural data to understand both visible and invisible aspects of another person/group/country/ culture.

———

4. Practice the Iceberg Self-Introduction (Small Group Exercise)

Divide participants into groups of four to five people and ask them to introduce themselves to one another, but add the iceberg concept of culture to deepen the experience. Instead of sharing only surface data, ask participants to share invisible data. It is essential to emphasize that participants share only data that they feel comfortable sharing. The invisible data can be related to sports or geography or any aspect of the life experience that they would like to share.

In addition to a self-introduction, participants are instructed to look for one invisible factor that all members of the group share. The goal is to find the common points among people who may look and sound very different from one another.

Explain by saying the following:

> During the exercise, listen carefully to one another and find something that everyone in the group has in common. Look for something specific rather than general. So, rather than saying, for example, "We are all human," look

for a specific hobby, sport, or life experience that is common to everyone in the group.

Seeing invisible data prevents reliance on stereotypes.

Without fact-based, first-person information, we are unable to correctly interpret what we see. We cannot make accurate assessments simply based on superficial information, especially when that information is connected to factors like race and ethnicity.

5. Create Awareness-Building Scenarios

The following four stories are designed to build awareness by describing real-life situations. Envision yourself as the leader or manager in each story and answer questions related to your options when faced with the opportunity to raise awareness of gaps among your workers. To build awareness in your organization, you can use these scenarios or create your own.

Justin is a twenty-year veteran at an entertainment company. He is put in charge of managing a new department that is staffed by five employees, including one newly hired woman, Sophie, who just graduated from college and has been working in the company for less than a year. The other employees have all been in the company for at least ten-plus years. During meetings, Sophie often checks her phone. She speaks with authority, challenging the way things are done in the office. She implies that corporate practices aren't environmentally conscious, such as their document printing methods. Justin notices that other staff seem put off by Sophie's style. He overheard one team member say, "She can't even walk down the hall without

checking her phone." At the same time, Justin values Sophie as a disruptor and innovator; their team has implemented some of Sophie's suggestions, saving time and
money as well as solving difficult problems.

Imagine you're in Justin's shoes and answer the following
questions:

1. A member of your team complains to you about Sophie,
   saying that she feels Sophie thinks she's "above" the
   rules that govern the team and that she is difficult for
   other team members to communicate with. How would
   you handle this situation?

   A. Commiserate with the team member and agree
      that Sophie's behavior is disruptive. Share that
      you noticed Sophie glance at her phone even
      during a meeting with the CEO.
   B. Consider transferring Sophie to another depart-
      ment so she is no longer your problem.
   C. Acknowledge the comment as an indicator that
      there may be an *Us versus Them* gap festering
      within the department. Give some thought to how
      to help team members recognize that the prob-
      lem may not just be with Sophie but their own at-
      titudes, beliefs, and norms.
   D. Shrug off the complaint and tell the team mem-
      ber to give Sophie a break because "she's young"
      and wait to see if any serious problems develop.
      Trust that things will improve naturally.

   The optimal WE-building answer is C. The easy answer would be to transfer Sophie to another team, but
   while that solves one problem, it may produce more serious ones, including a missed opportunity to build connections within the team. As a manager, Justin should

not commiserate or complain about her. Expecting things to improve naturally might work, but it's uncertain. Other team members may become more tolerant of Sophie once they realize they are as responsible for the gap as Sophie is.

2. Now that Justin is aware there could be a cultural division in his team, what steps should he take?

   A. Reflect on his firsthand experience with this generational gap.
   B. Evaluate whether he identifies with the *us* group in this generational dynamic.
   C. Do some online research to understand the generational gap.
   D. All of the above.

   The optimal WE-building answer is D. *All of the above.* As the leader of this department, Justin's first step should be to determine his own level of awareness regarding this particular culture gap so that he can be prepared to facilitate awareness in others.

3. Now that Justin has educated himself, what next steps should he take with others?

   A. Ask Sophie to prepare a presentation for the team on her generational characteristics.
   B. Nothing.
   C. Be on the lookout for additional signals that others notice a gap. Speak up if others complain and point out positive aspects of Sophie's style, including her quick response time to any email and her constant vigilance toward use of the department's resources.
   D. Facilitate a conversation about cultural differences and make his team members aware that culture

gaps can occur based on any aspect of a person's identity, including generational differences.

The optimal WE-building answer is C. As the leader, it is Justin's job to pay attention to potential problems in order to find solutions before issues turn into problems. Asking Sophie to make a presentation would not be appropriate and might make her feel even more like an outsider, which is the opposite of Justin's goal. It is not Sophie's job to educate her coworkers. It is Justin's job as manager to pay attention and help his team bridge gaps. You might think answer D would also be a good WE-building next step. Justin should only create a plan to narrow the gap if he makes the assessment that others in the department are also experiencing a gap.

Matthew is a veteran pilot with over twenty-five years' experience flying for a major airline. As is customary when he shows up for a new flight, one of the first things he does is introduce himself to the crew for that flight, which in this case includes one male copilot and three female flight attendants. He notices that one of the flight attendants is younger than the other two flight attendants and she is Black. Everyone else is white, which is common in the airline industry, where 92 percent of pilots and 73 percent of flight attendants are white.

1. When Matthew introduces himself, he notices that the young Black attendant has a slight accent and he doesn't catch her name. What should he do?

    A. Ask, "Where are you from?"
    B. Pause and say, "I want to make sure I'm pronouncing your name correctly. Do you mind telling me once more?"

C. Keep introducing himself to others and ask one of the other crew members later what her name is.

D. Nothing. He doesn't need to know her name.

The optimal WE-building answer is B. Asking "where are you from?" might deepen the divide that the attendant may (or may not) already be experiencing. Instead, Matthew should focus on simple bridging strategies, like knowing and using (correctly) another person's name. It might seem like a simple thing, but many people fail to grasp names that are initially hard for them to understand or unfamiliar. There is a common resistance to asking someone to repeat their name. But if Matthew chooses to do nothing or ask someone later, he would be defaulting to old paradigms that may or may not work out in his favor.

2. During a layover, Matthew notices the three white crew members discussing a plan to have dinner together at a well-known Mexican restaurant in the city that is their final destination. They tell Matthew their plans. The Black flight attendant is not present but later walks toward the area and sits down at a distance with a cup of coffee. What should Matthew do?

A. Continue chatting with all white members of the crew while the Black crew member sits separately and drinks her coffee.

B. Stop talking with the white crew members.

C. Ask one of the other crew members to tell her about the plans.

D. Matthew should tell the other crew members that he is going to make sure the other flight attendant, calling her by name, knows the plans. Then, calling her by name, Matthew should tell her the plans to make sure she knows she is invited.

The optimal WE-building answer is D. Continuing to behave as if there are no *Us and Them* dynamics at play might seem safe and easy for Matthew, but that behavior could be perpetuating a gap. Without knowing how the Black flight attendant feels, there is no harm in making sure she feels seen by saying her name to her directly in front of the other crew members. As a manager, it is essential to productivity to make sure all team members feel included. The fact that Matthew has encountered only a few Black professionals in his twenty-five years of flying is relevant information that he should not ignore. Matthew also recognizes that he is accustomed to working with mostly white people and therefore is aware that there may be invisible factors at play for the Black flight attendant of which he is not aware.

3. In our real-life scenario, Matthew did invite the Black flight attendant to dinner but she declined to join the others at the Mexican restaurant. The next morning on the van to the airport, the two white flight attendants chat the entire way, never including the Black flight attendant. The Black flight attendant is on her phone and does not speak to anyone. Matthew and the copilot are also on their phones. The flights that day proceed as usual. At the end of a long day, the crew goes to another hotel. When the elevator doors open, everyone except the Black flight attendant gets on. Matthew steps to the side to indicate there is plenty of room but she shakes her head *no*. She will wait for another elevator. When the four white crew members are then together alone in the elevator, what should Matthew do?

    A. Say nothing in the elevator. Check in with the Black flight attendant as soon as possible to ask if

there are any problems or concerns. Be prepared
to listen.

B. Consult with the other crew members to ask if
they noticed something is wrong.

C. Tell one of the other flight attendants to ask the
Black flight attendant if everything is okay.

D. Nothing.

The optimal WE-building answer is A. The incident
at the elevator could be nothing. It had been a long day
and everyone was tired. Matthew had never before encountered something like that, and it seemed such a
small thing that it would be easy to ignore. But it could
be a signal. Matthew should not talk with the other crew
members before talking directly with her. He should
also not ask someone else to talk with her. He's the
leader, and it is his job to engage in what could be a
difficult conversation. Talking with the other crew
members could exacerbate possible *Us versus Them* dynamics if they exist. It could also appear that Matthew
has some allegiance to the other white crew members
when that is not the case. As the head pilot, Matthew's
responsibility is to ensure the safety and productivity of
the entire crew. As a leader in any situation, Matthew
wants to know of potential problems sooner rather than
later so that he can help orchestrate solutions.

Janice is the manager of a customer service department
in her global company based in New Jersey. She is put in
charge of an outsourcing initiative to set up five call centers in the Philippines at a cost of $10 million. She has
never been to the Philippines nor has she known anyone
from there, but she has traveled to both China and Japan.
Janice is a talented manager with more than fifteen years
of experience. She will manage a team of ten people who

will support this effort. Ten years ago, Janice successfully set up new call centers for her company in Florida.

1. In preparation for this new initiative, what should Janice do?
   A. Focus on the metrics of success she used in the Florida experience.
   B. Assume that everyone in the Philippines speaks English, which must mean there will be little culture difference.
   C. Rely on her experiences traveling in Asia to help her make good choices as she leads her team.
   D. Recognize that there will be differences in Filipino workplace culture that she and her team do not yet understand, but which will be relevant in this project.

The optimal WE-building answer is D. If Janice only uses past metrics that helped her achieve success in the United States, it is highly likely that she will miss important cultural data that will be relevant in this new international venture. Assuming that sharing a language means sharing invisible cultural data is incorrect. It is probably useful that Janice has traveled to other Asian countries because this will likely have helped her develop higher awareness that cultural differences exist. But China, Japan, and the Philippines are very different in both obvious and invisible ways. Different countries must be understood and treated in ways that are appropriate for each.

2. Now that Janice is aware that cultural data is relevant, what steps should she take toward understanding it?

   A. Nothing until after the project is up and running.

B. Reflect on her own identity and her experience reading visible and invisible data.

C. Facilitate conversations with her team about cultural identity and how to access visible and invisible data.

D. Introduce the iceberg concept of culture and share examples of how it will be a useful tool in this project.

The optimal WE-building answers are both C and D. Others in Janice's group need to gain basic awareness of cultural issues. Facilitating this is part of Janice's job.

3. Now that Janice has helped her team understand that cultural data could be relevant, what steps should she take?

A. Encourage everyone to study up on the Philippines in their spare time.

B. Take everyone to a Filipino grocery store.

C. Make a training plan to specifically increase understanding of Filipino workplace culture, including a list of books, movies, and online resources, in-person training opportunities, and other face-to-face interactions.

D. All of the above.

The optimal WE-building answer is D. Going to a grocery store or encouraging employees to learn on their own is not bad, but Janice must prioritize cultural data in a way that is in alignment with the stakes of this initiative. Going going to a grocery store or familiarizing yourself with a different culture through reading might be appropriate before a vacation. But Janice is leading a $10 million initiative that demands that she place a higher priority on gathering cultural data as one of many metrics she and her team must use to achieve a successful outcome.

Michelle is the human relations manager in a manufacturing facility in the Midwest. This facility has been in production for twenty years, and during that time, the population of the workforce, about three hundred people, has diversified due to immigration from Somalia and other countries. The number of Muslim workers went from zero to 15 percent during that time. Most of the other employees either identify as Catholic or do not identify with any religion.

1. One day, a local employee approaches Michelle to complain about the smell of the food some of the Muslim workers bring from home and eat in the cafeteria. He says it is "gross" and complains that their food is "ruining the cafeteria." What should Michelle do?

   A. Tell the employee that she also finds their food offensive.
   B. Say that she understands his concern but tell him to be flexible. Suggest that he eat in another part of the cafeteria.
   C. Put up a sign in the cafeteria encouraging everyone to be aware of the strong aromas of their food.
   D. Acknowledge his complaint and take it as a sign that she needs to be proactive about bridging the gap between Somali employees and non-Somali employees.

   The optimal WE-building answer is D. As the human relations manager, Michelle must be on the lookout for warning signs of potential problems. Putting up a sign,

telling someone to eat elsewhere, or complaining herself will only cause further divisions.

2. Now that Michelle is aware there could be a cultural
division in the company, what steps should she take?

    A. Research Somali and Muslim culture on her own
and assess her own level of understanding.

    B. Identify people who know about Somali and Mus-
lim culture and seek their advice.

    C. Identify and reach out to Somali and Muslim em-
ployees who might be willing to share their observations and experiences with her so she can better
understand potential issues.

    D. All of the above.

The optimal WE-building answer is D. *All of the above.*
Any one of these actions is better than doing nothing at
all. Ethnicity and religion are sensitive and relevant topics in this organization and as such need to be understood by leaders like Michelle.

3. Now that Michelle has educated herself, what steps
should she take to address the potential *Us and Them*
gap?

    A. Consider creating a separate room for the Somali
employees to eat lunch.

    B. Make a rule that aromatic food must be eaten in
a different space.

    C. Nothing.

    D. Assess the gap between Somali and non-Somali
employees. If a significant gap exists, beyond that
one complaint, she should develop a plan, in co-
ordination with Somali community leaders and
employees, to narrow gaps and build connection
between Somali and non-Somali people.

The optimal WE-building answer is D. Creating a separate space for only one group or for people with strong-smelling food will not improve understanding and could exacerbate a gap that may already be growing deep and wide. Doing nothing is a weak choice because this complaint is providing a potential warning sign that there is more data below the surface. As the human relations manager, Michelle has a responsibility to build connections and not to wait until there is a huge problem. If Michelle is not an expert herself, she must rely on others to help her make a plan for improvement.

FIVE LEVELS OF AWARENESS

In the next chapters, we will begin the process of self-assessment, which involves selecting a relevant cultural group and measuring the level of integration and understanding. This process will be necessary when there is a wide gap. As a precursor, leaders can consider cultural groups that are relevant to their work lives and measure themselves on the scale below to determine how well integrated they are.

Select a target cultural group. How would you assess your level of cultural awareness with this group?

1. Almost nothing.
2. Vague familiarity, superficial, stereotypical.
3. Somewhat familiar, have logged time with people in this group, have purposely gathered information.
4. Quite familiar, have spent large amounts of time with people in this group, could list at least three examples of invisible data that I acquired myself.
5. An expert; can move fluidly between people who identify with this group and others; have built trusting relationships with people from this group.

5

CONDUCT AN *US VERSUS THEM* ASSESSMENT

LIKE MILLIONS OF smartphone users, I frequently use my iPhone to manage small daily tasks. I send emails to friends and colleagues, text my husband, locate my preteen, read news, check the weather, look at photos of nieces and nephews on Instagram, review updates on Facebook, and tweet. I always considered myself a light to moderate smartphone user until I saw a screentime usage report for the first time—1 hour 40 minutes on Twitter, 1 hour 36 minutes sending texts, picking up my phone over a hundred times in a single day. It was horrifying. Without that report, without seeing the visual evidence of the accumulated minutes and numbers, I would not have clearly understood the truth about my behavior.

The *Us versus Them* assessment is a measuring tool that provides a quick assessment of a person's level of integration and firsthand experience with a specific cultural group. Like a pitcher's ERA, it is just one number and does not tell you everything you need to know. But like the number on the scale when you weigh yourself or a screentime usage report, it provides data that enables people to make informed decisions moving forward.

Unlike a person's weight or number of minutes spent on Twitter, the *Us versus Them* assessment attempts to measure something amorphous—a person's level of integration and understanding of a specific cultural group. Since true understanding is very hard to measure, the assessment evaluates the number and types of interactions a person has had with someone from a specific cultural group. The questions are premised on the belief that face-to-face interactions of increasing depth are a path toward meaningful understanding, narrowing gaps, and eliminating dangerous stereotypes.

When people look at me—a slightly built, middle-aged, white woman—they never expect to hear me say, "私は日本で生まれました," which means, "I was born in Japan." I just don't *look* like a person who could do that. But, of course, it is impossible to look at another person and know what languages they speak. It's an example of the invisible data that we discussed in the previous chapter.

Just as it is critical to understand a person's invisible data in order to accurately understand and see the whole of another individual person, we must also seek out the invisible data to have a more complete understanding of groups of people as well.

We make assumptions about other people every day because there is so much information coming into our brains. Our neural receptors are so inundated that we cannot accurately filter and categorize all the data in a thoughtful manner. Instead, our brains sort data at a rapid pace that our conscious brains do not even register. This is the cause of unconscious or implicit bias, which is the unconscious attribution of positive or negative characteristics to a person or group in a way that is considered unfair. We glance up, see another human, and begin to categorize that person before we are even aware of it. Some of those assumptions may be accurate and others are not.

Stereotypes can be dangerous and are often connected to negative assumptions and harmful beliefs. Stereotypes cause division because they lend themselves to our *us* and *them* tendencies. The *Us versus Them* assessment is the starting point for disrupting stereotypes by measuring how much deliberate effort has been made to understand another cultural group.

My belief that face-to-face interactions of increasing depth are the path to disrupting *Us versus Them* dynamics grew out of my own experience and the experiences of thousands of professionals I have worked with over the years. It is also a well-researched academic principle in the field of social science called intergroup contact.[1] In 2006, two researchers amassed 515 studies across 38 nations and 250,000 people and found that 94 percent of the time intergroup contact reduced prejudices, including those associated with race, ethnicity, and cultural groups.

It's important to note that while in-person face-to-face interactions of increasing depth are the most important tool for building WE cultures, recent research demonstrates that using the internet or distanced interactions can be an effective tool, especially at the beginning of a relationship.[2] Using email or text-based interaction significantly reduces anxiety in many people. For some, starting with text, then gradually increasing communication to include images and video and then face-to-face contact, will lead to positive outcomes.

As many of us learned during the COVID-19 pandemic, not only were virtual meetings the only way to meet, but they became an effective vehicle for continued relationship growth during the crisis.

———

Bridging gaps starts with an honest self-evaluation of one's contact and understanding of the target culture.

———

IDENTIFYING *US VERSUS THEM* CULTURAL GAPS

The *Us versus Them* assessment is used by individuals to assess their level of familiarity with another cultural group. The selected culture can be defined by almost any factor and is highly flexible. It can be applied in a wide range of situations from playful to highly consequential.

A culture group might be an unchanging, visible identity factor like age or race. For example, we could identify the *them* group as people born before 1970. Alternatively, the group might be defined by invisible life-experience factors, like people who have been in the military. A culture can be broad, such as selecting a country like Nigeria or Japan, or it can be measured very narrowly by selecting one sports team or specific group of people, like St. Louis Cardinals baseball fans.

As we saw in Chapter 4, it is the job of leaders to determine which gaps are relevant. Leaders who pay attention to real interaction—like how people communicate and solve problems—will have the ability to identify the pertinent gaps. Sometimes, leaders need to pay attention to the signals generated by employees—and there are always signals—to determine if a gap warrants attention.

SIGNALS

All good managers know it is necessary to pay attention to various signals from their team in order to notice potential problems before they turn into complaints or worse. As many people who worked with people like Harvey Weinstein can tell you, long before there were formal complaints and lawsuits, there were whispers in Hollywood that were signals of the problems to come. Skillful managers take time to listen and notice what people are saying. They pay attention to patterns and notice where people sit and who has lunch with whom. A single negative comment or a group that enjoys having lunch together on a regular basis does not warrant attention. Some negative remarks turn out to be nothing but gossip, but a pattern of exclusionary behavior or a pattern of dismissive comments about a specific group may indicate a potential *Us and Them* problem.

Verbal Warning Signs

1. Derogatory comments about a specific group.

    "I can't believe those guys in accounting take so long to process my requests."

    "People in the LA office are on vacation half the time."

    "We'll never get an answer this year from the Tokyo head office."

2. Mentioning the name of a group causes eye-rolling and grumbles.

    "Our vendor in Mumbai asked for a deadline extension."

    "The newly graduated analysts will join our meeting tomorrow."

    "The engineering department has more questions about our proposal."

Behavioral Warning Signs

1. Strict divisions based on factors such as race, ethnicity, or religion in where people sit or with whom they eat lunch.

2. Voluntary participation at monthly gatherings, social events (official and unofficial):

> Who joins and where do they sit?

> Who hangs around to clean up?

> Who stays for the entire program?

SALES VERSUS ENGINEERS

Years ago, I worked with a company in Chicago in which the sales team had been viewed as the most important department. The engineering department was treated by the president and others as secondary since it was the sales team that brought in the money. These two groups constantly vied for attention and competed when they should have been cooperating. They viewed each other as rivals rather than allies.

The engineers in the company were, by training and character, rather careful and risk-averse. They took longer to make decisions and often required lots of data before moving forward. The sales team constantly teased them about their slow reaction time and chided them relentlessly. In a training session, I listened as a dozen adults, all of whom worked for the same company, participated in the TeamMachine exercise while putting each other down with snide remarks. The negative remarks were shared as though it were all in good fun, but the volume of insults was striking to me and may have betrayed their real thinking about the other group. It was a signal of a divide.

During the debriefing period, I mentioned my observation about their remarks and encouraged the participants to reflect on it. One member acknowledged in front of the others that he agreed that the teasing sometimes went too far. It was a surprising moment of self-reflection for a group that seemed to be on-guard with one another. These kinds of small but genuine

WE-building moments can be the starting point for building a more cooperative approach.

MEASURING GAP SEVERITY

The seriousness of the gap depends on many factors. Some culture groups, such as race, religion, and ethnicity, are sensitive and protected by law. Many leaders are reluctant to discuss topics related to these groups—afraid that even bringing up the subject will lead to complaints. The way to address sensitive topics without causing trouble is to never require anyone to complete an assessment about highly sensitive topics like race, religion, ethnicity, gender identity, or other protected characteristics. Instead, ask people to select the topic for themselves that is relevant or present in their lives. Participating in the assessment should always be 100 percent voluntary.

Working with experienced human relations staff or trained facilitators is another strategy for managing sensitive topics. Leaders who can speak from personal experience or who have training on how to facilitate sensitive or uncomfortable conversations are essential. When internal staff do not have these skills, working with an outside expert is best.

Leaders will need to model a genuine approach. You can say, "I'm committed to improving diversity and inclusion so I am going to challenge myself to learn more. I encourage you to do the same." Leaders should encourage their people to choose relevant cultural groups and work toward increasing their own firsthand experience with *them* groups.

FIVE RULES FOR ADMINISTERING THE ASSESSMENT

The *Us versus Them* assessment can be done individually with each person selecting a specific and relevant culture, or as a group focusing on one culture in particular. Either way, the assessment is always completed by an individual. The culture selected can be as specific or as broad as the participants decide to make it.

When administering the self-assessment, observe five rules of engagement:

Rule 1. Make It Voluntary

Don't force individuals to assess themselves. Do not insist that people go through the motions of assessment if they are not willing. If a person is not genuine about narrowing gaps, the exercise will not lead to growth. Instead, it will likely irritate the individual who does not want to participate. I have met people who were unwilling to bridge gaps for various reasons. Some did not see the benefit or felt it was a waste of time. Others were so triggered by words like race or ethnicity that they shut down. However, some of these same people were persuaded to participate once they understood that gaps were harming the company. Making friends is not the purpose of bridging gaps. The primary goal is to create a safe and welcoming environment for all employees in order to maximize productivity.

Rule 2. Ensure Privacy

Keep self-assessment scores private. Some people may be willing to share, and leaders should welcome this, but in order to encourage honest reflection, the score should not be public knowledge.

In some situations, especially when a group is measuring a single cultural group that is related to a specific geographical region, it is possible to do a group exercise that involves documenting the group results. Instructions for documenting group results appear later in this chapter.

Rule 3. Manifest Authenticity and Humility

To bridge gaps effectively, be authentic and humble. Accept that you do not have all the answers and that you can learn something new. Without this attitude, you'll come across as pandering or offensive when trying to bridge a gap. It would also be illegal in many cases to tell employees to purposely take an action to bridge a specific gap such as "talk with a Black person" or "invite a Muslim colleague out to lunch." Our laws will not permit that and it would not work anyway. The only way to meaningfully narrow gaps is to have a genuine wish to do so. Attempting to bridge a gap without a genuine wish to learn and understand another group can lead to more problems.

Rule 4. Stress Honesty

Communicate that you expect people to reflect honestly on their choices while completing the assessment. Without honesty, there is no way to accurately understand what is lacking and what steps can be taken to bridge gaps. Like any tool that attempts to measure something as amorphous as integration with a specific cultural group, it is entirely possible for a person to stretch and to revise the facts of their experiences in order to achieve a score as high as possible, or to view their experiences in a way that reflects an idealized but unrealistic version of themselves. Leave the decision about how to complete the assessment up to each individual and do not challenge their authenticity.

Real learning will take place when participants honestly reflect. The assessment provides a rare opportunity for participants to think deeply about their self-selected cultural group so that they may learn something about themselves. There will be people that are incapable or unwilling to do this. There will be people in denial about the real situations in their work lives. But hearing their colleagues reflect or watching others in the organization make choices to bridge gaps may provide inspiration.

Rule 5. Provide an Alternative

For those uninterested in building bridges, provide another option for the *Us versus Them* assessment. In these cases, I always offer an alternative, lighthearted choice, like sports. For example, I will ask what the local professional sports team is and then ask who is that team's biggest rival. If the person is not a sports fan, I will ask them to complete the assessment using the local team as the cultural group. If they are a fan of the local team, I ask them to complete the assessment using the rival team as the cultural group. Either way, the participant can participate in the exercise on some level.

Administering the Assessment

The self-assessment (see Figure 6) is always completed by all people in a group at the same time, but the topic each person chooses should be up to the individual. In this way, even people who do not feel comfortable or do not want to do the hard work of self-reflection can understand the questions one might ask when engaged in the meaningful work of bridging gaps.

Finally, before distributing the assessment, you should demonstrate how to use the self-assessment by selecting an innocuous topic like sports or geographical rivalry. Many cities have a historical rival that may be taken seriously or not. In preparation for a training class in Dusseldorf, Germany, for example, I learned that a rivalry over beer exists between Dusseldorf and the city of Cologne, located just thirty minutes away across the Rhine River.

People in Dusseldorf tend to favor a dark beer called Altbier while folks in Cologne prefer a light beer called Kolsch. Ohio State versus Michigan. Marvel versus DC. Cats versus dogs. There is no end to *Us and Them* examples.

"US VS THEM" ASSESSMENT

For _____ (please identify a specific cultural group)

Have you ever met a person who identifies with this culture?	NO	YES
Have you ever had a substantial conversation (more than twenty minutes) with a person who identifies with this culture?	NO	YES
Have you ever shared a meal or beverage with a person who identifies with this culture?	NO	YES
Have you ever deliberately researched or learned about this culture's history or values? (Do not count nonvoluntary school assignments.)	NO	YES
Have you ever observed or participated in an important event (holiday, tradition, custom) that is particular to this culture?	NO	YES
Have you ever been in a group (class, sport, worship) that met voluntarily on a regular basis where people from this culture were the majority? (Do not count work or school.)	NO	YES
Have you ever invited someone who identifies with this culture to your home or did you go to their home?	NO	YES
Did you ever or do you now have a trusting relationship with someone who identifies with this culture?	NO	YES
Have you ever deliberately spent twenty-four consecutive hours (vacation, shared experience, business trip) with a person or family that identifies with this culture?	NO	YES
Did you ever or do you now have a trusting relationship with someone who identifies with this culture that has lasted over five years?	NO	YES

TOTALS – circle the number of YES answers on the line below.

0   1   2   3   4   5   6   7   8   9   10

FIGURE 6

Interpreting Results

Providing a general analysis of an assessment score is the equivalent of a screentime usage report that gives the user a metric to view their own behavior. A higher score is desirable, obviously. The higher the score, the less likely one is to have problems when interacting with the other culture. The lower the score, the more likely someone is to cause problems, especially unintentional misunderstandings due to lack of familiarity and lack of skill in accurately interpreting visible data. Use the Cross-Cultural Continuum image from Chapter 1, combined with a scale representing the number of *yes* answers, to illustrate this concept (see Figure 7).

CROSS-CULTURAL CONTINUUM

	NEGATIVE CULTURAL IMPACT		POSITIVE CULTURAL IMPACT		
GAME-CHANGING	CONSEQUENTIAL	INCONSEQUENTIAL	INCONSEQUENTIAL	CONSEQUENTIAL	GAME-CHANGING
Significant, long-term negative outcome.	Measurable negative outcome.	Not meaningful enough to cause measurable negative outcome.	Not meaningful enough to cause measurable positive outcome.	Measurable positive outcome.	Significant, long-term positive outcome.
Damage caused is difficult or impossible to repair. Some permanent damage is done.	Time required rebuilding goodwill and trust. Money spent on solutions. Formal apology necessary.	Resources are not impacted. Register a moment of confusion.	Resources are not impacted. Register a moment of connection or clarity.	Achieve improved communication and relationships. Trust and goodwill established.	Achieve excellent communication and teamwork in culturally diverse group.

0   1   2   3   4   5   6   7   8   9   10

FIGURE 7

Next, look at the assessment score in relation to a combined image of the four stages of trust from Chapter 3 and the iceberg image from Chapter 4. This provides an immediate visual reflection of WE-building progress (see Figure 8).

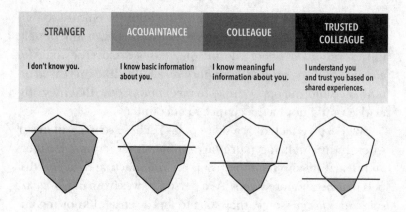

STRANGER	ACQUAINTANCE	COLLEAGUE	TRUSTED COLLEAGUE
I don't know you.	I know basic information about you.	I know meaningful information about you.	I understand you and trust you based on shared experiences.

FIGURE 8

Stage 1 is reflected by a score of zero. Without having any direct information or interpersonal contact with another person or cultural group, we are left with only superficial information that may or may not be accurate. Stereotypes flourish in Stage 1 and can be incredibly divisive.

Stage 2 is reflected by a score from 1–3, which occurs when some basic face-to-face interaction has occurred. Meeting someone from another cultural group and engaging with them for even a short time will provide basic data, which transforms a stranger into an acquaintance. Sharing a meal with someone could be anything from grabbing a quick coffee in the break room to an after-work dinner and drinks event. The depth and level of engagement will vary from person to person and event to event.

Sharing lunch at work is one of the best WE-building strategies, but also one of the most underutilized. Going out for drinks after work is not always an option, certainly not when social distancing is necessary. Spending money on dinner out can be a barrier. But everyone (or nearly everyone) eats lunch during the workday even when they are working from home. This means that time and money are already allocated to this activity. All that's required to elevate this activity to an effective WE-building experience is inviting a coworker from another culture to join you. Even with social distancing requirements, many people found ways to connect and in some cases discovered that the virtual meetups offered unexpected benefits like increased attendance and the opportunity to meet new people that they otherwise would not have a chance to encounter.[3]

Stage 3 is reflected by a score of 4–5. These scores will occur when individuals log more face-to-face interactions. Deliberately learning about a *them* group provides factual data and dispels inaccurate stereotypes. As a person moves from *acquaintance* stage to *colleague* stage, they start to feel a sense of knowing another person. This does not mean that people become friends. It does not mean that people like each other. It simply indicates that they have accrued more data and have gained deeper understanding of one another.

Reaching Stage 4 is the biggest challenge (see Figure 9). Most people stop in Stage 2 or Stage 3 because they don't think about it or don't want to put forth the effort to reach *trusted colleague* stage. But reaching trusted colleague stage is essential for

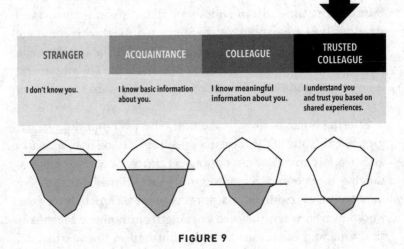

STRANGER	ACQUAINTANCE	COLLEAGUE	TRUSTED COLLEAGUE
I don't know you.	I know basic information about you.	I know meaningful information about you.	I understand you and trust you based on shared experiences.

FIGURE 9

leaders who want to limit gaps and enhance productivity in the workplace. There are no shortcuts to getting from Stage 3 to Stage 4. It will require time and effort.

The goal of WE-building is not to become friends with people from different backgrounds (though that does sometimes occur). The goals are to narrow gaps so that we operate with full understanding of others, not superficial stereotypes, and to eliminate costly damage to corporations and individuals inside those organizations. The more people who reach Stage 4 Trusted Colleague relationships with others, the better functioning the organization will be.

What Score Is Reasonable?

I once worked with a successful company in Texas that had just launched its first international venture in Japan. The people were motivated and determined to succeed. In over a dozen private conversations with leadership in the company, people told me that the success of the international venture was a very, very high priority. "It's a ten on a scale of one to ten," the vice president told me. But when I asked these same people to measure their level of integration with Japan, no one had a score over 3. When I conducted a training session in their Dallas office, I asked them to tell me the names of three colleagues in Japan. Not one single person could do it. I was shocked. One senior executive wanted credit for liking Japanese food. Sure, he had gone to many sushi restaurants but had barely paid attention to the real Japanese colleagues he and his company were depending on for success overseas. Perhaps he knew the difference between *chutoro* and *otoro*, two types of tuna, but he had not deliberately developed a trusted relationship with a real person from Japan. It was hard to understand how they all claimed this venture was of the highest priority but none of them had done any cultural work to enhance its success.

Exercise to Document Group Results

Needs: one large easel with paper, stickers, one copy of the *Us versus Them* assessment for each participant.

Draw a 1–10 scale on a large sheet of paper on an easel that looks like this:

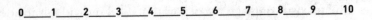

Give each person a sticker and explain that they will be asked to place their sticker on the scale to indicate their score. To demonstrate, place a sticker near the 2, 5, and 9 marks. These stickers, representing fake scores, will remain on the scale until after everyone has marked their own score with a sticker. Before having participants actually place their stickers on the scale, turn the easel around so that their placement on the scale will be hidden from view for the rest of the participants. Then invite people to place their stickers on the scale one at a time. By having a few fake scores on the scale from the beginning, people can keep their scores anonymous. If someone is embarrassed about their score or would prefer not to make it public, they can place their sticker after others have gone or not place their sticker at all. Once everyone has had a chance to place their sticker, remove the three fake stickers placed at 2, 5, and 9, then turn the easel around to reveal the results.

Seeing that others have a low score can be comforting to people who have not yet engaged in building their knowledge about a *them* group. At the same time, seeing that some people in the group have high scores can be inspiring because it demonstrates that anyone can get a high score.

How to Leverage Different Scores Within One Group

After members of a group have completed the self-assessment, provide a general analysis of the scores. Tell everyone that the goal for each person in the group is to reach a score of at least 4 over time. If someone has a low score today, that is acceptable. But emphasize that, three months from now, having the same low score will be inadequate.

Then, in an open discussion, ask for volunteers to share about their own experiences. Select a question from the self-assessment and ask if anyone answered *yes* and would like to share.

Emphasize that this is voluntary. Keep it positive and brief. The point is to utilize the firsthand experience of people in the group to provide real-life examples to teach others how to increase their scores. Real-life narratives from people inside the group tend to be interesting and are golden learning opportunities.

When Someone Has a Perfect Score

Achieving a score of 10 is great and rare. There will be people who have successfully bridged specific gaps in their profes-sional lives. People who have scored a 10 can be highly effec-tive resources for others if they feel comfortable sharing. Their personal narratives about how, when, and with whom they gained firsthand experience are one of the most effective learning tools.

When someone has achieved a 10, they can be challenged to select a new *them* group and start over. Once someone has the experience of building connection with a specific cultural group, they are often able to quickly adapt to bridge with other groups.

HOW TO USE THE SELF-ASSESSMENT RESULTS

The *Us versus Them* self-assessment is one measure of a person's level of integration with people outside their self-identified cul-tural group. It is a simple measurement and not intended to be comprehensive.

Here are three valuable outcomes.

Number One: Action Plan for Improvement

The *Us versus Them* assessment provides immediate feedback for anyone interested in bridging a specific gap because each question on the assessment is a potential action item. It can become a goal to transform each question that was answered with a *no* into a *yes*. Even if a person scores 0 on the assessment, there is a built-in solution to improving their score.

The first question on the self-assessment asks if a person has ever met a person from the other culture. Question 4 asks if the person has deliberately researched or learned about the other culture's history or values. If the answer is *no*, the solution is to open up a computer and type in a simple question such as "What is the history of X?" or "What are the cultural values of Y?"

Number Two: Conversion Experiences

Increasing face-to-face encounters with another cultural group can position people to have conversion experiences that can fundamentally transform the way they view a *them* group.

People who have engaged fully in the WE-building experience report having encounters that completely change the way they looked at a specific person or group, especially when those groups had previously been viewed in negative terms. These types of conversion experiences are not surprising to anyone engaged in the work of building connections. These are predictable occurrences that people seem surprised to encounter. History is full of meaningful episodes when a specific event or encounter led to someone rethinking old narratives and negative stereotypes.

The book *Best of Enemies*, by Osha Grey Davidson (and the movie by the same name), documents what happened in North Carolina between two unlikely allies. It is the true story of Ann

Atwater, a Black activist and single mother of two children, and C. P. Ellis, a white leader of the KKK and father of three children, who were selected to lead an integration initiative for the public schools in Durham.

Atwater and C. P., as he was called, had been on opposite sides of many arguments in Durham and were as surprised as others when they each were asked to be representatives at an intense ten-day process of community meetings called a charrette. The goal of the charrette was to come up with a proposal and vote on whether to integrate the schools. Over a hundred people participated. Atwater and C. P., enemies in every way, were forced to speak and listen to one another. They shared meals and spent hours of time in face-to-face meetings. They learned many things about each other that they had not known previously.

Atwater learned that C. P. had a son with disabilities. C. P. learned that Atwater had quit working as a maid because her employer considered Ann to be too outspoken. Throughout the ten-day process, they began to see each other differently and began to redraw the lines of belonging. As they did this, C. P. in particular began to see how he shared important factors with Ann Atwater, including the fact that they both suffered from being poor in Durham and that they both wanted better educational opportunities for their children. At the end of the ten-day period, C. P. Ellis disavowed his KKK membership and sided with Atwater on the decision to integrate the public schools. It was a dramatic conversion that occurred because they engaged in face-to-face interactions of increasing depth.

But the story didn't end there. In a documentary made when C. P. and Ann were both in their seventies, they spoke of their continued connection and the true friendship that developed, lasting for thirty years.

Number Three: Redrawing the Lines of Belonging

As we increase our engagement with another person or another cultural group, we will see invisible data. We will discover common factors that reside below the surface and find things we have in common with people who might look or sound different. We might discover, for example, that two people who don't look the same have the same love of cooking or that a common socio-economic status is a much more significant factor than racial difference. Finding these common points provides an anchor for redrawing the lines of belonging, which is an essential part of building a WE culture in any organization.

Leaders demonstrate how to redraw the lines of belonging by seeking and emphasizing broad points of connection. Rather than developing relationships based on race and ethnicity, as many people in their company did, LaVonda and Masa bonded over their experience of being parents. Rather than thinking of people as Muslims versus Christians, leaders can redraw a larger circle around people of faith.

Recently, in a group of about fifteen people from four countries who spoke four different native languages, I asked each person to introduce themselves with the usual professional information, including what type of work they did and their work history. I also asked people to share one invisible detail about themselves that they felt comfortable sharing with the group. The first person was a young woman who shared that she had recently gotten a puppy and that the experience had been a lot of work but also very joyful.

Then, to my surprise, every single person in the group made a comment related to dogs. Some shared that they, too, had a dog. One person shared that he had always wanted a dog. One person in the group even shared that his beloved dog had recently died. His was a brave moment of personal sharing that connected everyone in the room.

If you are a manager in a factory with a large population of people who practice a different religion, or you are a professional in a field that has historically been nearly all white, or you are involved in an international venture in a country you know little about, then conducting an *Us versus Them* assessment for yourself and facilitating this process with your team will start a WE-building process that can positively transform your organization.

6

CREATE A GAP-CLOSING ACTION PLAN

SEVERAL YEARS AGO, I was invited to do a WE-building workshop in Sao Paulo, Brazil, a place I had never before visited. Like most professionals planning to work in an unfamiliar foreign country for the first time, I was aware that the *Us and Them* gap was wide and deep. Since I had never before traveled to Brazil and had no close relationships with anyone from Brazil, I assessed that my level of integration was extremely low. So it was clear that I had to make a plan of action to improve my knowledge.

This was a fairly high-stakes opportunity for me since I work on my own and the client has offices all over the world. If the job was successful, it might mean more international work. If the job didn't go well, it might mean fewer jobs with the U.S. locations that I already had.

My action plan started with about two hours online researching Brazilian business culture. I learned that the *okay* sign is the equivalent of giving someone the middle finger and that many people in Brazil view time as flexible, so I should not consider it unprofessional if people arrived late to a meeting. Kissing is common as a greeting, and dressing well was considered important. I spent fifteen minutes or so learning some basic phrases in Portuguese including how to introduce myself. I gathered all this cultural data in a short amount of time for free.

Then I met with an acquaintance, Iara, who had grown up in Brazil. As I started to ask her about what adjustments I should make in my PowerPoint presentation, she said, "What about your shoes?"

I was confused. My concern was the PowerPoint deck and whether or not I should add Portuguese to the slides, or if I should start the training session with an inconsequential activity in case some people arrived late. I had not given any thought to my wardrobe.

I pulled my feet from under the table and showed her the shoes I wore every day: a pair of black leather, nearly orthopedic, loafers that easily could have been mistaken for men's shoes. I knew they were not fashionable, but since I stand when I work and because I had knee and foot pain for years, I almost always wore these unattractively supportive shoes. These shoes would never win any fashion awards, but I knew that my U.S. clients judged me based on the content of my presentation much more than the stylishness of my footwear.

Iara took one look at these gender-neutral, black loafers and said, "No! You cannot wear these shoes. Everyone will assume you are a nun!"

I glanced at Iara's feet under the table and noticed that she was wearing a delicate pair of wedge sandals with an open toe. The heel was higher than any heels I had worn in five years.

Iara then explained that many professional Brazilians care greatly about appearance because it is considered an indication of level of success. Hearing this from her confirmed one of the data points I had read online. "Brand-name clothing, handbags, and shoes are very popular in Brazil," she explained. Then she told me about a time early in her career when she rented an expensive car just to drive to a job interview, knowing that the kind of car she drove would make an impression. She got the job.

On Iara's advice, I took a pair of low one-inch-heel, open-toe, sling-back shoes to Brazil. On my first day of work in Sao Paulo, wearing my nicest silk suit, I carried the sling-back shoes to the office and quickly changed into them just before making my introductions. Later, as I was giving my presentation behind a large podium, I was able to switch back to a lower pair of very comfortable slip-on shoes so that by the end of the day I could still stand without pain. That evening, at a cocktail party given for all sixty participants in the Sao Paulo office, I switched shoes again. When I was asked to give a few impromptu remarks on a stage in front of the entire group, I walked up to the stage looking like I was going to a job interview. I greeted everyone in Portuguese and shared some remarks. No one mistook me for a nun.

Without action, there can be no meaningful progress.

BUILDING A GAP-CLOSING PLAN

Any action plan needs to be proportional to the gap you and your team are trying to close. In my case in Brazil, the stakes were consequential for maintaining my reputation and securing future work opportunities. Before building an action plan, refer back to the Cross-Cultural Continuum to assess how serious negative consequences resulting from the gap would be.

CROSS-CULTURAL CONTINUUM

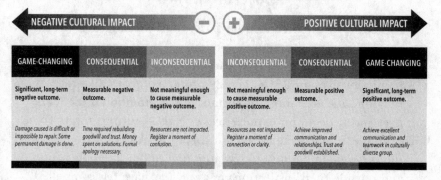

| NEGATIVE CULTURAL IMPACT | | | | | POSITIVE CULTURAL IMPACT | |

GAME-CHANGING	CONSEQUENTIAL	INCONSEQUENTIAL	INCONSEQUENTIAL	CONSEQUENTIAL	GAME-CHANGING
Significant, long-term negative outcome.	Measurable negative outcome.	Not meaningful enough to cause measurable negative outcome.	Not meaningful enough to cause measurable positive outcome.	Measurable positive outcome.	Significant, long-term positive outcome.
Damage caused is difficult or impossible to repair. Some permanent damage is done.	*Time required rebuilding goodwill and trust. Money spent on solutions. Formal apology necessary.*	*Resources are not impacted. Register a moment of confusion.*	*Resources are not impacted. Register a moment of connection or clarity.*	*Achieve improved communication and relationships. Trust and goodwill established.*	*Achieve excellent communication and teamwork in culturally diverse group.*

FIGURE 1

In the previous case studies, we can see a range from inconsequential to game-changing examples. In real life, there may be a situation involving a potential generation gap, like the one Justin was trying to bridge in his department. If there have been no formal complaints and measurable outcomes, then this situation would fit into the *inconsequential* category. Sometimes a specific *Us and Them* dynamic between employees will never turn into anything more than one colleague complaining about another's habits. But any culture gap has the potential to increase in severity, and for this reason, managers should remain watchful.

The *consequential* category generally includes situations where a lot of resources are at stake—like Janice, managing a new call center in the Philippines, and Michelle, managing a workforce in the United States, where there is friction between people from different religious or ethnic groups. Initiating a new project in another country will have an impact on the revenue of the organization. Managing ethnic and religious differences in the workplace is high stakes because they are both EEOC legally protected groups. These are also important because of the culture divides they represent in the workforce.

GAME-CHANGING

In real life, an inconsequential situation can turn into a game-changing situation very quickly. This is particularly important for managers to pay attention to if the *Us and Them* dynamic involves an EEOC legally protected group like race or religion. It is even more important to pay attention if the manager has little to no experience with this cultural topic. For example, many white leaders in corporate America are facing the very real imperative to pay attention to Black people inside and outside their institutions in a way few have felt compelled to do prior to the Black Lives Matter movement. This is a game-changing time and topic. Yet the reality is that the very people tasked with making decisions about diversity, equity and inclusion policies may themselves have little experience even talking about race.

WE-building Solutions

The WE-building Solutions Worksheet is a tool to prompt actionable ideas representing three levels of effort—safe, challenging, and radical. Whether a culture gap is inconsequential, consequential, or game-changing, the solutions can be reached by using the worksheet to generate ideas.

WE-BUILDING SOLUTION WORKSHEET

	SAFE— private, no vulnerability, no risk, usually low cost	CHALLENGING— face-to-face interaction, some vulnerability, some risk	RADICAL— ongoing face-to-face interaction of increasing depth, could make you uncomfortable, will feel risky
Individual			
Organizational			
Physical Space/ Policy/Visual Messaging			

The Solution Worksheet

There are nine categories of action for any *Us versus Them* gap. Safe Individual Actions, Challenging Individual Actions and Radical Individual Actions, Safe Organizational Actions, Challenging Organizational Actions and Radical Organizational Actions, Safe Physical Space/Policy Actions, Challenging Physical Space/Policy Actions, and Radical Physical Space/Policy Actions.

As indicated on the worksheet, some actions are suitable for an individual to take while others require an organizational approach. In addition, the policy/physical space category is a bit of a catchall so it can be used for a variety of ideas. For example, changes to seating arrangements or wall decorations belong in this category.

One client in New York deliberately redesigned an office space to foster interaction. Prior to the redesign, there were small closet-size pantries throughout the building where one or two people could stand while making a cup of coffee. The redesign created one larger gathering area with booths, a foosball table, and open space where more than thirty people could gather. In London, where pub culture is active, several clients purposely built bars with beer and other alcoholic beverages that could easily be accessed on certain days and for celebrations. A client in Ireland created a photo board imposed on a world map so when colleagues from other international offices came to visit they were invited to take an instamatic photo and attach it to the wall. A client in Tokyo with Muslim partners from the Middle East converted an empty office into a prayer room with an arrow pointing toward Mecca and a clock for monitoring prayer times.

Generating Solutions

The way to use this worksheet is to brainstorm possible solutions in as many categories as possible. This is a tool for individuals and groups to use as a framework for generating lots of ideas without concern for cost, effort and time. It is not important to worry about fitting each idea neatly into one category or another. It is important to think widely and broadly and in relation to the specific *Us versus Them* dynamic at hand.

Let's take a look at the three categories of action: safe actions, challenging actions, and radical actions.

Any WE-actions will contribute toward building a WE culture.

SAFE ACTIONS

Safe actions are ones you can do in private and do not require vulnerability. Many safe actions cost nothing but time. They are a good starting point for consequential and game-changing gaps. Taking safe actions will provide visible information about a target cultural group. The two hours I spent researching Brazilian business culture online is an example of this. Reading articles or books, viewing websites, or listening to podcasts about specific cultural groups are all easily accessible safe actions.

Online Tools

Several online resources have launched in the past few years to support professionals across the globe by providing country-specific information. Companies pay for a membership that allows their employees to access cultural data at any time. These sites are rich with country-specific information on making a good impression, forms of address, dress codes, business etiquette, structure of meetings and presentations, managing relationships, as well as overviews of the local economy, business, and politics, society, diversity, language, geography, travel, and more. Some sites offer learning paths and personal profile assessments on topics such as risk, communication, and decisionmaking tendencies.

Danger of Stereotypes

This is a good time to remind ourselves that individuals who identify with a particular generational cultural group or religious group or any defined cultural group *do not share* all cultural characteristics. Sharing an identity factor with another person (for example, you age, your race or your religion) does not mean that you share all other values and behaviors. Cultural tendencies exist when many people who share an identity factor also share a value or behavior. For example, many, but not all, Japanese people bow when they greet a stranger. Many, not all, Muslim people avoid eating pork as a religious practice. These are examples of cultural tendencies.

Stereotypes and cultural tendencies are similar in that they are both shortcuts to understanding another person or cultural group. Like stereotypes, cultural tendencies can be dangerous if they lead to uninformed assumptions about groups or individuals. Remember while doing your research that descriptions of any cultural tendency should not be interpreted to mean that any particular person who identifies with that cultural group is in agreement with that norm.

Safe Action Examples

In some low-stakes situations, like being prepared for a one-time business meeting with someone new, safe actions are enough. But generally speaking, safe actions alone are insufficient because they do not promote progress along the Trust-Building Scale.

Let's look at a concrete example. On December 18, 2015, at the Cargill Meat Solutions beef-processing center in Fort Morgan, Colorado, a supervisor denied a request from several Somali Muslim employees to use their break time to pray as they had done, with permission, for many years.[1] Somali Muslims had become a growing presence in Fort Morgan since 2005. Within a few years, they made up over 10 percent of the Cargill Meat Solutions workforce. Without any explanation, the shift supervisor incorrectly told the employees that the company policy that allowed them to pray during their break time (in order to reasonably accommodate their religious practice) had changed. Several years earlier, the company had set up a "reflection room" for prayers, and by all accounts, the arrangement was working to everyone's satisfaction. But on this day, the supervisor said no. About twenty workers staged an immediate walkout, which was joined by more than a hundred others in the subsequent days. On December 23, the company fired 150 employees due to their failure to show up for work for three days, during which they protested.

What happened at Cargill that December day? Was the supervisor new? Was it someone who disliked Muslims? Was this a coordinated effort by management? Or did this episode occur because the supervisor was uncertain about the company policy? The supervisor may have simply not understood the importance that salah, prayer has for many Muslim people. Rather than take cultural data into consideration, this supervisor made a decision that felt right at the moment.

Did Cargill management prepare this supervisor and others by taking safe actions to help them manage cultural differences, or were their workers left to figure things out on their own? Whatever the cause of the supervisor's decision that day, the result was a cultural catastrophe in the form of unexpected work disruption, negative publicity, low morale, and a $1.7 million settlement. These outcomes might have been avoided had anyone at the plant taken just a few simple safe actions.

Entering "Understanding Islamic workplace culture" into a web browser results in over two million hits in .57 seconds. One of these is an article in *Forbes* magazine titled, "Five Tips for Supporting Muslims in the Workplace." It would cost nothing for a manager at Cargill Meat Solutions to research and read this article. Anyone who took even ten minutes to try to understand this topic would have learned about the importance of prayers during the workday.

What if you are white like Matthew the pilot or one of thousands of white leaders confronting your own relationship to Black people and Black culture? What can you do to bridge this very high-stakes gap? Unlike a generational gap that has always confronted senior people, or a country-specific gap, race represents one of the most important and historically relevant *Us and Them* divides in the United States.

One choice is to basically ignore the situation and persuade yourself that the best thing to do with regard to race is to treat everyone equally. This colorblind approach has been used for decades. It is the standard go-to position of many well-meaning yet benignly uninformed white people.

I know this is true because I've been one of those well-meaning, benignly uninformed white people. I, too, subscribed to the common refrain, "Why can't I treat everyone as human?"

But I've learned through my own WE-building efforts that this approach does not work. First, pretending not to see a person's race or acknowledge their ethnicity means ignoring what is often an important factor of another person's identity and corresponding lived experience. A 2019 PEW research study revealed that 74 percent of Black adults, 59 percent of Hispanics, and 56 percent of Asians say that their race is very important to their overall identity.[2] When we don't see race, we fail to see an essential aspect of another person. If you do not see race there is no chance to see and dismantle racism.

Second, acting colorblind results in defaulting to a white-dominant norm. As we will look at in more detail in Chapter 8,

culturally dominant norms come with assumptions about behavior, such that the slightest deviation from the dominant
norm triggers suspicion and negative responses, ranging from
discomfort to suspicion to fear. We have seen repeated examples
in the news of white people endangering Black lives with
their inaccurate accusations. Defaulting to white cultural norms
results in the criminalization of Black people doing regular
things like having a BBQ, golfing, or lawfully driving down
the road.

So, what is a guy like Matthew to do? He does not see himself
as racist. He's never deliberately taken discriminatory action
against a Black person. He considers himself openminded. Matthew is the kind of guy that would most likely speak up if he saw
someone else being overtly racist. But outside of a few mandated
training sessions at work, Matthew has never thought deeply
about the experience of being Black in America or being Black
in the airline industry. He doesn't have to. (Though I can assure
you that the Black flight attendant has had to think about it in-
tensely and frequently.) Until people like Matthew, and me,
start taking active steps ourselves to narrow the racial gap, foundational change will not occur.

Not taking action is morally wrong. It is also a risky business
choice. Chances are high that Matthew and people like him are
going to have more and more interaction at work with non-
white people. The more informed and familiar Matthew is with
people outside his comfortable white world, the better prepared
he will be for the future.

The racial gap in America remains deep and wide because
people like Matthew and others in the dominant white culture
have not progressed along the Trust-Building Scale or taken
action to deliberately redraw the lines around a broad multiracial coalition. To the contrary—efforts to maintain and
deepen the racial divide are strengthened by unjust legislation,
racist policies like gerrymandering and voter suppression, biased law enforcement, disproportionate sentencing standards

and incarceration rates, and antagonistic actions of white supremacist organizations.

Once someone like Matthew becomes aware of the extreme gap that exists, there are many safe choices for him to make. Safe choices for any white person who wants to narrow this critical gap include taking the advice of comedian W. Kamau Bell, who writes about race in his book, *The Awkward Thoughts of W. Kamau Bell*. He directly advises white people to do more than block their racist Facebook friends. He writes, "Read books—actually read Ta-Nehisi Coates's *Between the World and Me* instead of just putting it on your shelf. Read Michelle Alexander's *The New Jim Crow*. Go to websites like The Root, Colorlines, Very Smart Brothas, Blavity."

―――――

Challenging actions may cause discomfort.

―――――

CHALLENGING ACTIONS

Challenging actions require human interaction. *Us and Them* gaps require individuals to engage in face-to-face interactions. As such, they are riskier and require a certain level of personal vulnerability. By engaging in challenging actions, you will learn both visible and invisible information that will help you navigate any *Us and Them* situation. My encounter with Iara was a challenging action because it involved face-to-face interaction with someone I had met only once. These types of encounters make up the fundamental substance of WE-building.

Face-to-face interactions of increasing depth are essential to any type of meaningful change. Unfortunately, these interactions are absent from most types of corporate diversity training. Online training can never replace the real work of engaging with another human, just like watching a lot of football will not turn you into a good quarterback. Online training can provide useful information that can contribute to the goal, but only if a person takes action.

Challenging actions require choices like inviting someone to lunch knowing that they might say no. Most people do not like rejection and so we avoid situations that *might* involve rejection. Facilitate these potentially vulnerable situations by advising your employees to follow two rules to increase the odds that others will respond in a positive way.

1. **Be genuine.** If you are taking action to relieve guilt or comply with a diversity rule, your actions will be superficial at best and offensive at worst. There is no benefit in searching for connection unless you are authentically interested in forming a relationship.
2. **Be humble.** The best way to demonstrate humility is to listen and learn. This can be difficult for people who identify with a cultural majority and who may be used to the role of speaker. But listening will result in useful data. It is not necessary to like or agree with everything you hear, but it is necessary to understand.

I have never once been rejected when I genuinely and humbly said to another person, "I would like to learn more about your culture if you would be willing to share." Many people are proud of their heritage and background, and if they feel that you are sincere, they are willing and even happy to help you learn.

When I wanted to speak one-on-one with someone who knew about Brazil, I started asking around my social network. Iara is the wife of an old work associate of my husband. She and I had met once in passing many years prior. When I explained to her via email my goal of understanding Brazilian business culture more deeply, she was happy to meet me.

Challenging actions range from no or low financial cost to medium cost, but they always involve face-to-face interaction, which may include virtual interactions. Challenging actions endeavor to advance people along the Trust-Building Scale. Some of these actions are less risky, like participating in a webinar or making a trip to a specific restaurant or grocery. More risky actions include attending a community meeting, visiting a congregation, or participating in a university lecture on a specific topic in person. Inviting someone to deliberately share time with you, like having coffee or lunch together, or scheduling a virtual conversation about a specific topic, are examples of challenging actions.

In Justin's journey to understand the generational *Us and Them* gap, safe action may be all he needs to take. But taking more challenging action will not hurt. Justin is a manager confronting generational friction with an employee from Generation Z, but eventually Generation Alpha will join the workforce. It is good practice for Justin and others in similar roles to understand the cultural norms of people that identify with all these generational groups.

Challenging actions for Justin might include deliberately having lunch with colleagues from the same generational group as Sophie. But Justin should not limit his encounters to people from work. He can look for opportunities outside the workplace, like joining a hobby or sports-affiliated group that attracts a younger generation, in order to advance his experience.

Let's consider a challenging action that Janice and Michelle could take. In both situations, they are seeking face-to-face interactions with a specific cultural group. Visiting a specialty grocery store or a restaurant is an easy challenging action. Another option is attending a culture-specific event or lecture at a local university.

Food is a great connector. Recently, several groups have leveraged this factor as a way to bridge culture gaps in communities. Tanabel and League of Kitchens are two organizations in

New York City through which immigrant women provide cooking lessons and/or meals inside their homes for a fee.[3] For the price of dining at a restaurant, someone like Janice or Michelle can engage face-to-face with people from a target culture and enjoy a good meal. Across the country, various organizations are using food and shared meals as a vehicle for connecting across difference. These include Cooking as a First Language in Tupelo, Mississippi; Sanctuary Kitchen in New Haven, Connecticut; The United Tastes of America in Montclair, New Jersey; Local Abundance Kitchen in Cleveland, Ohio; and Mera Kitchen Collective in Baltimore, Maryland.

Going to a new place or starting a conversation with someone from another culture is difficult for many people. Most likely there will be some unease involved because you are reaching out in new ways and you won't be able to predict exactly what will transpire. Building resilience to handle this discomfort is important.

If I had been a manager at Cargill Meat Solutions in Fort Morgan, Colorado, a challenging action would have been to seek out a Muslim person in the community and ask to have a conversation. Approaching a local mosque could have been another potential rescource. A quick online search shows that two cross-cultural groups, One Fort Morgan and Fort Morgan Cultures United for Progress, exist for the very purpose of these types of conversations and encounters.[4]

What if you are trying to build a multiracial social group? What if you are white and every important relationship in your life is also white? Matthew works in an industry that is overwhelmingly white and lives around other white people. What kind of challenging action can he take? How can he increase his face-to-face interactions with people in a racial group to which he might feel that he has limited access?

Poet and activist David Budbill, who died in 2016, faced a similar dilemma when he left New York City, where he had been deeply engaged in racial justice work, in the 1960s.[5] After moving to rural Vermont, he felt conflicted about his choice to live in a place with very few Black people. In response, he adopted what he called a personal affirmative action program. "If you want to live an integrated life, as a white person, you have to consciously and deliberately establish relationships with Black people. You can't just sit around and hope they will show up on your doorstep. I don't mean you have to befriend people just because they are Black. But sometimes, when you meet a Black person you might like to get to know better, you have to reach out and work at it. Otherwise, you'll miss a friendship that you might have had naturally in a country that was truly integrated. You have to make this artificial effort—to begin with, at least—because our lives are artificially segregated."

Author and Georgetown Law professor Sheryll Cashin provides practical advice in her book *Loving*. She writes that white people need to develop cultural dexterity, "an enhanced capacity for intimate connections with people outside one's own tribe, for seeing and accepting difference rather than demanding assimilation to an unspoken norm of whiteness."[6]

Activist and author Reverend Michael Eric Dyson suggests in his book *Tears We Cannot Stop: A Sermon to White America* that white people hire more Black people, pay them more, and even tip better. He calls it an IRA, Individual Reparations Account, to redistribute financial resources. He also calls on white people to make more friends with Black people. "The more Black folks you know, the less likely you are to stereotype us. The less likely you are to stereotype us, the less likely you are to fear us. The less you fear us, the less likely you are to want to hurt us, or to accept our hurt as the price of your safekeeping."[7]

What would this actually look like for a guy like Matthew? How does a middle-aged white man make Black friends? They are not going to show up on his doorstep.

Attempting this will be hard—that's why it's in the challenging category. Matthew will likely feel incredibly awkward and uncomfortable. To connect with Black folks means that Matthew needs to deliberately look for Black people in his orbit: for example, at his church and other places in his community. The process starts with learning people's names, having small talk conversations, and eventually sharing a meal. It means making small adjustments so that his proximity to Black people increases, which will increase his opportunity to interact. If Matthew doesn't have any Black members at his church, it means he might have to go to a Black church within his own denomination, as Reverend Dyson suggests. It might mean joining a choir or softball team or community group where Black people participate, as Sheryll Cashin suggests. It might mean going to parent meetings at your children's school or attending community events or other public gatherings and deliberately sitting with or near people of color.

Challenging actions must occur for real progress to take place. Some of these choices will lead to deeper conversations and genuine relationship development. Over time, if a deliberate and sincere effort is made, then progress along the Trust-Building Scale will take place. The transformations can be astonishing.

In his book, *The Awkward Thoughts of W. Kamau Bell*, Bell describes his white grandfather-in-law as a Fox News addict who was not enthusiastic when W. Kamau Bell married his granddaughter.

But, over time, this elderly Sicilian-American watched Kamau work hard to make a living and a life with his granddaughter. They brought two children into the world and, most importantly, Kamau writes, "I kept showing up." Then one day, years later, the grandfather said to Kamau, "I keep telling my friends that I can't keep up with my grandson. He's all over the place." It took a moment for Kamau to realize that the grandfather was speaking of him. "For a kid who grew up without any grandfathers it was a big deal."[8]

————

Radical actions are not necessary for
WE-building but will accelerate learning.

————

RADICAL ACTIONS

Radical actions are extreme steps designed to quickly improve knowledge and interaction. In some cases, radical actions are not necessary. Instead, consistent challenging actions will lead to foundational and meaningful change. But in some situations, either the stakes of the enterprise are so high or the gap so deep that radical actions are the best solution.

Radical actions speed up the process of Trust-Building. These actions require more vulnerability, a higher level of discomfort, and, sometimes, higher cost. The discomfort people feel will likely dissipate over time, but it is almost always an inherent part of taking radical steps. Individual radical actions require humility. They can be intense but will fundamentally change the understanding of *them*.

Radical organizational actions usually cost money and require a change from customary patterns, such as hiring or promoting historically marginalized people into positions where they have a strong voice. I have witnessed the positive impact these radical actions can make, one of which happened at Honda years after I left.

Like many foreign-based companies in America, most of the senior positions at Honda of America were initially held by Japanese people. The reason for this was language as well as the strong connections the leaders had with other Japanese people in Japan. In the 1990s, Honda of America Manufacturing, Inc., located in Marysville, Ohio, designed a multi-year, multimillion-dollar operation called the North American Task Group, whose mission was to send dozens of American workers and their families to Japan for several years at a time. American employees, their spouses, and their children lived and worked in Japan. They learned Japanese, made Japanese friends, learned how to cook Japanese food, and traveled throughout the country. Several dozen key employees, including a former colleague of mine named Tom Shoupe, participated in this program. The idea was to radically accelerate the knowledge, communication, and relationships of key English-speaking staff so that the entire organization could grow more quickly. Today, some of those North American Task Group participants are leaders of the organization, including Tom, who is now the Executive Vice President and COO of Honda of America.

If you are managing a generational gap, radical actions could be making a long-term commitment to join a group where you are the only participant not part of the generational group. If you are managing an international or ethnic gap, it could mean sponsoring a travel exchange or language class or creating a mentor program where participants make an ongoing commitment to one another.

One Christian group I worked with in Columbus, Ohio, organized a visit to a local mosque. Another organization with a new branch in Indonesia sent American employees for six-month rotations. A white person who wants to take radical action could take Reverend Dyson's advice to mentor Black kids, join a racial justice group, and participate in racial justice protests.

Step 1. Small Group Work

Using the WE-building Solutions Worksheet introduced earlier in this chapter, leaders provide a framework and an in-person or virtual group opportunity to complete the worksheet together. Small groups of individuals generate their action ideas and then share these ideas with the larger group.

WE-BUILDING SOLUTION WORKSHEET

	SAFE—private, no vulnerability, no risk, usually low cost	CHALLENGING—face-to-face interaction, some vulnerability, some risk	RADICAL—ongoing face-to-face interaction of increasing depth, could make you uncomfortable, will feel risky
Individual			
Organizational			
Physical Space/ Policy/Visual Messaging			

Management should not dictate solutions: They should challenge employees to honestly and genuinely confront issues. They should support employees on the front lines as they come up with their own solutions and participate in initiatives that make sense. Forced WE-building mandates are less likely to succeed because of lack of buy-in. Demonstrate the importance of WE-building by making commitments yourself.

Common *Them*

When an organization has a common target cultural group, such as Cargill Meat Solutions trying to bridge the gap with Muslim employees, or a French company operating in the United States, or a Jewish school trying to make Asian students feel more welcome, the gap can be addressed as a common one. But in other situations, the organization is working to build a more diverse environment and is not focused on a specific group. In these cases, individuals will choose their own *them* culture group.

Brainstorming

Ask small employee groups (between three and five people) to create ideas in every category during a twenty-to-thirty-minute period by answering the question: *What actions would foster a WE-culture?* Encourage employees to think broadly and without concern for budget and time restraints in order to generate creative solutions. Obviously, in the real world, budget and time are big constraints. But coming up with expensive or time-consuming solutions often provides access to ideas that can be adapted to real life.

When a group does not have a common *them* group but is working, for example, to diversify its homogeneous membership or population, the first step is to complete the solution worksheet on an individual basis rather than small group basis.

Step 2. Sharing Actions

Following the small group work, instruct each group to report their results and have a facilitator produce a master list (for Individual Action, Organizational Action, and Physical/Policy Actions). Use large easel paper and markers for easy sharing. One large easel paper will represent each of the three categories of action. Have the facilitator edit duplicate ideas. At the end of this step, the participants will have a master list of potential actions in each of the categories.

Step 3. Prioritizing

Ask participants to prioritize their top two action items. Give each person two stickers, which represent one vote each. Then, ask participants to vote for their highest priority items by placing a sticker next to the listed action. Complete this step in ten to fifteen minutes, depending on the size of the group. At the end of this step, you'll have an indication of the group's highest priorities, which can serve as a road map for action to bridge the *Us versus Them* issue.

Imagining New Solutions

If I had worked with a company that had a Muslim versus non-Muslim dynamic, I could image that employees there might have generated a list that looked like this.

	SAFE	CHALLENGING	RADICAL
Individual	Research online "how to support Muslim employees" YouTube practice saying "As-salamu Alaikum," the traditional greeting of Muslim people Read about etiquette with Muslim people	Say "As-salamu Alaikum," which means "May peace be upon you," to a colleague you know is Muslim (do not assume someone is Muslim) Purposely have lunch with Muslim employees	Visit a local mosque to learn about the religious customs and values of Muslim people
Organizational	Prepare a fact-sheet on Islam and Muslims in America to better understand their cultures, religious practices, holiday observances, tips on how to interact with Muslim colleagues and how to support and show solidarity to your Muslim colleagues during the month of Ramadan	Provide in-house training, invite speakers, sponsor culture opportunities for all Poll employees anonymously for feedback Start an ERG for Muslim employees	Hire advisor, contract with consultant for advice and training Include Muslim representatives in key decisions Promote Muslim employees to positions of power
Physical Space/ Policy/Visual Messaging	Create a prayer room Clock to monitor salah, prayer time Arrow toward Mecca Provide Halal food	Inform all employees about Ramadan including greetings to the Muslim peers such as Ramadan Mubarak (Blessed Ramadan) or Ramadan Kareem (May Ramadan be generous to you) Post Ramadan schedule	Adjust work schedule around Ramadan schedule Give Muslims the two Eid days as paid holidays like Christmas or New Years

	SAFE	CHALLENGING	RADICAL
Physical Space/ Policy/Visual Messaging *(continued)*	Print and post religious accommodation policy throughout building		

Best Practices

People who are engaged in firsthand experiences are in the best situation to generate solutions. The general list below is only a generic list to inspire ideas.

	SAFE	CHALLENGING	RADICAL
Individual	Research: online (e.g., culture tools, YouTube), books , movies podcasts Follow thought-leaders on Twitter, discover resources via Instagram	Invite someone to lunch Visit a new place Attend a club or activity for first time (e.g., international clubs, community groups, sports/hobby groups) University resources Festivals Take a class Take a tour of a new place	Make a commitment to ongoing meetings where you are a minority Travel to a foreign location for extended periods Deliberately put yourself in a situation where you are the minority in order to learn
Organizational	Diversity Council ERG Training on target cultures Inclusion Training	Diversity Council with budget and power Cultural Training Social events	Dedicated Task Force with power, time frame, accountability, and goals Hire people in target groups

Organizational (continued)		Off-site WE-building program	Support people in target groups
		Diversity Council with budget and power	Mentor people in target groups
			Promote people in target groups
		Cultural Training	
		Social events	Culture-specific intensive training
		Off-site WE-building program	Job Exchange
			International Exchange
		Language Lessons	
		Lunch and Learn	WE-building campaign
		Mixed TeamBuilding	ERG livestream learning
		ERG-sponsored activities	
Physical space/ Policy/Visual messaging	Clocks	Diversity and Inclusion Director	Diversity and Inclusion Director with power and budget
	Maps	Reorganize spaces	
	Desk arrangements		Build/construct spaces that promote connection
	Open social spaces	Reorganize seating arrangements	
	Inclusive calendars		Set goals for inclusion
	Photos of employee groups in satellite offices		

TAKE THE *US VERSUS THEM* CHALLENGE

The *Us versus Them* Challenge is like the Ice Bucket Challenge but it requires even more courage and has the potential to do more good (while still staying dry). Like the Ice Bucket Challenge, the *Us versus Them* Challenge requires a willingness to be uncomfortable. Unlike the Ice Bucket Challenge, it requires a willingness to be vulnerable and take a risk that may or may not get the results you expect.

Taking action is the most important part of creating real change. As popular and easy as online diversity training has become, it is too often ineffective because users do not have to take a risk or be vulnerable. People simply watch a video or click some boxes on a screen. Taking substantive action to make change is hard.

There are many reasons why people fail to take action, even when they genuinely care about an issue. Some people are busy, while others cannot tolerate the vulnerability required to take challenging actions. But the most frequent comment I hear among well-meaning people is, "I am not sure what the right action should be." By utilizing the Solution Worksheet, individuals and groups create a range of actionable items to address this common concern.

COMMITMENTS

Research shows that the simple act of writing down a goal makes you 42 percent more likely to achieve that goal.[9] For this reason, every participant engaged in bridging an *Us and Them* gap should write down one commitment they are willing to make to advance their knowledge and narrow the gap. At the conclusion of each of my training sessions, I ask every participant to privately complete the following card and then tell them to keep it as a reminder until they achieve their goal (see Figure 10).

In an effort to build connection across difference in my organization,
I commit to the following WE-building actions:

_____

_____

_____

_____

_____

www.laurakriska.com

FIGURE 10

ACCOUNTABILITY

Another strategy to enhance outcomes is to establish accountability by telling one other person your goal. Research suggests
that when people make some type of commitment to act it is
more likely to occur. One study found that a verbal commitment
to another person increases compliance by 65 percent. Success
rates of 95 percent were reported when those people agree to
meet on a regular basis and check on progress.[10]

Support employees by providing opportunities to set goals,
write goals, and share goals. Incentivize action by holding
WE-building follow-up meetings, for employees to report success stories and share their experiences.

FOLLOW-UP

Holding staff accountable and providing ongoing support
and encouragement is made easy with email surveys. The simple
act of seeing an email reminder asking if you have followed up

on your action can be a nudge to individuals who need support. Using anonymous online surveys is also a good way to gather data on efficacy. Technology provides many low-cost options to gather valuable metrics to measure the return on investment for various initiatives.

SECTION III

MOVING

FORWARD

7

OVERCOMING RESISTANCE AND APATHY

The Obstacles to Achieving Cultural Intelligence

AMY BLOCK HAS been an advertising executive in New York City for more than twenty-five years—so long that she remembers learning how to send contracts to clients by fax machine. Since those early days, the technological revolution has transformed the way Amy and millions of others communicate in the workplace—first email, then cell phones, and now smartphones. It seems to Amy that every week there is a new communication app she has to learn how to use: Slack, WhatsApp, Workplace. Once in a while she finds herself questioning the need for all these different apps. "Can't I just text?" she thinks.

Change is hard and many people resist change, whether it's to a new technology or a new brand of milk, especially when our current choices seem sufficient. Research and our life experiences show that once habits are set we are less likely to change.[1] People get familiar with certain ways of doing things and inertia sets in. Instead of seeing the potential benefit we might gain by doing something new, we look at the costs: too much time or too much effort. At work we all fall into patterns of behavior and communication—who we greet in the morning, what we drink at our desks, and where those beverages come from. In the absence of a painful encounter (interpersonal conflict, long line at the coffee shop, or malfunctioning beverage machine) most of us stick with what works. This is true on other levels as well. How and what we think about *Us and Them* dynamics in the company tend to remain the same unless there is pain in the form of complaints, lawsuits, or a social media crisis. Inertia and comfort with familiar ways of thinking and behaving are among the biggest barriers to WE-building in any institution.

CLASSIC DIVISIONS

Within a week of graduating from college, I was working on the assembly line in Marysville, Ohio, making cars. I had thirty seconds to place a piece of sand-colored putty into six specific locations of the steel chassis as it moved down the line. Like every other worker, I wore heavy, steel-toed boots, plastic safety glasses, and a white uniform with a red patch that said HONDA. I had never before worked in a manufacturing environment but quickly noticed differences compared to the office environments where I had done internships and had summer jobs. I heard people on the assembly line say *ain't*. They cursed occasionally and were less likely to be concerned about appearance. They tended to be louder, and when our white uniforms got dirty with grease or paint, nobody seemed to mind. Although I worked in the factory for only a month, it was enough to get a firsthand look at a timeless workplace culture gap—blue-collar versus white-collar work.

In the thirty years since I wore those steel-toed boots, I have spent time in hundreds of workplaces, from factories in the Midwest to executive suites in Europe. In every institution, I observed historical divides particular to each corporate environment. Sales versus marketing. Back office versus front office. Internal audit versus everyone. I've worked with thousands of professionals across the globe and virtually everyone I speak with can tell me a story about a time when they have suffered the consequences of a departmental *Us versus Them* rivalry.

Sometimes the consequences are mild and function as a type of initiation. When Susan started her first real job as a teller at a bank, the other, more experienced tellers completely ignored her for the first week. "After that, they started talking to me," she said.

But in other situations, the consequences have a long-term impact on the overall efficiency of the organization. Adam, an internal auditor, had difficulty getting his coworkers to return his calls and to behave in a civil manner toward him when he asked for basic documentation he needed in order to do his job, which was necessary to protect the company.

Maya worked in a tech company where engineers were treated like gods. If an engineer wanted information, it was considered high priority. If a non-engineer made the same request, they were put off. The engineers in the company ate lunch together and socialized together. Even though Maya, a non-engineer, was the same generation as many of the engineers, she was never included. Like many professionals, Maya resigned herself to the situation, believing that nothing would ever change, and started looking for a job where she would feel more central to the organizational mission.

Pete worked in administration in a prestigious New York City financial firm and saw how high-performing traders were allowed to flaunt the organizational rules that he was tasked with enforcing. In one case, the company had decided to cut costs by limiting first-class airline travel. It was Pete's job to explain this to a top-level trader who had requested a first-class ticket for an upcoming business trip. Rather than cooperate with Pete by either abiding by the company rule or working together to seek an exception from decisionmakers in the company, the trader attacked Pete. "Do you know how much money I make for this company?" Pete recalled the trader shouting at him. The trader eventually got his first-class airline ticket; Pete eventually left the company.

Some people might think that losing a lower-level administrative employee like Pete or a non-engineer like Maya is inconsequential. While the salaries of employees like Pete and Maya might represent a small fraction of the revenue generated by a successful trader or productive engineer, the *Us and Them* damage comprises more than just turnover cost. When different parts of the organization do not cooperate, there will be lost opportunities and costly inefficiencies. These costs are hard to measure because they represent new ideas, cooperative initiatives, and innovative opportunities that never materialize. The costs may be invisible, but the negative impact on the organization is real.

Us and Them gaps can cause serious damage.

THE COST OF DIVIDES

Why would engineers in Maya's company treat her as less important? Why do white-collar workers in a manufacturing company act superior to blue-collar workers? In most *Us versus Them* dynamics, there is an assumption that the *us* part of the dynamic is more important. White-collar work is generally viewed as better than blue-collar work. Engineers and financial traders have acquired specific skills that administrative workers have not. Wages are higher, working conditions are more comfortable, and usually there are advanced educational standards required to get these jobs.

While these factors may be true, it is also true that an organization is best positioned to achieve success when all employees are engaged and working toward the same goal. An easy way to think of this is to imagine everyone in a rowboat pulling an oar. If everyone pulls in the same direction, together, the boat is going to move faster. Deviation by even one person will disrupt the momentum, speed, and chance of reaching the goal.

When an *Us versus Them* dynamic negatively impacts communication, relationship building, and teamwork, it's also harming the efficiency, productivity, and overall competitiveness of the organization. As a result, people will be under greater stress, miscommunicate more often, and encounter other problems. This can lead to the organization being less competitive in the marketplace by negatively impacting market share, revenue, and staffing.

Old-School versus New-School

In 2015, Brad was hired by the new owners of a company that had been a successful start-up before being purchased by (and becoming a subsidiary of) an international conglomerate. The people in the company were accustomed to doing business in an informal manner, relying on long-term relationships and old-school ways of doing business, like handing a salesperson an unmarked envelope of cash after a particularly lucrative deal was secured. When Brad joined the organization, he was viewed as an outsider, even though he was experienced in the field and had many contacts in the industry.

Everyone from the original employee team looked at Brad as an enemy, despite the fact that they were working for the same company and ostensibly working toward the same goals. Employees would not share data with Brad, and they delayed responding to his emails. In 2017, Brad proposed the development of a product that could open up a new revenue stream, but senior leaders shut it down without any due diligence. For two years they flatly rejected any idea or suggestion from Brad. Meanwhile, a competitor company began developing the exact same product and within a year had established the very same revenue stream Brad had proposed.

Historical divides, like blue-collar versus white-collar, or front office versus back office, or management versus administration, are often viewed as permanent, "natural" divides grounded in class, education, and socio-economic factors and perpetuated by policies and longstanding behavioral norms. Rather than challenging the divisive norms, some leaders acquiesce and assume nothing can be done to change them. Other leaders actually encourage *Us versus Them* dynamics, mistakenly believing that these divisions will promote "healthy" competitiveness.

But the reality is that the front office cannot operate without a back office. Management needs non-management employees to do the daily work of the organization. Even the most successful financial traders need administrative staff to execute and support the big deals they make. White-collar employees in the automotive industry might have impressive degrees in marketing and excellent experience in sales, but if the manufacturing teams are treated as inferior, this will be reflected in the products they make—and the company will eventually suffer.

PRIORITIZE, DON'T MARGINALIZE

The great myth of the *Us versus Them* mentality is the belief that the only way to prioritize some people is by marginalizing others. This is wrong. Retaining your top performers by making sure they feel appreciated and allocating resources to support those performers is part of any manager's job. Paying higher salaries to highly productive employees is standard business practice around the world. It rewards and incentivizes performance and reminds those top employees that they are important to the organization. But achieving this sense of importance by allowing high performers to flaunt rules or treat others poorly can have a negative impact on the whole organization as it did in Pete's company.

Achieving a sense of importance by marginalizing blue-collar or administrative colleagues is bad business and will compromise the competitiveness of the organization. When leaders fall into *Us versus Them* ways of thinking in the workplace, they are buying into a dangerous hierarchy where resources (power and money) are concentrated among the *us* group, rather than a more equitable distribution among all.

Prioritize and Recognize

The solution is to prioritize and recognize at the same time. Every leader must prioritize staff, tasks, and use of resources. But they can prioritize *and* recognize the contributions of others. They can pay higher salaries to high-performing people *and* make sure to engage lower-paid employees in their jobs through equitable policies and verbal encouragement. They can keep the employment of the more skilled workers *and* affirm the contributions of people with less experience and talent. Although financial resources are usually limited, a leader's ability to promote WE-building within an organization through his or her communication and behavioral choices is not. Most employees seek secure employment, and this can be accomplished by maximizing the competitiveness of the organization. This maximum competitiveness is much more likely to occur when all employees are pulling their oars toward the same goal.

Inspire others to make change.

WE-BUILDING LEADERSHIP

The difference between organizations that have big, damaging gaps and ones that don't experience these gaps is leadership.

When leaders are aware of *Us and Them* culture gaps and assess their own ability to successfully manage these gaps, they can take meaningful action to narrow them. There are three categories of action: policy, communication, and behavior. Let's take a look at each category and examine specific strategies in each.

WE-BUILDING POLICY STRATEGIES

Policies that promote equitable work tend to promote cohesion. Wearing uniforms, having similar vacation policies, and work-from-home rules can promote connection. However, these strategies are not always possible to implement given industrial demands. In a factory, you cannot have assembly-line employees working from home. In a New York City bank, it is unlikely that a company uniform would be welcomed. But any organization can promote equity with policies that make sense for their organization.

When I worked at the Honda factory in Marysville, Ohio, in the 1990s, I saw firsthand how the gap between blue- and white-collar workers was addressed through policies and use of space in order to limit the differences between roles. For example, in most automobile manufacturing organizations in the United States, people in the executive office wear suits and ties, but at Honda in Ohio people who worked in the office, including everyone from clerks to the president, wore the same white jumpsuits as the people working in the factory. Having a water bottle or coffee on your desk was not allowed in the office because workers on the assembly line were not allowed to have nonessential items while they worked. The parking lot was first come, first park, with no executive spots. The cafeteria was the same; there was no such thing as an "executive" dining room. In addition to these rules, there was frequent rotation of personnel and physical movement between the factory floor and the office space. These standards supported a WE culture at Honda in Marysville, Ohio, and were written about widely because they were so different from the way any other automobile facility in the United States operated.

Equitable Pay

When companies share the profits of their success, they enhance retention, productivity, and morale. But there has been a trend toward pay inequity in the past fifty years in the United States. In 1987, CEOs earned approximately thirty times the salary of the average worker. In the intervening years, CEO pay has increased by 937 percent, so that today, the average pay disparity between a CEO and the typical worker's salary is 300 to 1.

Engaging all employees through equitable distribution of income is a choice any company can make. But it's hard to find an example in the United States today of a company that values equitable distribution. Ben & Jerry's ice cream famously maintained a 5:1 ratio of CEO pay to average worker salary, but that only lasted until 1994 when a replacement for retiring Ben Cohen could not be found.[2] They increased to a 7:1 ratio, then to a 17:1 ratio by 2000. Once the company was purchased by Unilever in 2000, the salaries were no longer public information. Dr. Bronner's, a personal care company specializing in organic soaps, is one of the few U.S. companies committed to a 5:1 compensation ratio.

Support WE-building by being an
equitable workplace.

Recognition Programs

Compensation and benefits are always important, but these costly factors are not the only ways to engage employees.

Recognition programs are a cost-effective way to reward good performance and promote employee engagement. Programs that are ongoing are more effective than once-per-year recognition. Don't be stingy by limiting recognition. If more than one employee has achieved a notable goal or earned recognition, they all should be acknowledged. Authentic and detailed recognition will usually require more than presenting an employee with a standard certificate, so be thoughtful and take time to articulate what is being recognized.

Inclusion Policy

Written inclusion policies provide affirmation to all employees that they are safe and welcome in the workplace. These written affirmations can be particularly meaningful to anyone who represents a historically marginalized voice in the organization. Building a culture of belonging occurs when policies are clear and behaviors support those written policies.

An example of one company's approach is Salesforce's five core principles of inclusive leadership.[3]

1. Lead with equality.
2. Have brave, authentic conversations.
3. Practice inclusive meetings.
4. Be fair in assignments and promotions.
5. Celebrate and bond with everyone in mind.

Building a WE culture that can tolerate predictable economic and personnel changes requires establishing WE policies like written inclusion statements and equitable income distribution. These policies will fortify the day-to-day WE behavior and will contribute to establishing a sustainable WE culture.

Establishing an equitable workplace is part
of building a WE culture.

WE-BUILDING COMMUNICATION STRATEGIES

WE-statements that emphasize the whole rather than separate parts of an organization can be an effective tool. Comments that articulate the larger goal will promote a WE culture. Leaders should also clearly keep in mind that the real competition is outside the organization, not inside.

WE-Language Tips

Simply replacing *I* or *you* or *they* statements with words like *we* or *us* or *our* can reframe the message shared by leaders. Using derogatory phrases like *losers* or *awful* or other cutting words is an effective way to cause immediate division, not cohesion.

WE-building Positive Feedback

Leaders who notice and acknowledge key performers through genuine positive feedback are applying one of the most underutilized tools in business. Praising an employee for their performance is free. It costs nothing but a bit of time. If a top salesperson has great results, then telling that salesperson you see and notice those results provides encouragement and affirmation. But also noticing and acknowledging those who support and execute those big sales made by the salesperson is a way to make sure that all contributions are recognized.

In addition to praising business results, praising specific WE-building behavior like collaboration and cooperation is another way to use positive feedback to promote WE-building.

Acceptable Feedback	WE-building Positive Feedback
The sales team is on track to hit their targets for 2021.	Thanks to good results from *our* sales team, *our* company is on track to hit *our* targets for 2021.
The marketing team is great.	*We* have the best marketing team in *our* industry.
Jeff is the most talented salesperson in the organization.	Jeff's great contributions have helped *us* reach *our* company targets.
The Houston office secured new business in Mexico.	*Our* team in the Houston office has secured new business in Mexico, which is good for *our* company.

WE-building Negative Feedback

Constructive negative feedback is an extremely useful tool for any organization. Pointing out problems is critical to growth and improvement. Using WE-language when sharing negative feedback is a way to clearly point out problems while also promoting unity in the organization. It is not an attempt to sugarcoat bad news or shy away from real problems. Instead, WE-language firmly keeps the focus on outside competition and on the shared goals of the organization.

Examples:

Us versus Them language	WE-Language
There is no way the sales team will make their sales targets for the first quarter.	*We* need to discuss ways to support *our* sales team because *we* are not on track to meet *our* first-quarter sales targets.
The marketing team is awful.	*We* need to improve *our* marketing team so that *we* can be more competitive in *our* industry.
Jeff doesn't know what he's doing.	Jeff needs support to be more knowledgeable so *we* can leverage his contributions.
The losers in Houston failed to secure new business in Mexico.	*Our* team in Houston failed to secure new business in Mexico, which is bad for *our* company.

No Tea, Please

"What's the tea?" My teenagers once taught me that this phrase is how Generation Z refers to gossip (though I've learned that their language changes quickly so this may no longer be true). Every generation, every culture, and every company engages in gossip because generational groups and cultures and companies are composed of people. People are social and curious. Humans are hardwired to react when we perceive signals of conflict, as evidenced by the automatic reaction people have to look when they hear the sound of screeching tires or raised voices.

Studies of gossip in the workplace demonstrate that it almost always has a negative impact on morale, productivity, and efficiency.[4] It contributes to lower job satisfaction, higher turnover, and undermines integrity in the workplace. Credibility is undermined by gossip because it erodes trust among individuals. Without trust, individuals inside an organization cannot reach the most productive *trusted colleague* stage of a professional relationship.

Having constructive conversations about problem employees or problem behavior with the appropriate people is not the same as gossip. For example, HR professionals are trained to manage employee problems without undermining trust. Demonstrating integrity by not engaging in gossip is a hallmark of any strong leader.

It is true that gossip, especially if it involves someone's personal life, can feel irresistible to listen to and then share. But gossip incites conflict and perpetuates *Us versus Them* dynamics. Gossip is a direct threat to building and maintaining a WE culture. Leaders will never completely eradicate gossip in the workplace, but limiting it is central to WE-building efforts.

Unfortunately, even leaders have a hard time resisting this tendency. I recall meeting the president of a company who started to complain to me within minutes about certain people in his organization. "No one can stand him," he said of another senior leader. My role at his company was to promote

WE-building and to facilitate activities that promoted connection. Within minutes of meeting him, he showed me one reason his organization so desperately needed outside help.

Tips for Managing Gossip

1. **Never Gossip.**

   Set an example by never engaging in negative gossip about individuals or groups in the company. If you wouldn't say a comment in front of the other person, then don't say it behind their backs. Instead, rephrase your comment. There is a difference between saying "John is the worst!" and "John's results last quarter are unacceptable. We need to help him improve because he is 15 percent below his target."

2. **When You Hear Others Gossip, Take Action.**

   Walk away. People who trade in the misfortune of others need listeners, so without listeners they are less able to gossip.

   Redirect the conversation by changing the subject or by offering a neutral or positive spin on what has been said. For example, if you hear an employee say, "The new guy Bob has no idea what he is doing." A neutral response might be, "I remember when I first started out, I had no idea how this company operated. It took me weeks to become functional." A positive spin might be, "Bob seems well connected in our industry. If we help him out, he might help us attract new customers quickly."

   Stop it. The hardest response to gossip is to shut it down directly. "I don't want to hear that kind of comment." Or, "Talking that way about a colleague can undermine our productivity."

WE-BUILDING BEHAVIORAL STRATEGIES

When leaders expand the definition of WE to include everyone in the organization, independent of specific roles, rather than perpetuating *Us and Them* divisions, new norms of inclusion begin to take shape.

There are five specific behavioral strategies leaders can use to overcome apathy and resistance. Let's take a look at each of these categories and understand the reasons behind them. Leaders should:

1. Show enthusiasm for the entire team
2. Assume they are not above cultural data
3. Prioritize cultural data before there is a crisis
4. Broaden the definition of culture
5. Bust the false narrative that proximity = integration

1. Show Enthusiasm for the Entire Team

Showing enthusiasm for the entire team is essential. Leaders must be aware of the different mandates that people and departments have. Leaders also must advance the belief that every department and every person in the organization has a specific role to play in achieving overall goals. Spending time via formal meetings or informal conversations reflects the value a leader places on different people and departments. Making an effort to distribute time and attention across the entire organization contributes to a stronger sense of WE.

Leaders must also demonstrate that they are broadly connected throughout the organization, rather than only with a small group of like-minded people. If, for example, a leader only has lunch with a particular few, then they may be viewed as prioritizing some over others. Even knowing people's names and using those names is a way to recognize a broader group of contributors.

2. Assume They Are Not Above Cultural Data

"Okay, Boomer," is a phrase that resonated with many people immediately because it captured the *Us versus Them* dynamic between the older and younger generations. This gap is timeless, because no matter what decade or century you are living in, listening to people from a younger generation is difficult for older people, and understanding the mindset of older generations is hard for younger people. Every sixty-year-old has been twenty-five. When it relates to the workplace, we older folks firmly believe that we know what it's like to be young. We also firmly believe that our additional thirty-five years of experience is valuable. Like generations before us, these years of experience translate into an assumed superiority in our own minds. But in reality, a sixty-year-old in 2021 often has little firsthand understanding of what twenty-something consumers or employees want, because so many societal factors have changed. As any young adult can tell you about their own parents, "they just don't understand my generation." No matter what the era, those with more years of experience tend to look down on those with fewer years of experience. People who identify with the younger group look at the older group as "out of touch" and "outdated." But generational gaps, like other culture gaps, can be bridged with deliberate effort.

For Tim Morton, music and film provided an important connection with the younger generation.[5] Tim started his career in sales when typewriters were still the norm. As the decades passed, he moved from being the young guy in the office to being the oldest person in his organization. Tim feels the generational gap every day and works to narrow it. Instead of rolling his eyes at the way younger employees multitask during meetings, Tim finds ways to incorporate the use of smartphones into his presentations by utilizing a platform called Kahoot. This platform engages participants in meetings by linking every smartphone in the room to his visual presentation, which then displays group feedback. Instead of complaining about how entitled Generation Z employees act, he seeks their advice about new apps and joins after-work gatherings, always paying with the latest peer-to-peer payment apps. When Instagram and Snapchat became popular, Tim got accounts and became familiar with how they functioned. Tim's own teenage children were impressed with his effort to stay informed.

Now that Tim is the most senior person in his workplace, he makes a consistent effort to stay connected to the younger generation and considers it part of his job. He discovered that the arts, particularly music and film, can be unifying topics. He makes it a practice to ask, "What music are you listening to?"

Tim discovered that one of his twentysomething colleagues, Evan, was a cinema studies major in college. He and Evan could talk about many films that Tim had seen when they were initially released and that Evan had viewed as part of his film history studies.

Tim's investment in the younger generation has paid off in many ways. For example, he often conducts interviews and used to spend many hours transcribing his tape recordings before writing reports. Evan suggested an AI transcription app that Tim could use. Instead of investing hours transcribing, the app automatically transcribed the interview in realtime and Tim was able to generate his report within half an hour.

3. Prioritize Cultural Data Before There Is a Crisis

Weeks after D&G's fiasco in China, fashion icon Prada released *Pradamalia*, a series of seven collectable charms, and neglected to notice that one of the charms, Otto, was outrageously insensitive due to its blackface imagery.[6] After a swift public reaction, Prada denounced racism in a statement and promised to remove all charms from the marketplace. Adidas's inclusion of an almost all-white tennis shoe called "Uncaged" in celebration of Black History month in 2019 was also called out as insensitive and removed from the marketplace.[7]

Leaders of corporations in any industry need to prioritize cultural data *before* they are in the middle of a catastrophe by recognizing that culture is a relevant factor in everyone's life. Finding ways to see cultural norms, especially when those norms are different from your own, is essential. Using the iceberg concept of culture (introduced in Chapter 4) provides a mechanism for seeing invisible data that may be hard to access if you are inexperienced interacting with a relevant cultural group. As leaders improve their understanding of different cultural norms, both visible and invisible, they will also begin to understand what constitutes a violation of those norms.

They will learn, as Prada did, that blackface imagery is highly sensitive and not an appropriate motif for a charm. They will learn, as Adidas did, that launching an all-white shoe called "Uncaged" in honor of Black History month triggers suspicion about what the company thinks about Black History. Leaders prioritize cultural data by both recruiting and supporting diverse decisionmakers and by educating themselves. When a diverse and educated leadership team makes culturally informed decisions about products, campaigns, and other business initiatives, they are more likely to prevent a crisis from developing in the first place.

Tips for continual awareness of cultural data:

- Assume cultural norms are always at play, even if you cannot see and hear them.
- Actively use the iceberg concept of culture to access invisible data.
- Proactively seek advice and counsel from people who understand or come from different relevant cultural groups.
- Actively include input from individuals from underrepresented and relevant cultural groups.

Benefits of Cultural Awareness

Jeff Layton is a successful engineer who worked for many years at Google.[8] In 2013, he was hired by a Korean company to head up a start-up division in New York. Jeff, who looked very much the technology hipster geek, with a full beard and shaggy haircut, possessed the awareness to recognize that his shaggy appearance might be viewed differently at his new company. When he began working in their New York office, he noticed that none of his Korean colleagues had a beard or facial hair of any type. A short time into his job, he was asked to visit the headquarters in Seoul to secure funding for his project.

Before the trip, Jeff thought about his appearance and deliberated over whether he should wear a tie or not. A Korean friend told him that some people in Korea consider facial hair unrefined and associated beards with people who are homeless. This was clearly not the image Jeff had in mind for his first meeting. Although no one in the company suggested that Jeff alter his appearance, he made the choice to shave off his beard to optimize his goal of making a positive first impression. It worked. His funding was approved.

Shaving his beard is not what made Jeff culturally aware. Knowing that his beard might be viewed differently in Korea is what made him culturally aware. I do not advocate that people like Jeff always follow the rules and norms of another cultural group. If the norms are in conflict with your own personal values, then simply knowing that a difference exists is useful information. There is no obligation to follow another culture's norms. Rather, I advocate that we always learn what the rules and norms are through research, firsthand experience, and listening to those who know more about those cultural norms. Then, even when the norms are in conflict with our own values, we are aware that the gap exists.

_____

Culture difference does not only refer to
different countries, it can be a difference
based on any factors of identity.

_____

4. Broaden the Definition of Culture

Some organizations literally see culture in black and white.
They don't look beyond the most obvious factors, such as nationality, and recognize the wide range of differences that can
create culture clashes. It is much easier to identify a culture gap
when it corresponds with a national boundary or a different
language. But culture gaps occur due to differences over any
aspect of identity. Prada and Adidas had problems because they
failed to deeply understand aspects of Black culture. The #Me-
Too movement is a result of decades of inequity, disrespect, and
mistreatment of women. The phrase "Okay, Boomer" revealed
the cultural discord between an older generation, who complain about the entitled, overly confident, gender-fluid, tech-
savvy younger generation, and those younger people who value
their work-life balance and have little tolerance for the regres-
sive, inflexible mindset of those old folks. Cultural catastrophes
occur because people fail to recognize that culture is broadly
defined by any factor of identity.

A Chinese client, Zhou, complained to me about a culture
gap in his Shanghai office because some of the employees had
grown up in Shanghai and others had grown up outside of
Shanghai. Those who were originally from Shanghai spoke
Shanghainese to one another and looked down on those who
did not. Another client in Indonesia explained that the biggest
culture gap in his manufacturing company was related to workers who came from the countryside to work in the factory and
those from the city who also worked in the factory but saw

themselves as superior. It is important to recognize that many factors contribute to a person's cultural identity, and consequently, cultural gaps and conflict can appear anywhere.

5. Bust the False Narrative That Proximity = Integration

Joe is a middle-aged white man working in the entertainment industry as a lawyer. His law school class was more diverse than any in the history of his university, yet Joe's experience as a lawyer has been homogeneous. Over a twenty-year career, his bosses have always been white men. The law firm where he worked after law school was 70 percent white, and the only discernible diversity among the 100 percent white partners was a small number of female lawyers—also all white.

Joe considers himself open minded and unbiased. He has acquaintances from many racial, ethnic, and religious backgrounds. One of his closest friends is a gay man, also white. And like millions of other well-meaning leaders in American business, Joe has bought into a false narrative that he and his company are diverse and are inclusive because they have hired non-white people. While they do have non-white lawyers in the firm, none of them are in a position of authority. Although he doesn't want to broadcast this, he has noticed that the most high-profile cases and most important clients are assigned to white men. He has bought into the illusion of inclusivity when only proximity exists.

Despite the fact that more Black students graduate from law school today than ever before, the increase of Black partners in law firms nationwide from 2009 to 2018 changed from 1.7 percent to 1.8 percent. Black lawyers have shared that they feel unwelcome and not supported when they look at all-white partner teams. One Black professional told me that he felt like a *them* every day in his white shoe New York City law firm.

Lawyers of color encounter othering experiences that white lawyers like Joe could never imagine. In March 2019, attorney

Rashad James, a Black man, was detained in a courtroom by a white officer from the Harford County, Maryland, sheriff's office on suspicion of impersonating a lawyer. James was in the courtroom that day to represent a client, also a Black man, who did not show up. The complaint filed by James alleges that the officer suspected James of impersonating an attorney on the basis of his race. James was the only Black attorney in the courtroom that day.

Attorney and social activist Bryan Stevenson writes in his best-selling book, *Just Mercy*, about an episode that happened to him in an Alabama courthouse. Stevenson, a Black man, had arrived early to prepare for an appearance on behalf of a client. When the judge and prosecutor, both white men, entered the nearly empty courtroom, the judge took one look at Stevenson and told him to go outside and wait for his lawyer because he was not allowed to be in the courtroom alone.

For the first twenty years of my career, I worked exclusively with the American branches of Japanese organizations that on paper looked like diverse workplaces with high numbers of both Japanese and American employees. However, I saw firsthand that these two groups were not well integrated at all. In fact, proximity to one another was as far as integration got in some cases. In one company, a Japanese manager, Mr. Taguchi, who spent hours and hours working every day within a few feet of five American employees, never had more than a simple conversation with any of them in over three years. When I spoke with Mr. Taguchi in Japanese, he was personable and warm. We discussed many topics including baseball, his family, and opera, which he loved. But Mr. Taguchi made no effort to speak about non-work topics in English with his staff. His failure to engage prevented him from developing a trusting relationship with his colleagues.

In order to overcome resistance, leaders
must ask if they're congratulating
themselves for fostering diversity and
inclusion when in fact all they've fostered is
better-looking logistics.

ONGOING PROCESS

Apathy and resistance will never disappear entirely. Fostering a
WE culture requires ongoing vigilance, somewhat like achieving a weight goal requires monitoring on a regular basis. But
just like establishing healthy eating, once best practices are in
place, the maintenance of the desired outcome is a lot easier.

And just like trying to lose weight, there will be ups and
downs when it comes to adjusting past behaviors. Change is
hard for leaders, too. Leaders should be vigilant, but they don't
have to be perfect. Sharing your struggles with *Us and Them* gaps
can be inspiring to others because they, too, will struggle. Celebrating collaborative efforts, big and small, will motivate others
because enthusiasm over successful outcomes is contagious.

When leaders demonstrate that proximity alone is not
enough to bridge gaps and broaden the concept of culture, they
will establish new norms of behavior. Instead of waiting for a
crisis to motivate change and recognizing that culture differences show up in many forms, leaders will redefine a new paradigm for the twenty-first century.

8

HOME TEAM ADVANTAGE

Why the Traditional Majority Culture Must Take the Lead

ON AN UNSEASONABLY warm day in January 2020, I was on a short break from facilitating a WE-building workshop for a group of thirty professionals in a New York City financial institution where I had worked many times in the past. The group was diverse, with thirteen different languages spoken (Mandarin, Hindi, Arabic, Bengali, and more). At least a quarter of the group identified themselves as nonnative English speakers. No particular race or ethnicity made up a majority, and collectively, there were more people of color than white people. This room was fairly reflective of the percentage of the white population in New York City.

I was looking through a stack of yellow index cards on which the participants had anonymously written answers to a question I had asked earlier: "When in your life have you experienced feeling like a *them*?" It is a question I ask thousands of people every year, and it is a question that many people can answer very quickly.

"Having immigrant parents that spoke with very thick accents and growing up in a very American neighborhood."

"Being the only Jewish kid in my class."

"I was in an insurance role transitioning to a credit role and working with several colleagues with backgrounds in credit."

"Being one of the few vegetarians in my group. Sometimes I cannot eat with my colleagues when they go to meat-based restaurants."

"I was the only female on the executive team."

"In elementary school, my parents came to eat lunch with me and brought a traditional Mexican meal for us to eat. My friends thought the food was weird and said it was gross."

"I went to business school at age twenty-six after being in the military and was surrounded by younger kids."

"The first time I visited my 'homeland' of China at eight years old and was put in Chinese day care with my younger sister. The other kids made fun of us for speaking 'gibberish' despite the fact we finally looked the part to fit in."

"Working in a Midwestern bank and I was the only New Yorker."

"Being gay in high school and not going to prom because of it."

"In first grade my teacher couldn't pronounce my name and made a joke about it."

Everyone has felt like a them.

Asking this simple question, "When did you feel like a *them*?" provides an opportunity to remember our own experiences of not feeling included. Remembering what it is like to be a *them* reminds all of us how awful it can feel. These episodes also provide specific ideas for bridging *Us versus Them* encounters. Since everyone knows what this feels like, each of us also knows what to do about it. A welcoming gesture, a proactive introduction, making the effort to say another person's name correctly or the simple effort of pulling up an extra chair can make a huge difference in those moments.

The answers to this customary WE-building workshop question always intrigued me, and I was often struck by how personal some of the statements were. As usual, the responses ranged from feeling slightly left out to memories of significant experiences that clearly had a lifelong impact. But of all the cards I reviewed that day, one card stood out. On the pale-yellow card, written in black wispy script, was the phrase, "Can't think of anything."

I had occasionally encountered this response in the past, in part because I told my audience it was an option: "If you really cannot think of a situation where you felt like a *them*," I would say trying to sound genuinely neutral, "you can write that you can't think of anything."

Despite giving permission for this type of response, my experience tells me that almost everyone has felt like a *them* at some point in their lives. President Obama felt like a *them* because of his mixed-race heritage. Laura Bush felt like a *them* as an only child growing up in Texas, because most of her friends had siblings and she did not. Steve Jobs famously felt like an outsider having been adopted as an infant. These were among the examples I often shared when preparing participants to anonymously write their own examples on colorful index cards. Independent of a person's background and identity, the feeling of not belonging is universal. Even straight white men, America's favorite punching bag when it comes to conversations about privilege and race, have had times when they felt like they didn't belong.

I looked around the room, wondering who in this group of thirty chose to write this neutral response. Was it someone who just didn't feel like digging deep or revealing anything personal even though the answers were anonymous? Or was it someone who genuinely had never felt like an outsider?

If the person could not recall a time feeling like a *them*, it would seem likely that this person had always felt like part of the cultural majority in his or her community. I guessed that this person had grown up surrounded by people who looked, sounded, ate, dressed, and prayed in the same way.

The idea of living and growing up around people who looked, sounded, and behaved in a similar manner tends to be rare in the United States due to our heritage as a country established by immigrants from all over the world. Even in the early days, before there was a United States of America, white European immigrants and Indigenous People interacted across differences in language and culture. But the notion of growing up surrounded only by people who looked alike, spoke alike, and shared a similar culture reminded me a lot of another country—Japan.

HOMOGENEITY AS A LIABILITY

Although diversity has increased slightly in big cities like Tokyo, Japan is nearly 98 percent Japanese people. Non-Japanese people were so rare when I was an exchange student that seeing another non-Asian foreigner on the street often warranted a silent nod of recognition. In addition to the common ancestral and racial identity, Japan fosters uniformity in other ways including a strong emphasis on rule-following in school and throughout one's life. Unlike other highly populated countries like China and India, for example, there is only one standard language in Japan and it is used and understood by 125+ million people. Textbooks and educational standards set by the Ministry of Education are followed nationwide. These common factors do not result in a population of people who are all the same. But it does result in a large body of shared culture and experience among all people who grow up in Japan.

This strong sense of common community and identity translates into an impressive ability to focus resources and people toward the same goals. This is one of the many characteristics of Japanese culture that I deeply admire. The whole world saw evidence of this in 2011 as the population in Japan responded with unrivaled cooperation to the catastrophic impact of the tsunami and Fukushima nuclear disaster that took more than sixteen thousand lives. People waited in long orderly lines to receive a fair distribution of water and food. Instead of looking out for individual needs, they worked together. Despite limited access to basic necessities, there was virtually no looting.

But in an increasingly diverse global marketplace, this homogeneity is also a liability. During the first twenty years of my career working primarily with U.S. subsidiaries of Japanese companies, I saw firsthand how many hardworking, intelligent Japanese people were fundamentally ill-prepared to be successful interacting with non-Japanese people. Their homogeneous backgrounds and limitations speaking English caused an inability to understand alternative cultural norms. All of them lived outside Japan, but the majority continued to live a Japanese life, which meant that they spent nearly all their time, both at work and outside work, with other Japanese people. As a result, their skill at interpreting differences was low, as was their ability to adjust to other behavioral norms.

These professionals represented the dominant culture, or home team, in their organizations. They often held all the top jobs and they made the important decisions. They had access to power and money within the organization. But instead of recognizing that dominant Japanese cultural norms were prioritized in the office, these members of the cultural majority unintentionally moved throughout their work life carrying an invisible set of expectations that put all the non-dominant people at a disadvantage. Many of the Japanese professionals lacked awareness of their position and of the implicit expectation that non-Japanese employees should assimilate to their unspoken norms.

For example, in many U.S. subsidiaries of Japanese companies, there is tension around the way people greet one another each morning. There is a cultural tendency in U.S. corporate culture to verbally greet people you encounter as you walk through a lobby or office or manufacturing space. It is considered basic courtesy. At a minimum, simply saying "Good morning," is the norm. While I have encountered Japanese professionals who quickly adapted to these norms, some Japanese staff struggled to adjust. The Japanese cultural tendency to be deferential combined with insecurity about using English resulted in Japanese colleagues walking right by English-speaking colleagues without saying a word. Sometimes the Japanese colleagues would put their heads down or simply act as though the other person did not exist.

This behavior made some local employees furious. "It's like I'm not even there!" one woman exclaimed. "He acts like I am not a human," she said, referring to a particular executive in the company.

When I spoke with the Japanese executive about his lack of greetings, he was genuinely perplexed. He confessed that he was not entirely sure of how to greet others and had chosen not to speak, hoping that this was the safer choice. I explained to him that by ignoring others and not offering even a simple greeting, he was causing a problem. As someone who identified with the home team, he had been unaware that his dominant cultural norm exacted a cost.

The home team is often determined by who controls the money and power.

HOME TEAM ADVANTAGE

Home team players in any setting have an advantage. They know the territory, the language, the visible and invisible rules. In any sporting event and in life in general, having connection, experience, and familiarity with a place or a culture provides access to people and information. Being an insider in a company can provide access to power and money. Simply put, being on the home team gives you a leg up.

Identifying with a home team, particularly if it relates to your appearance, should not work against you. But at the same time, those who belong to a home team must recognize the inherent advantages they have simply due to their similarity to those in power.

When you look, sound, and share many identity factors with your boss or with the culturally dominant group in your department, your behaviors are constantly affirmed by the presence of those others. Your clothes, your words, even the food you eat for lunch are seemingly inconsequential commonalities, but they can matter to people who do not share these factors. As we have discussed, when culturally dominant norms are standardized and prioritized, then deviations from these norms can trigger negative responses like racial profiling. Unfair assessments can occur because home team players apply their own cultural norms.

People who belong to a culturally dominant home team may not have necessary skills to build trusting relationships with people from different backgrounds.

Just like my Japanese colleagues, many smart, hardworking, and well-meaning straight white men live segregated white lives, and this can make them less aware of their privilege. As a result of their limited firsthand experience with people who are different, they may be less skilled at interpreting behavior in the workplace. Their ability to accurately read situations may be dull. They may be unaware of the importance of building trusting relationships with people outside their cultural groups. As a result, they create false narratives to explain behavior they do not understand and negatively mischaracterize people outside the dominant group. This can result in powerful people acting in ways that range from benignly oblivious to criminally ignorant.

Consider the example of women as a minority presence when they started to enter the workplace in greater numbers and in more professional roles. So often, men treated them in ways that were not appropriate—everything from using irritating nicknames to overt discrimination. Ask any professional female over fifty years old and you're likely to hear at least one example of an inaccurate narrative perpetuated by men.

For example:

False: She never complains when I call her "sweetie" or "honey," so she must like it.
True: Diminutive nicknames are unprofessional and marginalizing.

False: If she is wearing a low-cut top, then she wants me to compliment her appearance.
True: Women can dress how they like. Compliments can be viewed as hostile and may be unwelcome.

False: She has kids so I'm sure she's not able to accept this promotion that will require long hours and travel.
True: She is deserving of a promotion and it must be offered without consideration of her personal circumstances. It will be up to her to decide if she can manage long hours and travel.

False: Putting a woman on our board will make her uncomfortable since she will be the only one.

True: Boards should be comfortable places for all their members.

False: She agreed to meet for dinner/drinks, so this means she wants to have sex with me.
True: She agreed to meet for dinner/drinks to discuss business.

False: She agreed to meet in my hotel room, so this means she wants to have sex with me.
True: She agreed to meet in the hotel room because she has no power to refuse.

Most people on any home team enjoy their status at the top. They may or may not give thought to how and why they got there. In the United States, there is a definitive and historical racial hierarchy that places white people at the top, yet until Black Lives Matter protests swept the world, most white people I know rarely talked about being white. Despite the fact that the United States is increasingly non-white (racial and ethnic minorities make up almost 40 percent of our population), many white people live segregated white lives. A recent study revealed that roughly one in five respondents rarely or ever had an interaction with someone of a different race.[2] We eat lunch with similar colleagues, consult with one another in meetings, and spend nearly all our free time with other folks who grew up and look just like we do.

Sure, many white people can tell you about a person of color in our orbit, a colleague or fellow parent. We hope that knowing a person of color will demonstrate that we are not prejudiced. We eagerly talk about Black athletes that we follow and Black musicians we listen to. We are delighted to talk about the great Asian or Mexican or whatever cuisine we happen to love as a sign of our open minds. We are quick to mention how diverse our city is becoming, and don't forget, we voted (even campaigned!) for a Black president.

At work we might nod in agreement or even voice our approval for Diversity and Inclusion Initiatives, ERGs, and other efforts to build a multiracial and multiethnic coalition. But meanwhile, the reality of our segregated daily lives means that we fail to gain accurate understanding of different cultural norms. Our segregated lives lead to false narratives to explain behavior we don't understand and facts we cannot compute.

Many of us, myself included, have lots of acquaintance-level or even colleague-level relationships (from the Trust-Building Scale introduced in Chapter 3) with people of color in our lives. But when it comes to cultivating Stage 4, *trusted colleague* relationships, fewer white people have made an effort to expand their circle.

Growing up white meant that I almost never thought about my race, much less discussed it openly. Even now, if I simply name race as an observation in any setting, such as "There are a lot of white people here," many white people I know get uncomfortable. Author Sheryll Cashin accurately describes people like me with the following statement in her book *Loving*: "Being raised not to acknowledge race means they lack the tools to deal with it or talk about it when it arises."[3]

People who belong to a home team often are unaware of the privileges they have.

Living in a culturally homogeneous bubble provides a racially and ethnically stress-free environment for those, like me, who can often walk through life without ever naming race as a relevant factor. Surrounding yourself with other home team members provides a constant source of tacit approval for the oversimplified manner in which many of us approach any diversity topic. Rather than engage in the uncomfortable work of examining our privileged home team status, we take refuge behind an inadequate binary system that identifies anyone who is not actively racist or openly bigoted as good and fair.

We don't acknowledge the negative factors of living in a homogeneous world. We pretend that we are integrated even though the imbalance of white advantage is obvious and on display in every corner of our communities. We deny and pretend and make excuses because once we name the racial home team advantage for what it really is, we come face-to-face with a deeply uncomfortable truth. There has been a heavy thumb on the scale of opportunities and resources in favor of white people. Once this fundamental imbalance is seen, we can never again view the scales as fair.

FIVE COMMON PITFALLS

I've spent much of my career encouraging people on the home team to take action by asking leading questions. As a result, I've heard a great many excuses. These excuses correspond with the five pitfalls leaders from a dominant culture face.

1. Unaware and oblivious
2. Aware but scared
3. Aware and unaccountable
4. Aware and seeking organic approach
5. Aware, willing to act, but unsure

1. Unaware and Oblivious

Question: "What would you say is the biggest *Us versus Them* gap in your company?"

Unaware and Oblivious Answer: *"Our company doesn't have any diversity problems. We all get along."*

The #MeToo movement was a reaction not just to egregious harassers who abused their power, like Harvey Weinstein, but also to men who did not intend to diminish or marginalize women in the workplace but did so nonetheless, because they were oblivious and perhaps benignly ignorant. These are the type of men who worked in mostly male spaces and who thought nothing of remarking on a woman's appearance. Some of these men likely thought their compliments were welcome, and in a few cases, I suspect they were.

But for decades, too many men perpetuated an *Us and Them* dynamic in the workplace, because they did not understand that their comments and behavior were unwelcome. When people in a dominant group are surrounded by others from that same dominant group, it is easy to miss clear signs of distress. Most members of a home team assume that everything is fine so long as there are no complaints.

Actions for Unaware and Oblivious

- Look around!
- Make a list of the people you've shared lunch with in the past week.
- Make a list of the three people you trust most in your business.
- Analyze the representation of people from non-dominant cultures in your organization/in positions of power in your organization.
- Read this list from Robin DiAngelo's book *White Fragility* (2016–2017 data).[4]

Category	Percentage white
Ten richest Americans	100%
U.S. Congress	90%
U.S. governors	96%
Top military advisors	100%
President and vice president	100%
U.S. House Freedom Caucus	99%
Current U.S. presidential cabinet	91%
People who decide which TV shows we see	93%
People who decide which books we read	90%
People who decide what news is covered	85%
People who decide which music is produced	95%
People who directed the one hundred top-grossing films of all time, worldwide	95%
Teachers	82%
Full-time college professors	84%
Owners of men's professional football teams	97%

2. Aware but Scared

Question: "Have you ever tried to have a meaningful conversation about the *Us versus Them* dynamic around race, ethnicity, sexual orientation, or other divides?"

Aware but Scared Answer: "No way. That is way too risky and would lead to legal trouble for sure!"

Ironically, this fear gets in the way of honest self-assessment. Without self-assessment a workplace may be more at risk. Fear of breaking laws can prevent people from recognizing their complicity in maintaining a dominant culture. Laws that mandate equal employment do so by preventing employment decisions made on the basis of sex, race, age, national origin, disability, religion, sexual orientation, veteran status, genetic information, and citizenship. But the laws are not meant to prevent conversation to tackle these problems in comprehensive ways. It's always important to seek out and listen to the advice of counsel regarding these issues, but doing nothing is also often a bad option. There are times when inaction creates an environment that exposes an organization to other liability. Inaction perpetuates the status quo. The goal is to take action to make things better, not remain passive out of fear that we might do or say the wrong thing.

The laws as affirmed by Supreme Court decisions over the years create great uncertainty in the marketplace, because there is frequently no clear and definitive rule. This is complicated by state laws that sometimes differ from federal laws and apply in different parts of the country. Consulting with experienced employment counsel before starting conversations will help you make sure you understand what laws apply to you. The overall message is that everyone has the same rights. A company should not give preferential treatment to employees based on race or other protected factors. And at the same time, companies should work toward establishing a diverse workforce that reflects our increasingly diverse population.

Given the sensitivity and importance of these issues, it is understandable that many people want to avoid discussing identity topics like race and ethnicity, because they are afraid of possible outcomes. But change will only occur when the dominant group leverages its power and privilege and takes action.

Actions for Aware but Scared

- Align yourself with non-dominant people.
- Seek the counsel of more knowledgeable people inside your organization.
- Seek the counsel of knowledgeable people outside your organization.
- Listen to people from marginalized groups inside your organization.
- Listen to people from marginalized groups outside your organization.
- Read *them* websites.
- Follow *thems* on Twitter.
- Read books and articles by *thems*.
- Read more books and articles by *thems*.

3. Aware and Unaccountable

Question: "Have you ever participated in a group that met on a voluntary and regular basis in which people from another cultural group were the majority?

Aware and Unaccountable Answer: "I have not attended, but we sponsor many ERGs and we have an excellent Diversity Committee."

After working in Japan, I returned to Ohio at age twenty-five and continued working for Honda by supporting supplier companies from Japan that had relocated to the Midwest. These suppliers made transmissions, carburetors, engine mountings, brakes, tubes, hoses, and many other parts that go into a car. Some of these companies were suppliers to Honda in Japan and had set up factories in America to supply the factory in Ohio.

There was a pattern in these companies that looked like this—the homogeneous all-Japanese management team would hire one American in the role of Human Relations manager and outsource the hiring and management of local staff. Of course, this approach made sense for Japanese executives who were not comfortable with English and unfamiliar working outside Japan. But instead of looking at this strategy as a temporary approach to dealing with difference, many of the Japanese teams viewed this outsourcing as a permanent solution. Rather than developing their own, firsthand experiences with non-Japanese people, the leaders in the companies, whether they lived in Indiana or Ohio or Michigan, lived almost entirely Japanese lives.

This same outdated approach to diversity is common among leaders of major American companies. Rather than expand their own firsthand experiences with people outside the cultural majority in their organizations, they outsource the job of "diversifying" to people of color, Directors of Diversity, or lawyers.

Actions for Aware and Unaccountable

- Stop shirking and show up.
- Go to ERG meetings.
- Join Diversity Council meetings.
- Engage with people from marginalized groups face-to-face.
- Listen to people from marginalized groups inside your organization.
- Listen to people from marginalized groups outside your organization.
- Read *them* websites.
- Follow *thems* on Twitter.
- Read books and articles by *thems*.
- Read more books and articles by *thems*.

4. Aware and Seeking Organic Approach

Question: "Have you ever joined a group outside the workplace that will provide exposure and firsthand experience to a relevant *them* group?"

Aware and Seeking Organic Approach Answer: "No.
That would be artificial. I am interested in connections that
develop naturally and are built in a more organic way."

The Chautauqua Institute of New York, founded in 1874, is a
gated summer retreat dedicated to the arts, education, recre-
ation, and religion. Every year, thousands of people gather near
the shores of Lake Chautauqua to hear lectures and to be enter-
tained and educated by important speakers and artists from
around the world. The institute spawned a movement of smaller
Chautauquas around North America in the early twentieth century, with a peak of about twelve thousand communities hosting
temporary assemblies or establishing permanent facilities in
1915. Today, a dozen of these institutes remain. The Chautauqua Institute in New York as well as the other remaining institutes, are magical, exclusive and very white places. Day passes to
the grounds range from $15 just to walk around to $99 for an
all-day pass with access to entertainment and lectures.

The whiteness of Chautauqua has been called into question
by many, including invited guest speakers. In August 2018, Reverend Irene Monroe, the resident chaplain, spoke directly to the
thousands of visitors in attendance that week. "You are overly
traditional in your religious training, your white privilege, and
your class traditions."[5] She acknowledged that the institute had
always invited speakers and entertainers of color to perform,
but that the community itself was ambivalent about race. "One
person of color is always okay, but two might create a trend."

This wasn't the first time race was called into question.
Twenty years earlier, in a 1998 *New York Times* article, the official
historian at Chautauqua, Alfreda Irwin, said, "Because the society is diverse, we aim to be like society. Chautauqua is very open
and would like to have all sorts of people come here and participate. I think it will happen, just naturally."[6]

The "natural" or organic progression toward a more inclusive
community has not happened at Chautauqua or at other

institutions. There are too many intrinsic barriers—where people live, how much they earn, and access to education to name just a few. WE-building is a deliberate antidote to centuries of purposeful segregation. Redlining, voter suppression, and hiring discrimination are all twentieth-century examples of orchestrated acts of marginalizing minorities. After centuries of discrimination and segregation, there is no "natural" process that will narrow gaps at the necessary pace. WE-building is deliberate integration across any aspect of identity difference with the goal of establishing trusting relationships over time.

Actions for Aware and Seeking Organic Approach

- Stop waiting for someone else to do the work.
- Start taking action to bridge *Us and Them* gaps.
- Listen to people from marginalized groups inside your organization.
- Listen to people from marginalized groups outside your organization.
- Read *them* websites.
- Follow *thems* on Twitter.
- Read books and articles by *thems*.
- Read more books and articles by *thems*.

5. Aware, Willing to Act, but Unsure

Question: "Have you ever invited someone from this *them* group to lunch?"

Aware, Willing to Act, but Unsure Answer: "They don't want to have lunch with me. I don't want to offend anyone by pressuring them to have lunch with me."

Companies cannot force employees to confront racial, ethnic, sexual orientation, religious, or other differences, but they can invite them to participate in WE-building initiatives where individuals are invited to reflect on *Us and Them* gaps of their own choosing. They can be encouraged to complete the WE-building solutions worksheet (from Chapter 6) with other colleagues. They can support voluntary participation in WE-building actions described in Chapter 7. But it is equally important that leaders who identity with the dominant cultural group in their organizations also pay attention to their own daily interaction with others

Actions to broaden inclusion:

Don't List

1. DO NOT make jokes or use humor around identity factors, especially when first meeting someone.

   "What is a Jew doing in the middle of Ohio?"

   "Hola, señor!" said in an exaggerated accent (to a Latinx person).

   "I sure hope you don't have the coronavirus!" (to an Asian person).

2. DO NOT overtly bring attention to differences in identity.

   "Where are you from? I mean *really* from?"

   "We've never had anyone Black work here before."

   "I'll introduce you to Maria. She's also Hispanic."

3. DO NOT other people who may not identify with the culturally dominant norm.

   "What are you? What's your ethnicity?"

   "I'm so glad we finally have a Latinx person on our team!"

   "Are you from Puerto Rico or the Dominican Republic? I can never keep them straight."

4. DO NOT make stereotypical remarks.

"You look like you are a good basketball player" (to a Black person).

"You must be in IT" (to an East Asian person).

"Which do you speak better, Cantonese or Mandarin?" (to an Asian person).

5. DO NOT make comments about or related to appearance.

"You remind me of Beyoncé."

"I love Mexican food" (to a Latinx person).

"You guys sure do stay in good shape" (to a gay person).

Do List

1. DO guide the conversation to shared or common factors.

"How long have you lived in _____ (name the current location)?"

"Are you originally from _____ (name the current location)?"

"I've been working _____ (name the current location) for ___ years."

2. DO use the conversation to seek common factors and make a connection.

"I'm thinking about going to visit _____ (name a local public place like a park, botanical garden, zoo, museum, or other well-known destination). Have you ever been there?"

"I am thinking about visiting Chicago. Have you ever been there?"

"I used to live in Washington, D.C. Have you ever been there?"

3. DO share information about yourself that may be invisible but is important to your identity (that you are comfortable sharing).

"I've got three teenage kids and one dog."

"I like to play golf but rarely find the time."

"I'm really into a band called BTS from Korea. They sing in four languages."

Strategies for Limiting Gaps

Small talk comments can be the yellow flags that trigger bigger problems. For this reason, being more mindful of offhand remarks, especially when using humor, is a simple technique that can limit rather than perpetuate gaps.

Using examples from the beginning of this chapter, we can see in the chart below how just a slight adjustment in a remark can make a big difference.

Examples of Feeling Like a *Them*	Comments/Jokes That *Perpetuate* Gaps	Comments That Limit Gaps
"In first grade, my teacher could not pronounce my name and made a joke about it."	"That name sure is a mouthful! I'll never be able to say that!"	Politely say, "I want to make sure I am saying your name correctly. Is this right?"
"Being one of the few vegetarians in my group, sometimes I cannot eat with my colleagues when they go to meat-based restaurants."	"How could you give up eating bacon? Everybody loves bacon!"	"What is one of your favorite vegetarian dishes?"

Examples of Feeling Like a *Them*	Comments/Jokes That *Perpetuate* Gaps	Comments That Limit Gaps
"Working in a Midwestern bank and I was the only New Yorker."	"Oh, here's the fancy guy from Manhattan."	"How long did you live in New York?" or, "I've always wanted to visit."
"I went to business school at age twenty-six after being in the military and was surrounded by younger kids."	"At ease, Sergeant."	"Would you mind telling me which branch you served in the military?"
Person of color.	"Are you bummed that Black History Month is over?" "Do you know Kung Fu?" "Now that you work here, can we all take a siesta?"	Make no comments about race. Seek inclusive common factors.
"Being the only Jewish kid in my class."	"You don't look Jewish."	Make no comments about religion or ethnicity. Seek inclusive common factors.
"I was the only female on the executive team."	"Finally, we have some beauty in the room."	Make no comments about gender. Seek inclusive common factors.
"Being gay in high school and not going to prom because of it."	"My cousin is gay."	Make no comments about sexual orientation. Seek inclusive common factors.

INCLUSIVE TOPICS

- **Food.** It's universal and almost always a topic people from different backgrounds can talk about. Pairing a specific food with the geographical location is a great conversation topic. "What is the best pizza around here?" Be mindful of not falling into discussion around foods associated with another culture because you assume the person you're talking to identifies with that culture (e.g., don't ask the Asian person where to find the best Chinese food in town because they're Asian).

- **Arts.** Music, movies, and other arts are topics that can be shared across cultures and languages. Popular movies and artists are generally known even if a person has not experienced them firsthand.
- **Travel/Geography.** Talking about common destinations such as the Grand Canyon or Disneyland can be good topics. More local destinations, such as the city zoo, a local park, or a nearby body of water, are even better.
- **Sports.** Whatever major league sport is currently in season is a time-tested topic for businesspeople worldwide. Learning what sports and teams a person follows is an excellent bonding topic. I don't care much about sports, but always make a point to see how the local team performed when traveling and meeting new people for work. Inevitably, someone will be very interested to tell me more about last night's game, and before long we've segued into other topics in which I'm more interested.
- **Pets.** In any group of twenty people or more, I can almost always find connection through pets. If I ask the simple question, "Who has a photo of their pet on their phone?" I am guaranteed to see many beloved animals.
- **Current geographical location.** The current location may be someone's hometown or maybe a destination for a first-time visitor. Either way, that geographical location is a common point. Asking someone "What do you like best about _____ (place)?" never fails to get conversation going. Asking for advice, "Where is the best _____ in _____?" is another.

9

ON BEYOND DIVERSITY

The Need for Building Internal Infrastructure

AT THE END of a lecture to a group of students at the NYU Stern School of Business, a young Asian woman raised her hand to ask a question. She said that her parents had emigrated from China and that she had grown up in the United States in a Mandarin-speaking household. She brought up the idea of the Perpetual Foreigner—the racialized and xenophobic tendency to perceive native-born citizens like her as being foreign because they belong to a minority group. Then, with her voice slightly shaking, she said, "I worry that people will look at me like this, especially when I am looking for a job." Her comment resonated. I've met so many people like her—people who didn't fit the false assumption that being American meant being white. These are people who regularly hear the question, "But where are you *really* from?" They are people who, because of the way they look or the spelling of their names or the way they dress, elicit a range of reactions from curiosity to fear.

Studies of the Perpetual Foreigner syndrome show that it causes a lower sense of belonging.[1] Generations of immigrant families and their descendants have dealt with this unfair categorization for decades, though, as I told her, I noticed a change on the horizon. As a potential employer, instead of questioning whether she belonged, I would view her as a strong candidate. Not only would she have a degree from NYU Stern School of Business, but she was fluent in the two languages that represent the world's two biggest economies, the United States and China. I could see that the Perpetual Foreigner label had burdened her and many others in the past, but I looked at her not as lacking, but as having a valuable advantage. She was culturally fluid.

Cultural fluidity can be game-changing.

Culturally fluid people are WE-building's secret weapons— they are folks who have strong firsthand experience in two or more *Us and Them* cultural groups. They are people who can see and understand more than one perspective; they have an identity or experiences in life that provide insights that others do not have. They can maintain unbiased points of view and tend to avoid false assumptions because of their firsthand experiences. Culturally fluid people disrupt the homogeneity of an organization. They can relate well to different groups of people and can be a powerful tool to facilitate the integration of others. They often have multiple languages so they can communicate directly and smoothly between *Us and Them* groups. They may be multiracial or have grown up in a household that practiced different religions. Having culturally fluid people on your team can help your organization be more profitable and innovative. They may also help you successfully access hard-to-reach markets.

CULTURALLY FLUID

A culturally fluid woman named Hana Tajima made a game-changing positive impact on Uniqlo's bottom line, helping make it the world's number one clothing retailer.[2] Uniqlo started in 1984 with twenty stores in Japan and grew quickly from there. In 2015, they opened their first store in Malaysia, a country with an over 60 percent Muslim population. Uniqlo's bright-colored, simple clothing was popular, but it did not always accommodate Islamic norms that include covering the head, arms and legs. In response to customer needs, Uniqlo partnered with a Muslim designer named Hana Tajima, a half-Japanese and half-British woman who had converted to Islam at the age of seventeen. Together they launched a collection called "modest wear" in Malaysia in 2015, which included items such as hijab head coverings and kebaya tunics. The next year, the collection expanded to the UK. One year later, the "modest line" products were available in the United States and could be purchased online. Now, in their sixth year, the line continues to dominate the growing hijab couture market, estimated to be in the billions of dollars by 2025.

Anyone can become culturally fluid.

Many culturally fluid people are born into their role: people like Hana Tajima or President Obama, who have parents of different nationalities or spent time growing up in more than one country. Third Country Kids (TCK), those who are raised in a place other than the culture of their home country or their parents' country, are another example of those born into cultural fluidity. Tayo Rockson is one such person who grew up the son of a Nigerian diplomat and shares this experience in his book, *Use Your Difference to Make a Difference*. TCK can include kids whose parents are in the military, diplomatic corps, or are missionaries. But this isn't the only way to become a culturally fluid person.

Being born into and raised in a homogeneous family or belonging to a dominant cultural group does not preclude you from becoming culturally fluid. A person's life experience, viewpoint, personality, and values all contribute to shaping one's character and influence anyone's ability to move between distinct cultures. Working at closing an *Us and Them* gap until you become culturally fluid is possible for anyone.

WE-building is the antidote to decades of artificial separation between people from different backgrounds.

MOVING IN ONE DIRECTION

It is my life's mission to encourage leaders to WE-build as an ongoing practice and to cultivate their own understanding of *Us and Them* dynamics. I want to inspire leaders to move away from cultural ignorance and toward cultural awareness and positive outcomes. I want leaders to inspire their employees and colleagues and suppliers and B2B partners to move in a constructive direction. It is my great hope that the ten simple questions on the *Us versus Them* self-assessment will become an often-used reflection point for well-meaning people who agree that building barriers and other fear-based, protectionist actions are not a viable long-term path to thriving in our increasingly diverse and deeply interconnected world.

The most effective way to connect across difference is through face-to-face interactions of increasing depth. Spending time gathering cultural data and looking below the surface to learn invisible information will eliminate dangerous stereotyping and false assumptions. As a person's score on the *Us versus Them* self-assessment increases, they are more likely to get positive outcomes. Moving away from unintentional negative consequences and toward intentional positive results is the goal of WE-building.

CROSS-CULTURAL CONTINUUM

NEGATIVE CULTURAL IMPACT ⊖			⊕ POSITIVE CULTURAL IMPACT		
GAME-CHANGING	CONSEQUENTIAL	INCONSEQUENTIAL	INCONSEQUENTIAL	CONSEQUENTIAL	GAME-CHANGING
Significant, long-term negative outcome.	Measurable negative outcome.	Not meaningful enough to cause measurable negative outcome.	Not meaningful enough to cause measurable positive outcome.	Measurable positive outcome.	Significant, long-term positive outcome.
Damage caused is difficult or impossible to repair. Some permanent damage is done.	Time required rebuilding goodwill and trust. Money spent on solutions. Formal apology necessary.	Resources are not impacted. Register a moment of confusion.	Resources are not impacted. Register a moment of connection or clarity.	Achieve improved communication and relationships. Trust and goodwill established.	Achieve excellent communication and teamwork in culturally diverse group.

0   1   2   3   4   5   6   7   8   9   10

FAILING TO INTEGRATE

Put-in-Bay is a small island located just off the Ohio coast in Lake Erie. Only five miles long and less than three miles wide, it is home to fewer than four hundred year-round residents. But in warmer months, Put-in-Bay is a lively tourist destination known for its wineries and bars. Put-in-Bay actively promotes its reputation as a place to party, especially for young adults. Their tourism website lists events nearly every weekend, starting in mid-April with the Whiskey Lighting Celebration at the famous Roundhouse Bar that kicks off the tourist season. Revelers are welcomed to celebrate recognizable holidays, such as Memorial Day and the Fourth of July, as well as invented holidays, including Half-way to St. Patrick's Day.

It was another invented holiday—Christmas in July—that led to an *Us versus Them* cultural conflict on Put-in-Bay. The event, which started as a casual celebration, grew over the years into a weeklong Mardi Gras–like party with Christmas decorations, a parade with bikini-clad young women wearing red and white Santa hats, and a contest for the best Christmas lights on a boat. Maumee State Park in the area promoted hayrides with Santa. Local tour bus operators organized trips specifically for the event. The number of visitors to the island for Christmas in July weekend grew from hundreds to thousands and it became one of the most lucrative business weekends of the season.

In 2018, an estimated 35,000 people visited the island to celebrate the made-up holiday.[3] For a tourist community that generates most of its profits during the summer, this would seem like good news. But Put-in-Bay had a homogeneity problem. Like many places in the United States, it was very white and had few culturally fluid people. From its early days in the 1800s as a destination for steamship vacationers, the home team demographics had not changed much. Meanwhile, the minority population of Ohio had risen to over 20 percent. For more than two hundred years the racial and cultural demographics of Ohio and the rest of America was diversifying—but that diversity had not made its way to Put-in-Bay.

The tour buses brought in a new kind of clientele: African Americans from Cleveland, Sandusky, and Detroit. This was a "them" tourist segment that the nearly all-white island had not experienced in large numbers, and the outcome wasn't good. News sources reported that twenty-seven people were arrested and seventy-five citations were handed out that weekend for violations like drinking alcohol in public.[4] Residents complained about visitors smoking weed, driving golf carts recklessly, and fighting. The local news characterized the event as chaotic and blamed tour bus visitors for causing havoc. Put-in-Bay village council president Jessica Dress stated the obvious: "It's a different type of customer than the island is accustomed to."[5]

Few would openly say that race was the factor in the overwhelming negative response and media coverage. Instead, they hid behind complaints about too many intoxicated tourists. But

Put-in-Bay is a small tourist island with more than twenty-five bars. They are geared toward encouraging partiers and managing large numbers of intoxicated tourists. They were not accustomed to welcoming large numbers of Black tourists. As a community, Put-in-Bay was ill-prepared to welcome large numbers of people who didn't look like them.

Local business owners were prepared for a small number of tourists who looked or sounded different—they were quick to talk about Spanish-speaking families who increasingly came to visit. But when the tourists were Black and the numbers were large, the *Us and Them* dynamic fundamentally changed. The white home team *Us* became the minority, outnumbered by *Them*. The local residents were not used to this, and some of them really didn't like it.

This experience triggered intergroup anxiety among many in the white population. This is the feeling of discomfort and fear that we discussed in Chapter 3 that can happen whenever anyone is in a new and unfamiliar situation. It is normal to feel stress around strangers. This often happens when a person starts a new job or goes to an unfamiliar new place. Our heart rates increase and we get sweaty palms. Researchers have discovered that the stress hormone cortisol becomes elevated.[6] Many non-white people feel intergroup anxiety on a regular basis when they are the only person of color in an office, a classroom, or even a social gathering. I felt this when I first lived in Japan. My Japanese clients felt this when they arrived in Houston or Chicago. It's the feeling, often untrue, that we are unwelcome and don't belong.

The fact that many white people in Put-in-Bay were uncomfortable and perhaps even fearful when thousands of Black visitors arrived was predictable, but the problem wasn't the number of Black tourists. It was the lack of diversity and the lack of firsthand experience with Black people among the home team folks in Put-in-Bay. My guess is that many of the white residents had few meaningful firsthand experiences with Black people, and even fewer trusted relationships with Black people, so they felt unease.

People who have lived homogeneous, home team lives are more likely to feel apprehension when they engage with people who don't look, sound, or pray like them, especially in large numbers. Unlike my Japanese clients, the folks in Put-in-Bay did not travel thousands of miles by plane. They didn't even leave their hometown. Their experience of being a *them* happened suddenly when the *Us* and *Them* roles were unexpectedly reversed. Rather than any of them choosing to be in a more diverse area, diversity came to them. This same phenomenon has been happening and continues to happen, perhaps more slowly, in small communities across America and throughout the world. Despite increasingly diverse demographics in the United States, many destinations like Put-in-Bay, the Chautauqua Institute, or other organizations and businesses remain extraordinarily homogeneous and white. One reason for this is that many white people don't see a problem with the homogeneity and the historical marginalization of non-white people. If questioned about why there are few, if any, people of color in their communities and organizations, they might shrug their shoulders with genuine wonderment and act as though these circumstances are acceptable.

An Unseen Problem in Broad Daylight

The Missouri Athletic Club in downtown St. Louis is a private club and defining institution where only men could be members until 1973. If you go to their website, you'll see the following phrase: "Since 1903, the Missouri Athletic Club's mission has been to be the premier athletic, dining, and social club for business, professional, and civic leaders and their families in the St. Louis region." The language sure sounds inclusive. But if you scroll through the photos of MAC events or go visit the club (with a member, of course), what you will see is a whole lot of white people. I know because I've been there many times. My first visit was in 1997 with the people who would become my in-laws. Due to my own lack of awareness, it took me years before I even noticed that the only Black people I saw there were working.

More than fifty years since the passage of the Civil Rights Act and still the MAC's motto might as well read, "Since 1903, the Missouri Athletic Club's mission has been to be the premier athletic, dining, and social club for *white* business, professional, and civic leaders and their families in the St. Louis region." While St. Louis has a particularly insidious history of racial segregation and division, the MAC is like numerous other private athletic and country clubs throughout the United States. Membership to traditionally underrepresented groups remains limited.

The MAC, like many other institutions in the United States, claims inclusion but practices exclusion. My guess is that the majority of members and guests do not recognize any problem with the situation at the MAC. I didn't see a problem for many years. It took a tragedy nearby for me to take notice.

On August 9, 2014, only twelve miles from the MAC, a young, unarmed Black man named Michael Brown was shot and killed by police officer Darren Wilson.[7] The subsequent protests and investigations motivated me to start questioning things about St. Louis that I had never before considered. It was part of what started the examination of my own complicity and ignorance of race. Upon recognizing the deep-rooted racial inequality in the city's social structure, reflected in institutions like the MAC, I realized the extent to which I had been participating in and benefiting from these unjust systems. I had eaten many enjoy-able meals and attended beautiful weddings and other celebra-tions at the MAC. These were opportunities that have not been as available to Black families in St. Louis, despite the laudable words comprising the MAC's mission statement.

VISIBLE COMPLIANCE

Part of the ongoing *Us and Them* problem in the United States is that virtually every tourist destination and business publicly and enthusiastically states, "Everyone is welcome!" but few are really prepared to live up to this claim. Saying you are compliant with the 1964 Civil Rights Act or posting the federal EEOC code is easy. It is more challenging to do the work to ensure that people from different races, religions, and backgrounds are represented. It takes real commitment to do the work to learn about and increase your understanding of another group.

When the Americans with Disabilities Act (ADA) became law in 1990, it required most businesses, schools, and government buildings to become accessible to people with disabilities. When the law went into effect, thousands of organizations spent considerable time and money making visible, concrete adjustments to establish accessible parking spaces, build ramps, and provide closed captioning. These changes were intended to fundamentally break down the *Us and Them* gap between those without disabilities and people who live with disability. Unlike civil rights laws, it was easy to see who had and who had not actually complied with the new law by building infrastructure.

INTERNAL INFRASTRUCTURE

Far too many organizations proudly claim inclusion through slogans yet fail to do the work to achieve the stated goal. Following the Black Lives Matter protests, many organizations released impressive statements of solidarity, which were encouraging. But I remain skeptical. Words alone do not effect change. Saying what you think your customers, employees, and the public want to hear is different from building the internal infrastructure that would make places like Put-in-Bay, the MAC, or the Chautauqua Institute more diverse and genuinely inclusive.

For foundational progress to occur, we need home team leaders to build an internal infrastructure—to accumulate real-life experience interacting with people who are different on a *trusted colleague* basis. Until that is achieved, no slick slogan or public relations mission statement is going to make a measurable difference.

Any objective measure of minority representation in the workplace reveals that words are not enough. The data is indisputable. In her excellent book, *Diversity, Inc.*, Pamela Newkirk closely examines real metrics. She writes, "Despite decades of handwringing costly initiatives, and uncomfortable conversations, progress in most elite American institutions has been negligible."[8] To be sure, there are specific pockets of progress, but overall, the evidence is clear that we have not succeeded.

A solid internal infrastructure can lead to a genuinely inclusive WE culture. Without it, there is no opportunity for self-reflection when problems occur. Instead of looking inward, folks will look outward and point the finger of blame at others. It's like claiming on your website that your building is ADA compliant without building any ramps. Then, when a person using a wheelchair shows up, you blame them for expecting the fair access that you advertised.

The process of building an infrastructure needs to happen on an internal basis for home team players throughout America's institutions. Building WE cultures means interacting face-to-face with people who are different from you until you have built a trusted colleague relationship. Then you keep repeating this process with more and more people. Don't stop. Don't stop even when you realize that your intergroup anxiety is no longer triggered. Don't stop when you achieve benchmarks or are praised for your progress. Don't stop because there will always be gaps to close and your effort to keep building an internal infrastructure will make you a more interesting, successful, and empathic person. It will also make the world a better place.

Following Black Lives Matter protests, the Chautauqua Institute began the work of building internal infrastructures. They started a characteristically intellectually vigorous initiative called the Mirror Project. Leaning on their history of religious inclusivity and in partnership with the African American Heritage House on the grounds, the thoughtful project welcomed participants to reflect on race by responding to a series of written prompts such as: How has your thinking about racism evolved since national protests and related media coverage began? Are you discussing racism in your family? What are you reading regarding race?

Videos of thought leaders including Clint Smith and Dr. Tricia Rose were posted for participants to view and respond to. They started a series of virtual lectures, available to anyone for free, with leading speakers on race, including the Reverend Robert M. Franklin and Iyabo Onipede. A curated online gallery of responses reflected a genuine interest in becoming a more diverse and inclusive place. One such response was this: "I struggle with the lack of diversity at Chautauqua and feel that this should be one of our key focuses. We must as a community not only welcome people of color but help the African American community feel like they belong here. There is a difference between 'being welcoming' and a sense of 'belonging.' I believe we must address white fragility and the history of racism before we can move forward. BLM is a movement that Chautauqua must support: Black Lives Matter, Black voices matter, Black cultures matter, Black stories matter."[9]

I've watched thousands of professionals take on the challenge of developing their internal infrastructure. It can be done. I've supported many by suggesting small gestures to begin the process. I've experienced this myself when I worked to bridge myriad gaps in both my personal and professional life. You, too, can become a WE-builder by following the steps laid out in this book.

Following the negative Christmas in July events, the Chamber of Commerce in Put-in-Bay was looking for solutions. The question was not: Why did so many white people feel uncomfortable and respond in the way they did? The question was: What were they going to do about it? I advised the Chamber to partner with non-white people to think about solutions. I sent them the ten-question self-assessment, advising each member of the business community to reflect on their own lived experiences.

But rather than reflect on their homogeneous roots and consider how to become a more genuinely inclusive destination, they decided to do damage control. Claiming they were unhappy that the family-friendly concept of the faux holiday had morphed into a party scene, they voted to cancel Christmas in July moving forward. They also established the Safe Island Task Force and recruited two off-island members, both African American men from nearby communities, to join.[10] This was an encouraging action. Some members worked with tour operators and negotiated to have fewer buses at any one time in the future. They also discussed increasing law enforcement and posting new signs throughout the island to remind visitors about the rules. Local business leaders alleviated their immediate problem, but they seemed to do little to address the systemic issues that gave rise to their concerns. As they later learned, this was a big mistake.

FACE OF AMERICA

In a rare example of a home team leader recognizing and naming the lack of diversity as a serious economic problem in the United States, prior to the Black Lives Matter protests, former CEO of PGA of America, Pete Bevacqua, advocated for fundamental change by suggesting that golf must become more accessible and diverse in order to stay relevant in the future. "I think we would all agree, or most of us would agree, that the face of this game has to change if it's going to grow. It needs to look more like the face of America."[11]

Pete Bevacqua was born onto the American home team as a straight white man. There is no fault in this: straight white men are not the problem. The problem is any person on a home team who acts like they have no advantage and does nothing to bridge *Us and Them* gaps.

Alexis Ohanian, cofounder of Reddit, is another straight white male who not only recognized his advantages but took action in response to Black Lives Matter protests. In addition to making supportive statements, Ohanian resigned from the Reddit board and asked the company to replace him with a Black candidate.[12] A week later, Black tech mogul Michael Seibel joined Reddit's board. Ohanian also committed to ongoing financial contributions to serve the Black community.[13] He encouraged others to consider big change, saying, "We need diversity at the highest levels of business now more than ever."

When people in the majority like Pete Bevacqua and Alexis Ohanian advocate for foundational change in an institution by broadening the identity of who "belongs," they are deliberately using their home team advantage to build a WE culture. This is an action any leader can take, but it is particularly effective when these actions are performed by leaders who identify with the home team in their organizations.

As our demographics continue to diversify, all businesses and corporations need to advance toward a broader definition of WE in order to look more like "the face of America." It is in every organization's economic interest because it will avoid costly problems and help them stay relevant. It is also the right thing to do.

Anyone can build an internal infrastructure.

NEW PARADIGM

Developing a WE culture is an ongoing process. Don't wait for a catastrophe to force you into taking action. Take action now. Fortunately, there are many cost-effective ways for leaders to expand the definition of who belongs in their organizations. Here are ten actions leaders should take right now to make sure they are continuously aware.

1. **Look for *Us and Them* gaps.** The old paradigm had many of us thinking that when we talked about "culture difference" we meant differences between countries and languages. To be sure, these differences remain, but the gaps can reside anywhere people come together and may be related to differences in age, race, ethnicity, or any factor of identity.

2. **Increase awareness of marginalizing behaviors, especially if you identify with the home team.** Estimates place the cost of corporate diversity initiative in the billions, yet there has been little measurable progress when it comes to the number of non-white people in positions of power in corporate America.[14] One reason for this is that home team players do not fully and deeply understand the experience of being a minority. The lived experience of many home team people prevents them from seeing that marginalizing behaviors perpetuate pernicious *Us and Them* gaps.

3. **Ask for input from marginalized voices.** When you do not have the lived experience of being a minority, it is important to educate yourself and increase your own understanding. But no amount of study and listening can translate into knowing what it is like to live and work as a minority. Getting honest input from trusted people who represent voices different from your own is a foundational requirement for any WE organization.

4. **Make a deliberate effort to move toward trusted colleague status with individuals from historically marginalized groups.** So often, well-meaning home team people establish acquaintance-level or colleague-level relationships and then stop doing the work to move forward to trusted colleague–level status. There are many reasons for this failure, including limited time, uncertainty, and privilege, but none is sufficient justification for not taking action. Make this a priority.

5. **Notice when behavior seems unusual to you.** Instead of immediately reacting to experiences in which another person or group behaves in a way that seems out of the ordinary to you, be prepared to pause and consider culture difference. Ask yourself, "Is there invisible data that explains this behavior that I'm not considering?" The simple act of pausing to seek information requires awareness, patience, and curiosity—all freely available resources.

6. **Be sensitive and aware when a person from outside the cultural majority is present.** Notice language, race, ethnicity, religion, and other differences. A new paradigm for inclusion requires that we overcome an outdated "colorblind" approach. The new model requires that attention be paid to topics like race, ethnicity, and religion. Solutions to narrowing any *Us versus Them* gap will only arise when dominant cultural groups reconcile their role in longstanding narratives of exclusion and this starts with seeing, not ignoring, difference.

7. **Assume there is cultural data you cannot see and seek to find it.** Cultural data such as beliefs, values, and assumptions circulate around us like the air we breathe, informing choices we make on conscious and unconscious levels. Rather than waiting for a crisis to trigger reflection, assume that there is invisible and meaningful information around you at all times, just waiting to be seen.

8. **Build your own internal infrastructure.** Use the ten questions of the *Us versus Them* assessment as a measuring tool for your own development. Build your knowledge and firsthand experience with a person or group with whom you have a cultural difference, whether that gap is related to differences in generations, race, sexual orientation, nationality, or any factor of identity.

9. **Become Culturally Fluid.** Over time, accumulate insights and firsthand experiences so that you eventually reach a score of 10 with a *them* group. Then repeat.

10. **Inspire others to become WE-builders.** Utilize your position of authority to provide encouragement and support to others in their own journeys toward building understanding and firsthand experience.

MOVING FORWARD AS A TEAM

I was invited to Put-in-Bay to meet with the Chamber of Commerce to discuss ways to make the island more welcoming to all tourists. But not everyone showed up to the meeting. Those who did clearly fell into the "Aware, Willing to Act but Unsure" category discussed in Chapter 8. Others belonged in the "Unaware and Oblivious" category, unwilling to attend a meeting about an issue they didn't consider particularly important. Those members did not see increasing diversity as an opportunity to expand their knowledge and benefit their business. When I asked who had not shown up for the meeting, one of the members said, "It's the same people who have racist lawn jockey statues in their yards."

The WE-minded contingent of the Chamber had proposed inviting the tour bus operators to visit the island for face-to-face meetings, leveraging their common goal to foster safe and profitable tourism. But the *Us versus Them* members said no. Instead, they suggested having more heavily armed police. When I asked about the two African American off-island task force members, they told me that only one member remained. The WE-minded team told me that the old-school business owners listened to longtime customers who threatened to take their business elsewhere if they encouraged more non-white visitors to the island.

The 2019 season progressed with no notable trouble. This may have been a result of reports that some tour bus operators were harassed on social media and decided to cancel their trips. Some residents mistakenly thought the goal was to limit the number of Black tourists (it's understandable how they would draw this conclusion) and congratulated members of the Chamber. The WE-minded members felt discouraged. Instead of being part of a unified group with a common goal, they saw a disparate group of small businesses unlikely to work together.

Following the Chamber's decision to cancel the Christmas in July event, I stayed in touch with the folks in the "Willing to Act" group, encouraging more WE-building solutions. I wrote to say that I understood their short-term decision to cancel the event but warned them that they could not cancel the increasingly diverse tourist demographics. Canceling the event and limiting tour buses was a Band-Aid approach. The long-term goal was to create a safe, inviting, and profitable destination that truly is welcoming to all visitors, no matter their race, ethnicity, or background. Like so many other organizations in the United States that want to stay relevant and survive in business, Put-in-Bay had to acknowledge and combat this specific *Us versus Them* racial gap.

As the community prepared for the 2020 season, the COVID-19 pandemic hit hard. Like summer destinations everywhere, instead of gearing up for thousands of visitors, they held off hiring seasonal workers. Worried about the spreading virus, and following state and local restrictions, the community canceled its usual spring opening. A strong statement from local authorities suggested that only residents and essential workers travel to the island. For a community that earns most of its annual income during the summer months, the economic impact was worrisome.

Then, just as Put-in-Bay opened up for business in June, there was another incident.[15] What started off as a misdemeanor triggered by too many people riding on a golf cart turned into two white officers pulling their guns on unarmed Black people and putting nine of them in handcuffs. In the process, officers used Tasers on two individuals. Six men spent the night in jail accused of aggravating a riot and inciting violence.

Over the next twenty-four hours, news of the arrests and video clips of the event spread quickly. A small group peacefully protested at the local courthouse and cheered as each of the six men were released. Days later, the county prosecutor reviewed video from police body cameras and dropped all charges.[16] The prosecutor then released footage to the public, which revealed that police officers unnecessarily escalated the situation. Two officers resigned and the local police chief was put on leave. The Ottawa County prosecutor asked the FBI to investigate officer misconduct and racism.[17]

Body cam footage of the incident reveals the underlying racial divide. Immediately before to pulling over the Black tourists, the two white officers had pulled over a separate group for the exact same reason—too many people on a golf cart.[18] This group, however, was all white. The officers were in the process of writing a citation to the all-white group when they saw the golf cart with Black people. They made a decision to give the white group a warning, rather than a citation, and to go after the Black group, later claiming that the Black driver was operating the cart recklessly.

It was a deeply disappointing start to the season. The events revealed to me that the overall community had not done the hard work of self-reflection. Some in the community tried to create positive change. I knew they were genuine and well-meaning people, but it was not enough.

———

WE-building rejects the notion that inclusion is a zero-sum game.

———

MINDSET

It's not location that determines behavior; it is intention. A person can fly halfway around the world and still have an *Us versus Them* mindset. It is time for a new paradigm that rejects fear-based behaviors like building walls, limiting tourist buses, and increasing law enforcement. These protectionist behaviors are not a viable long-term solution because we are too deeply interconnected to survive without one another.

The simple questions each leader must answer are these: Are you trying to limit or broaden the definition of who belongs? Are you seeking connection or perpetuating division? Are your choices highlighting shared factors or fanning flames of division? We answer these important questions with our own behavioral choices in every encounter, every meeting, and with every decision we make.

SMALL UTOPIAS

During the unsettled time of the COVID-19 pandemic, I observed the creation of more "small utopias," a phrase conceived by author Sheryll Cashin in her book *Loving*. She describes them as "places open to all, with new norms for inclusion, where people can build trust and be culturally dexterous."[19] Cultural dexterity is a concept she describes as "an enhanced capacity for intimate connections with people outside one's own tribe, for seeing and accepting difference rather than demanding assimilation to an unspoken norm of whiteness."

The scientific community became a small utopia, working across different languages and nationalities and abandoning competitive practices like keeping laboratory findings to themselves. Instead, researchers immediately shared important laboratory findings so that other scientists around the world could access the data. Among my clients, I heard many examples of how colleagues from different backgrounds stepped up to the challenge. Samuel in Kenya wrote to say that now that they worked from home, they had more regular virtual meetings and shared information more openly and readily, because maintaining business was essential to their economic survival. The Chautauqua Institute in New York started work toward becoming a Small Utopia with the Mirror Project.

Small utopias can be created anywhere.

THE FUTURE

WE-building is a purposeful effort to close real-life *Us versus Them* dynamics that exist in Put-in-Bay, in the PGA, the NFL, and in every office, factory, and business where people from different cultural backgrounds have not developed trusted colleague–level relationships with others. This deliberate approach is necessary to correct the segregated lives so many of us have experienced.

I don't know if Put-in-Bay can become a small utopia. What I do know is that Put-in-Bay is, like many communities around the country, struggling to navigate a diverse landscape with outdated tools at a pivotal time. Despite having had an opportunity two years earlier to confront their failure to live up to the claim that everyone is welcome, the good intentions of a few were not

enough to create the change they need.[20] When I last communicated with the folks on the island, they told me that the Safe
Island Task Force was engaged again and had reached out to
several African American thought-leaders who were attending
their meetings and trying to find solutions.[21] They hired an in-
terim police chief, a Black man with twenty years of law-enforce-
ment experience. It is encouraging to see more inclusive action
by the Put-in-Bay community but frustrating that it took an incident involving arrests, resignations, and an FBI inquiry to
make this happen.

There is a better, less costly way to address difference in our
increasingly diverse times and it is WE-building. People from
different backgrounds are the future of tourism at places like
Put-in-Bay and for businesses everywhere. If the community in
Put-in-Bay decided to embrace WE-building to improve inclusion, the prescription is straightforward. They need to follow
the three-step approach for closing the gap.

First, the local white community would need to gain **awareness** of their own complicity in creating a tourist destination
that is not as inclusive as it can and should be in the twenty-first
century. They would need to see how their all-white advertising
and imagery on the website and in town reflect a narrow, white
experience. The members in the community would need to examine and take responsibility for the ways in which they have
made non-white people feel excluded and unwelcome, including the way law enforcement has behaved.

Second, every business owner would need to honestly **assess**
their own level of engagement with Black culture and Black people with the *Us versus Them* assessment. They would need to reflect on what their scores say about their choices and life
experience so far and see that building an internal infrastructure is necessary and achievable.

Third, these folks would start taking **action**. They would begin
building their own racial literacy and relationships with

non-white people, to the point that every single one of them understood, for example, that lawn jockeys are viewed as demeaning relics that caricature Black people and promote the theme of servitude. They would get rid of all lawn jockeys voluntarily.

With humility, they would take more safe actions to start educating themselves, perhaps reading one of the books suggested in the Recommended Reading section, or following some of the other suggestions from Chapter 8, like following Black voices on Twitter. They could read "100 Things White People Can Do for Racial Justice."[22] They could go to Open Yale Courses on the internet and in four clicks be watching one of twenty-five free lectures by Professor Jonathan Holloway on African American history from Emancipation to the present.[23] Next, they would select actions from this list or create their own challenging actions, which would include interacting with more people of color. They would humbly seek the council of nearby NAACP leaders and other people of color who have experience and insight that they do not have. They would make changes to the police department and start building trust with non-white visitors. They would listen and learn. Business owners would go out of their way to start hiring Black people to work, not only as bouncers and back in the kitchen, but in front-facing jobs and with decisionmaking power.

Transformation is possible when individuals honestly reflect on their own life experience. Residents of Put-in-Bay could encourage one another and get the help of others with more experience. With lots of effort and little expense, they could fundamentally alter their trajectory and become a more inclusive, and profitable, destination. Over time, some of them would develop cultural fluidity, which would facilitate communication, relationship building, and integration in the community. This would be good for business. This would be good for business *and* the right thing to do.

LEGACY

I know from my interactions with folks on Put-in-Bay that many of the people there have roots that go back for many generations. They are devoted to this magical and beautiful place. I believe these folks genuinely want the best for the future and want to be successful stewards of their beloved town.

I believe NFL commissioner Roger Goodell genuinely loves football and wants to foster a long and healthy future for the game. The same goes for every CEO who made a public statement committing to racial justice and condemning silence. These statements are unprecedented in their forcefulness and clarity. They are a welcome departure from the overwhelmingly neutral voices of the past. Yet, as we have discussed throughout this book, slogans and verbal commitments are not enough to close any gaps, particularly one as important and historically charged as the Black versus white racial divide.

So the questions for the folks in Put-in-Bay are the same questions for any leader who looks toward the future: What is the legacy you want to leave? Will you risk a social media firestorm or legal action because you failed to embrace the diversity that exists in our communities and will continue to grow? Will you risk economic failure because you were not willing to self-reflect and not successful making a wide range of customers or employees or business partners feel welcome?

Whether you are a business owner on a small island in Lake Erie or a leader in a multinational conglomerate, if you really care about succeeding in the future you will prioritize WE-building as though your organizations depend on it. Outrage expressed during Black Lives Matter protests is evidence that people—many types of people—will no longer accept outdated, unjust conditions.

The world is a fundamentally different place as a result of the COVID-19 pandemic and the protests. We should take the positive lessons from these experiences with us as we move forward and navigate our diverse and deeply interconnected economy. A WE-mindset offers access to an untapped resource right in front of us. The gaps between any *Us versus Them* dynamic in the workplace represent underutilized energy, innovation, and productivity. With committed leadership, this time can be an opportunity to work through many *Us versus Them* gaps in order to create small utopias with new norms for inclusion, where people can build trust and develop intimate connections with people outside their own tribe.

Will this happen on Put-in-Bay? Will this happen in your department or your organization or your community? Will leaders be successful making their organizations more equitable and enable them to stay relevant by looking more like "the face of America"? Will NFL commissioner Roger Goodell do more than publicly state that he wants to be part of a solution?[24] Will there be meaningful and measurable change?

None of us really knows how this is going to play out in the years and decades ahead. Many factors will inform the choices leaders make that will impact financial markets, social structures, and individual well-being. What I know for sure is that maintaining the status quo will no longer work and will leave us ill-prepared for the future ahead. Legal action or violence against people of color must not be the reason home team people take action and crisis-response cannot be the only remedy to our failures to build WE communities.

Here's the thing: many of us already have what we need to change the trajectory away from division and toward connection. The most important requirements to establish a new paradigm in which diversity is valued and people have the skills to build connection across any differences are free and available to anyone—the willingness to be both genuine and humble and the desire to close gaps. Using the tools in this book, it is possible to move forward toward a truly integrated culture in which only inconsequential *Us and Them* dynamics remain. Working together, I believe in a path forward where consequential and game-changing *Us versus Them* gaps no longer exist, where there is only WE.

I hope to meet you there.

RECOMMENDED READING

Books

All You Can Ever Know by Nicole Chung. Chung's memoir about her experience being adopted and raised by a white family provides valuable insight into race and family identity.

Becoming by Michelle Obama. Obama's book speaks to the importance of bridging gaps in our society through her rare life experience as first lady.

Becoming a Man by P. Carl. P. Carl's memoir is a rare account of a person's experience of being both female and male.

Between the World and Me by Ta-Nehisi Coates. Coates writes about his experience with race in America and growing up as a Black man in this iconic book.

Born a Crime by Trevor Noah. Noah's thoughtful and humorous memoir describes his childhood in South Africa and the experience of being the child of a Black mother and white father.

Diversity Inc., by Pamela Newkirk. Newkirk documents the failure of diversity initiatives in corporate America, the entertainment world, and academia.

Dying of Whiteness by Jonathan M. Metzl. Metzl's thoroughly researched book examines the devastating consequences of right-wing policies and how they hurt the same people that support these policies.

Eloquent Rage by Brittney C. Cooper. Cooper writes frankly about being a Black feminist in America, sharing personal insights while also challenging the notion that Black women's anger is a destructive force.

Good and Mad by Rebecca Traister. Traister examines women and the important role that anger has played historically in social change.

Hillbilly Elegy by J. D. Vance. Vance's memoir of growing up poor and white provides insight into this culture.

How to Be an Antiracist by Ibram X. Kendi. Kendi writes from a personal and analytic perspective on how to move beyond awareness of racism to an actively antiracist position that requires policy change.

Inheritance by Dani Shapiro. Shapiro's memoir describes the life-changing results of a DNA test showing that her identity is not what she had assumed it was all her life.

Just Mercy by Bryan Stevenson. Stevenson's book is about his work as a social justice activist as cofounder of the Equal Justice Initiative and his important work on behalf of people falsely imprisoned.

Leading While Muslim by Debbie Almontaser. Almontaser examines the experiences of American Muslim principals following 9/11.

Loving by Sheryll Cashin. Cashin's thoroughly researched and important book examines the long history of integrating loving relationships and the positive impact this can have on society.

My Accidental Jihad by Krista Bremer. Bremer writes about her marriage to a Muslim man from Libya and the culture differences they encounter as they make a life together in North Carolina.

Quiet by Susan Cain. Cain's book provides insight into the importance of introverts and the traditional American marginalization of introverts.

Rising Out of Hatred by Eli Saslow. Saslow chronicles the life of Derek Black, son of the founder of Stormfront, as Derek challenges racist notions and ultimately denounces white supremacy.

Saving the Race by Rebecca Carroll. Carroll examines W. E. B. Du Bois's iconic book *The Souls of Black Folk* through conversations with influential African American thought leaders.

So You Want to Talk About Race by Ijeoma Oluo. Oluo writes clearly about race providing both insight and a framework for deepening one's understanding and ability to talk about this important topic.

Stamped From the Beginning by Ibram X. Kendi. Kendi's nonfiction book on race in the United States examines the many disparities throughout history.

Tears We Cannot Stop by Michael Eric Dyson. Dyson writes from a personal perspective to challenge readers to think more deeply about racism in America and the moral urgency we all carry to address it.

The Awkward Thoughts of W. Kamau Bell by W. Kamau Bell. Bell writes with humor and sincerity about his life as a self-described Black nerd, his path toward becoming a comedian, his experiences with racism, and many other stories.

The Best of Enemies by Osha Gray Davidson. Davidson chronicles the story of KKK leader C. P. Ellis and Black activist Ann Atwater and their unlikely partnership in North Carolina to lead public school integration.

The Broken Heart of America by Walter Johnson. Using St. Louis as a central character, Johnson examines racism and white supremacy through history to the inevitable divisions that exist today.

The Culture Map by Erin Meyer. Meyer shares cultural dimensions to help explain differences in the way people from different countries do business and interact.

The New Jim Crow by Michelle Alexander. Alexander takes a deep look at the way America has unjustly criminalized Black people, creating mass incarceration.

The Real Thing by Constance L. Hays. Hays examines the real story behind Coca-Cola, which includes problems with racial discrimination.

The Souls of Black Folk by W. E. B. Du Bois. Published in 1903, Du Bois's discussion of Black Culture is relevant today as Americans continue to struggle with race and issues of identity.

The Warmth of Other Suns by Isabel Wilkerson. Wilkerson's book examines the Great Migration when millions of Black Americans left the South to seek better opportunities in the North.

Unorthodox by Deborah Feldman. Feldman writes about her life growing up in a strict orthodox Jewish community in Brooklyn and her decision to leave it.

Use Your Difference to Make a Difference by Tayo Rockson. Rockson writes about his experience growing up as a TCK—Third Culture Kid—and shares lessons on building awareness of culture difference.

Waking Up White by Debbie Irving. Irving shares insights about her awakening to white privilege.

We Were Eight Years in Power by Ta-Nehisi Coats. This book is a collection of essays originally published in the *Atlantic* by Coats examining the Reconstruction era to the Obama presidency.

When I Was White by Sarah Valentine. Valentine explores identity and race through her experience of being raised white and later learning that her biological father is Black.

White Fragility by Robin DiAngelo. DiAngelo's book is an important resource for people who want to understand racism by understanding how white privilege and white fragility are barriers to dismantling racism.

White Like Me by Tim Wise. Wise writes about his reckoning with racist systems in America and his own path toward becoming an activist.

Why Are All the Black Kids Sitting Together in the Cafeteria, 20th Anniversary Edition, by Beverly Daniel Tatum. Tatum's seminal study of the psychology of racism examines how racial identity operates as children grow into teens and how they are viewed in the world.

Online Culture Resources

These are learning and development platforms that provide country-specific data on a wide range of places. These resources are useful for specific-country business and international organizations with teams made up of people from different countries.

Country Navigator   https://countrynavigator.com

GlobeSmart   https://www.globesmart.com

Culture Wizard   https://www.rw-3.com

Cultural Orientations Framework   https://www.cof-online.com

The Culture Map by Erin Meyer   https://www.erinmeyer.com/tools

NOTES

Introduction

1. Kurt Streeter, "Kneeling, Fiercely Debated in the N.F.L., Resonates in Protests," *New York Times*, June 5, 2020. Accessed at https://www.nytimes.com/2020/06/05/sports/football/george-floyd-kaepernick-kneeling-nfl-protests.html.

2. Aliza Chasan, "See It: One of NYPD's Top Cops Kneels, Hugs Protester," PIX 11, June 1, 2020. Accessed at https://www.pix11.com/news/local-news/see-it-one-of-nypds-top-cops-kneels-hugs-protester; "See Police Officers Kneel in Solidarity with Protesters," CNN, June 1, 2020. Accessed at https://www.cnn.com/videos/us/2020/06/01/police-kneel-solidarity-protesters-george-floyd-death-es-vpx.cnn; "Portland Police Take a Knee with Protesters, *Oregonian*, May 31, 2020. Accessed at https://www.youtube.com/watch?v=8WFqP_Yb3yI.

3. "Officers in N.J. Take a Knee with Police Brutality Protesters," NJ.com, June 1, 2020. Accessed at https://www.youtube.com/watch?v=CjCszfmgRiw.

4. Mark Berman and Emily Wax-Thibodeuax, "Police Keep Using Force Against Peaceful Protesters, Prompting Sustained Criticism About Tactics and Training," *Washington Post*, June 4, 2020. Accessed at https://www.washingtonpost.com/national/police-keep-using-force-against-peaceful-protesters-prompting-sustained-criticism-about-tactics-and-training/2020/06/03/5d2f51d4-a5cf-11ea-bb20-ebf0921f3bbd_story.html.

5. Kate Brumback, "6 Atlanta Police Officers Charged After Video Shows Them Forcibly Removing Protesting College Students from Car," *TIME*, June 2, 2020. Accessed at https://time.com/5846652/atlanta-police-officers-charged-protest/.

6. Ana Sandoiu, "Racial Inequalities in COVID-19—The Impact on Black Communities," Medical News Today, June 5, 2020. Accessed at https://www.medicalnewstoday.com/articles/racial-

inequalities-in-covid-19-the-impact-on-black-communities#What-explains-the-disparities?-And-how-does-racism-play-into-it?-.

7. Matt Apuzzo and David G. Kirkpatrick, "COVID-19 Changed How the World Does Science, Together," *New York Times*, April 1, 2020 (updated April 14, 2020). Accessed at https://www.ny-times.com/2020/04/01/world/europe/coronavirus-science-re-search-cooperation.html.

8. Patrick Wintour, "U.S. Stays Away as World Leaders Agree Action on COVID-19 Vaccine," *Guardian*, April 24, 2020. Accessed at https://www.theguardian.com/world/2020/apr/24/us-stays-away-as-world-leaders-agree-action-on-covid-19-vaccine; Damien Cave, "New Zealand Lifts Lockdown as It Declares Virus Eliminated, for Now," *New York Times*, June 8, 2020. Accessed at https://www.nytimes.com/2020/06/08/world/australia/new-zealand-coronavirus-ard-ern.html; Pablo Gutiérrez, "Coronavirus World Map: Which Countries Have the Most COVID-19 Cases and Deaths?" *Guardian*, July 2, 2020. Accessed at https://www.theguardian.com/world/2020/jun/12/coronavirus-world-map-which-countries-have-the-most-covid-19-cases-and-deaths.

Chapter 1

1. Joseph Guzman, "Walmart CEO Pledges $100 Million to Address Systemic Racism," *Hill*, June 5, 2020. Accessed at https://thehill.com/changing-america/respect/equality/501396-walmart-ceo-pledges-100-million-to-address-systemic-racism; Jessica Snouwaert, "Companies Like Netflix, McDonald's, and Target Are Speaking Out Amid the George Floyd Protests—And Some Are Actually Taking Action," *Business Insider*, June 2, 2020. Accessed at https://www.businessinsider.com/george-floyd-protests-companies-responses-actions-apple-tar-get-mcdonalds-nike-2020-6#mcdonalds-president-joe-erlinger-wrote-a-post-on-linkedin-expressing-the-companys-commitment-to-inclusion-and-its-ceo-said-it-would-hold-a-town-hall-4.

2. Chloe Melas, "NFL Commissioner Roger Goodell Says League Was Wrong for Not Listening to Players Earlier About Racism," CNN, June 6, 2020. Accessed at https://edition.cnn.com/2020/06/05/sport/roger-goodell-responds-nfl-stron-ger-together-video/index.html; "Roger Goodell Disagrees with Colin Kaepernick's Actions," *Boston Globe*, September 2, 2016. Accessed at https://www.bostonglobe.com/sports/pa-triots/2016/09/07/roger-goodell-disagrees-with-colin-kaeper-nick-actions/hGtwLR0g3duTTfPqeCOgBP/story.html.

3. "Michael Jordan Speech," YouTube, uploaded August 24, 2014 by Rhene Vic. Accessed at https://www.youtube.com/watch?v=DOuNIyv_W7U.

4. "40 Michael Jordan Quotes (about Teamwork, Basketball, Goals . . .)," UpJourney, September 13, 2019. Accessed at https://up-journey.com/michael-jordan-quotes.

5. Greg Mitchell, "Factbox: What Changes Are Companies Making in Response to George Floyd Protests?" Reuters, June 11, 2020. Accessed at https://www.reuters.com/article/us-minneapolis-police-companies-factbox/factbox-what-changes-are-companies-making-in-response-to-george-floyd-protests-idUSKBN23I-2TA; Mike Ozanian, "How CrossFit Became a $4 Billion Brand," *Forbes*, February 25, 2015. Accessed at https://www.forbes.com/sites/mikeozanian/2015/02/25/how-crossfit-became-a-4-billion-brand/#212da05f1f96.

6. Daniel Bentley, "The Fall of CrossFit Founder and CEO Greg Glassman, Who Resigned After Racist Remarks," *Fortune*, June 9, 2020. Accessed at https://fortune.com/2020/06/09/crossfit-ceo-greg-glassman-resigns-founder-tweet-protests/; Hannah Gold, "CrossFit CEO Resigns After Saying 'We're Not Mourning for George Floyd,'" The Cut, June 10, 2020. Accessed at https://www.thecut.com/2020/06/crossfit-ceo-greg-glassman-resigns-after-racist-remarks.html.

7. "Uber: Co-founder Travis Kalanick to Resign from Board of Directors," *Guardian*, December 24, 2019. Accessed at https://www.theguardian.com/technology/2019/dec/24/uber-co-founder-travis-kalanick-to-resign-from-board-of-directors.

8. Joshua Rhett Miller "Road Rager: Racist Meltdown 'Ruined My Life,'" *New York Post*, July 31, 2018. Accessed at https://nypost.com/2018/07/31/racist-contractor-whines-that-road-rage-encounter-ruined-his-life/.

9. Phile Wahba, "The Number of Black CEOs in the Fortune 500 Remains Very Low," *Fortune*, June 1, 2020. Accessed at https://fortune.com/2020/06/01/black-ceos-fortune-500-2020-african-american-business-leaders/.

10. Pamela Newkirk, *Diversity, Inc.: The Failed Promise of a Billion-Dollar Business* (Bold Type Books, 2019), p. 5.

11. Tim Rosten and Max A. Cherney, "Here's How Much It May Cost Starbucks to Close 8,000 Stores for an Afternoon," MarketWatch, April 18, 2018. Accessed at https://www.marketwatch.com/story/what-starbucks-said-the-last-time-it-closed-its-stores-for-an-afternoon-2018-04-17.

12. "History of Dolce and Gabbana," Dragon Horse Agency, August 8, 2019. Accessed at https://www.dragonhorseagency.com/history-of-dolce-and-gabbana/.

13. Marc Bain, "Chinese Web Users Have Shunned Dolce & Gabbana Since Its Racism Controversy," Quartz, July 19, 2019. Accessed at https://qz.com/1670526/dolce-gabbana-still-shunned-online-in-china-after-racism-controversy/.

14. "The Chinese Are Burning, Dumping Their Dolce & Gabbana Products," *New Straits Times*, November 24, 2018. Accessed at https://www.nst.com.my/world/2018/11/434101/chinese-are-burning-dumping-their-dolce-gabbana-products.

15. "Financial Health & Reputation: D&G May Suffer Ripple Effect for Years in China After Racism Ad Row," *Times of India*, November 27, 2018. Accessed at https://economictimes.indiatimes.com/magazines/panache/financial-health-reputation-dg-may-suffer-ripple-effect-for-years-in-china-after-racism-ad-row/articleshow/66825493.cms?from=mdr.

16. Dexter Filkins, "James Mattis, A Warrior in Washington," *New Yorker*, May 22, 2017. Accessed at https://www.newyorker.com/magazine/2017/05/29/james-mattis-a-warrior-in-washington.

17. Michael Ray, "James Mattis," *Encyclopaedia Britannica*. Accessed at https://www.britannica.com/biography/James-Mattis.

18. Cpl. Gabriela Gonzalez, "CAOCL Closes Cultural Gap," Marine Corps Base Camp Pendleton, January 9, 2009. Accessed at https://www.pendleton.marines.mil/News/News-Article-Display/Article/536773/.

19. Christine Simmons, "Paul Weiss Vows to 'Do Better' After Partner Promotions Stir Diversity Debate," Law.com, December 18, 2018. Accessed at https://www.law.com/newyorklawjournal/2018/12/18/paul-weiss-vows-to-do-better-after-partner-promotions-stir-diversity-debate/.

20. Christine Simmons, "170 GCs Pen Open Letter to Law Firms: Improve on Diversity or Lose Our Business," Law.com, January 27, 2019. Accessed at https://www.law.com/americanlawyer/2019/01/27/170-gcs-pen-open-letter-to-law-firms-improve-on-diversity-or-lose-our-business/.

21. Kate Sullivan, "Former Starbucks CEO Howard Schultz: 'I Honestly Don't See Color,'" CNN, February 13, 2019. Accessed at https://www.cnn.com/2019/02/13/politics/howard-schultz-see-color/index.html.

22. Kate Taylor, "Howard Schultz Reveals How He Decided to Launch Starbucks' 'Embarrassing' and 'Tone-deaf' 'Race To-

gether' Campaign Despite Internal Concerns," *Business Insider*, January 29, 2019. Accessed at https://www.businessinsider.com/howard-schultz-failed-race-together-campaign-2019-1.

23. Austin Carr, "The Inside Story of Starbucks's Race Together Campaign, No Foam," *Fast Company*, January 15, 2015. Accessed at https://www.fastcompany.com/3046890/the-inside-story-of-starbuckss-race-together-campaign-no-foam.

24. Kate Taylor, "Howard Schultz Reveals How He Decided to Launch Starbucks' 'Embarrassing' and 'Tone-deaf' 'Race Together' Campaign Despite Internal Concerns."

25. Fiona A. White, Rachel Maunder, Stefano Verrelli, "Text-based E-contact: Harnessing Cooperative Internet Interactions to Bridge the Social and Psychological Divide," *European Review of Social Psychology* 31, no. 1 (2020), pp. 76–119, DOI: 10.1080/10463283.2020.1753459.

Chapter 2

1. Greg Winter, "Coca-Cola Settles Racial Bias Case," *New York Times*, November 17, 2000. Accessed at https://www.nytimes.com/2000/11/17/business/coca-cola-settles-racial-bias-case.html; "How Abercrombie Ended Up Being Sued by 250,000 Employees," The Fashion Law, January 30, 2018. Accessed at https://www.thefashionlaw.com/how-abercrombie-ended-up-being-sued-by-250000-employees/; "Sprint Nextel to Settle Age Discrimination Suit for $57 Million," *Mercury News*, May 18, 2007. Accessed at https://www.mercurynews.com/2007/05/18/sprint-nextel-to-settle-age-discrimination-suit-for-57-million/.

2. Greg Winter, "Coca-Cola Settles Racial Bias Case."

3. Steve Greenhouse, "Abercrombie & Fitch Bias Case Is Settled," *New York Times*, November 17, 2004. Accessed at https://www.nytimes.com/2004/11/17/us/abercrombie-fitch-bias-case-is-settled.html; "Abercrombie & Fitch Pays Out $71,000 to Settle Lawsuits Over Hijabs," *Guardian*, September 23, 2013. Accessed at https://www.theguardian.com/world/2013/sep/23/abercrombie-fitch-lawsuits-hijabs-head-scarves.

4. "USA: Morgan Stanley Pays $46 Mlln. in Gender Discrimination Lawsuit," Business and Human Rights Resource Centre, April 25, 2007. Accessed at https://www.business-humanrights.org/en/usa-morgan-stanley-pays-46-mlln-in-gender-discrimination-lawsuit.

5. Constance L. Hays, *The Real Thing: Truth and Power at the Coca-Cola Company* (Random House, 2004), pp. 205–207.

6. Nikhil Deogun, "Suit Is Filed Against Coke by Current, Past Employees Who Allege Racial Bias," *Wall Street Journal*, April 26, 1999. Accessed at https://www.wsj.com/articles/SB925075-898646132761.

7. Elsa Brenner, "Texaco Accused of Bias in Suit by Blacks," *New York Times*, July 14, 1996. Accessed at https://www.nytimes.com/1996/07/14/nyregion/texaco-accused-of-bias-in-suit-by-blacks.html; Thomas S. Mulligan and Chris Kraul, "Texaco Settles Racial Bias Suit for $176 Million," *Los Angeles Times*, November 16, 1996. Accessed at https://www.latimes.com/archives/la-xpm-1996-11-16-mn-65290-story.html.

8. Davan Maharaj, "Coca-Cola to Settle Racial Bias Lawsuit," *Los Angeles Times*, November 17, 2000. Accessed at https://www.latimes.com/archives/la-xpm-2000-nov-17-mn-53405-story.html.

9. Jonathan D. Glater and Greg Winter, "Coca-Cola Selects Former Labor Secretary to Lead Diversity Task Force," *New York Times*, March 16, 2001. Accessed at https://www.nytimes.com/2001/03/16/business/coca-cola-selects-former-labor-secretary-to-lead-diversity-task-force.html.

10. Anne D'Innocenzio, "Racism and Fashion: Why Top Brands Keep Producing Products That Prompt Backlash," Global News, February 17, 2019. Accessed at https://globalnews.ca/news/4970809/racism-fashion-products-backlash/.

11. Lacey Louwagie, "City's Lawsuit Accusing Wells Fargo of Racist Lending Advances," Global Courthouse News, June 15, 2018. Accessed at https://www.courthousenews.com/citys-lawsuit-accusing-wells-fargo-of-racist-lending-advances/; David Folkenflik, "Fox News Pays $10 Million to Settle Racial, Gender Bias Suits," NPR, May 16, 2018. Accessed at https://www.npr.org/sections/thetwo-way/2018/05/16/611504340/fox-news-pays-10-million-to-settle-racial-gender-bias-suits; "Wal-Mart Settles Racism Lawsuit for $17.5 Million," Industry Week, February 23, 2009. Accessed at https://www.industryweek.com/leadership/companies-executives/article/21955378/walmart-settles-racism-lawsuit-for-175-million.

12. "Researchers in Pittsburgh, Paris and Vienna Win Grant for COVID-19 Vaccine," PittWire Health, University of Pittsburgh, March 25, 2020. Accessed at https://www.pittwire.pitt.edu/news/researchers-pittsburgh-paris-and-vienna-win-grant-covid-19-vaccine.

13. Kelsey Piper, " How the Coronavirus Is Changing Science," Vox, May 22, 2020. Accessed at https://www.vox.com/future-perfect/2020/5/14/21252024/coronavirus-science-peer-review-preprints-grants-medrxiv.

14. "1942: Navajo Code Talkers," Office of the Director of National Intelligence. Accessed at https://www.intelligence.gov/index.php/people/barrier-breakers-in-history/453-navajo-code-talkers.

15. "Demonstration in California, 1942," Cline Library, Northern Arizona University. Accessed at http://archive.library.nau.edu/digital/collection/cpa/id/44718.

16. Sebastian Edwards, "How Effective Is Foreign Aid," World Economic Forum COVID Action Platform, November 28, 2014. Accessed at https://www.weforum.org/agenda/2014/11/how-effective-is-foreign-aid/; "Why We Do It," World Connect. Accessed at https://www.worldconnect-us.org/about-us.

17. "Poorly Executed Programs," GiveWell. Accessed at https://www.givewell.org/international/technical/criteria/impact/failure-stories#Poorly_executed_programs.

18. "Water and Sanitation in Dassilame Soce," World Connect. Accessed at https://www.worldconnect-us.org/projects/water-sanitation-dassilame-soce-boutilimite-saroudia.

19. Interview with Pamela Nathenson, March 7, 2019.

20. https://qcss.wordpress.com/2011/06/20/over-94-of-fortune-500-companies-outsource/.

21. Amar Gupta, *Outsourcing and Offshoring of Professional Services: Business Optimization in a Global Economy* (IGI Global, 2008), p. 181.

22. Ravi Aron and Jitendra V. Singh, "Getting Offshoring Right," *Harvard Business Review*, December, 2005. Accessed at https://hbr.org/2005/12/getting-offshoring-right.

23. Nils Moe, Darja Smite, Geir Hanssen, and Hamish Barney, "From Offshore Outsourcing to Insourcing and Partnerships: Four Failed Outsourcing Attempts," *Empirical Software Engineering* 19 (2013). DOI: 10.1007/s10664-013-9272-x.

24. Ismail Nizam, "Why Walmart Failed in Germany? An Analysis in the Perspective of Organizational Behaviour," *International Journal of Accounting & Business Management* 4 (2016), pp. 206–215. DOI: 10.24924/ijabm/2016.11/v4.iss2/206.215.

25. Phoebe Jui, "Walmart's Downfall in Germany: A Case Study," *Journal of International Management*, May 16, 2011. Accessed at https://journalofinternationalmanagement.wordpress.com/2011/05/16/walmarts-downfall-in-germany-a-case-study/.

26. "Allyship at All Levels: How Organizations Can Support Black Employees Right Now," Paradigm webinar. Accessed at https://info.paradigmiq.com/wod-allyship-at-all-levels?utm_campaign=Allyship%20Webinar&utm_medium=email&_hsmi=89439248&_

hsenc=p2ANqtz–xdlaH1-K7xHwuCccuQMaFfFVDbuydFVSgNs-
JpAbtOhIKfdh2ATQYzAArC_bp9wzKT-0kTPL-EX-n-uDPbEQx-
dGQKOIg&utm_content=89439248&utm_source=hs_email.

27. "Titan Fast Pitch 2018 Recap," CSUF Entrepreneurship, November 14, 2018. Accessed at https://csufentrepreneurship.com/
titan-fast-pitch-2018-recap/.

Chapter 3

1. "Charge Statistics (Charges filed with EEOC) FY 1997 Through
FY 2019," U.S. Equal Employment Opportunity Commission. Accessed at https://www.eeoc.gov/enforcement/charge-statistics-
charges-filed-eeoc-fy-1997-through-fy-2019.

2. Betsey Guzior, "EEOC Sexual Harassment Lawsuits Up 50 Percent," BizWomen, October 10, 2018. Accessed at https://www.bi-
zjournals.com/bizwomen/news/latest-news/2018/10/eeoc-sex-
ual-harassment-lawsuits-double.html?page=all.

3. https://www.forbes.com/sites/geristengel/2020/06/17/black-
lives-matter-protests-moves-corporate-di-initiatives-into-the-spot-
light/.

4. https://www.bizjournals.com/bizwomen/news/latest-news/
2020/07/diversity-inclusion-jobs-rebound-racial-protests.htm-
l?page=all.

5. Rodolfo Mendoza-Denton and Amanda Danielle Perez, "Racism and the Narrative of Biological Inevitability," Othering &
Belonging. Accessed at http://www.otheringandbelonging.org/
racism-and-the-narrative-of-biological-inevitability/.

6. Mark Levine, Amy Prosser, David Evans, and Stephen Reicher,
"Identity and Emergency Intervention: How Social Group Membership and Inclusiveness of Group Boundaries Shapes Helping
Behavior." Accessed at http://citeseerx.ist.psu.edu/viewdoc/
download?doi=10.1.1.210.5348&rep=rep1&type=pdf.

7. https://www.youtube.com/watch?v=AvRuYrH5rjs.

8. See, for instance, https://scholar.google.com/scholar?q=gordon
+allport+intergroup+connection&hl=en&as_sdt=0&as_vis=
1&oi=scholart.

9. Kristin Davies, Stephen C. Wright, Arthur Aron, and Joseph Comeau,
"Intergroup Contact Through Friendship: Intimacy and Norms,"
chapter 9 in Gordon Hodson and Miles Hewstone (eds.), *Advances
in Intergroup Contact* (Psychology Press, 2013). Accessed at https://
books.google.com/books?hl=en&lr=&id=8NSYO5J-a5AC&oi=f-
nd&pg=PA200&dq=gordon+allport+intergroup+connection

+not+all+conditions+necessary&ots=BnocoSRp7T&sig=mcti_
XGIbR4W9WHRmBGBx_VYt1w#v=onepage&q&f=false.

10. Salma Mousa, list of working papers. Accessed at https://www.
salmamousa.com/research.

11. Interview with Pete Diehl, Columbus, Ohio, April 1, 2000.

12. "Charlotte L. Beers," Office of the Historian. Accessed at https://
history.state.gov/departmenthistory/people/beers-charlotte-l.

13. "Biography of Farah Pandith," U.S. Department of State archive.
Accessed at https://2001-2009.state.gov/p/eur/rls/or/83085.htm.

14. Farah Pandith, *How We Win: How Cutting-Edge Entrepreneurs, Polit-
ical Visionaries, Enlightened Business Leaders, and Social Media Ma-
vens Can Defeat the Extremist Threat* (Custom House, 2019), p. 8.

15. Jim A. C. Everett, "Intergroup Contact Theory: Past, Present,
and Future," *Inquisitive Mind* 2 (2013). Accessed at https://www
.in-mind.org/article/intergroup-contact-theory-past-present
-and-future.

Chapter 4

1. "Edward T. Hall's Cultural Iceberg Model," from Edward T. Hall,
Beyond Culture (1976). Accessed at https://www.spps.org/cms/
lib/MN01910242/Centricity/Domain/125/iceberg_model_3.
pdf.

2. "P&G Detergent Pulled in Germany over Neo-Nazi Code Found
on Packages," NBC News, May 9, 2014. Accessed at https://www.
nbcnews.com/business/consumer/p-g-detergent-pulled-germa-
ny-over-neo-nazi-code-found-n101526.

3. Interview with Jenna Fischer, April 27, 2019.

4. See, for instance, https://scholar.google.com/scholar?q=ac-
ademic+study+of+saliency+in+identity&hl=en&as_sdt=0&as_
vis=1&oi=scholart.

Chapter 5

1. Thomas F. Pettigrew and Linda R. Tropp, "A Meta-analytic Test
of Intergroup Contact Theory," *Journal of Personality and Social
Psychology* 90, no. 5 (2006), pp. 751–783. DOI: 10.1037/0022-
3514.90.5.751.

2. Yair Amichai-Hamburger and Katelyn Y. A. McKenna, "The Contact Hypothesis Reconsidered: Interacting via the Internet," *Journal of Computer-Mediated Communication* 11, no. 3 (April 1, 2006),
pp. 825–843. DOI: 10.1111/j.1083-6101.2006.00037.x.

3. Josia Nakash, "Connecting with Total Strangers," Medium, April 6, 2019. Accessed at https://medium.com/the-ascent/zoom-meet-up-with-total-strangers-8d7ff753cf2d. Accessed at https://www.businessinsider.com/unexpected-benefits-of-working-from-home-2020-4.

Chapter 6

1. Emilie Rusch, "Cargill: Tried to Resolve Issues before Firing Colorado Muslim Workers," *Denver Post*, December 31, 2015 (updated February 2, 2017). Accessed at https://www.denverpost.com/2015/12/31/cargill-tried-to-resolve-issues-before-firing-colorado-muslim-workers/.
2. Juliana Menasce Horowitz, Anna Brown, and Kiana Cox, "Race in America 2019," Pew Research Center, April 9, 2019. Accessed at https://www.pewsocialtrends.org/2019/04/09/race-in-america-2019/.
3. See https://www.tanabel.com and https://www.leagueofkitchens.com.
4. See https://www.onemorgancounty.org and https://cndc.org/fort-morgan-cultures-unite-for-progress/.
5. See https://davidbudbill.com.
6. Sheryll Cashin, *Loving: Interracial Intimacy in America and the Threat to White Supremacy* (Beacon Press, 2018), p. 10.
7. Michael Eric Dyson, *Tears We Cannot Stop: A Sermon to White America* (St. Martin's Press, 2017), p. 198.
8. W. Kamau Bell, *The Awkward Thoughts of W. Kamau Bell: Tales of a 6' 4", African American, Heterosexual, Cisgender, Left-Leaning, Asthmatic, Black and Proud Blerd, Mama's Boy, Dad, and Stand-Up Comedian* (Dutton, 2017), p. 264.
9. "The Science behind Setting Goals (and Achieving Them)," Forbes Books. Accessed at https://forbesbooks.com/the-science-behind-setting-goals-and-achieving-them/.
10. Barrerr Wissman, "An Accountability Partner Makes You Vastly More Likely to Succeed," *Entrepreneur*, March 30, 2018. Accessed at https://www.entrepreneur.com/article/310062.

Chapter 7

1. Adi Jaffe, "Why Is It So Hard to Change Bad Habits?" *Psychology Today*, March 26, 2019. Accessed at https://www.psychologytoday.com/us/blog/all-about-addiction/201903/why-is-it-so-hard-change-bad-habits.

2. Jim Edwards, "Occupy Wall Street: Why Ben & Jerry's Endorsement Rings Hollow," CBS News, updated October 10, 2011. Accessed at https://www.cbsnews.com/news/occupy-wall-street-why-ben-jerrys-endorsement-rings-hollow/.

3. "Cultivate a Culture of Equality with Inclusive Leadership," Trailhead, Salesforce.com. Accessed at https://trailhead.salesforce.com/en/content/learn/modules/inclusive-leadership-practices/cultivate-a-culture-of-equality-with-inclusive-leadership.

4. Ming Jong, "Effect of Perceived Negative Workplace Gossip on Employees' Behaviors," *Front. Psychol.* 12 (July, 2018). DOI: 10.3389/fpsyg.2018.01112.

5. Interview with Tim Morton, December 15, 2019.

6. Fiza Pirani, "Prada Pulls Monkeylike Products after 'Blackface Imagery' Backlash," *Atlanta Journal-Constitution*, December 14, 2018. Accessed at https://www.ajc.com/news/world/prada-pulls-monkeylike-products-after-blackface-imagery-backlash/FBXJuMvGVstGKopaKgRRaK/.

7. Kevin J. Ryan, "The Worst Designed Products of 2019," *Inc.*, December 4, 2019. Accessed at https://www.inc.com/kevin-j-ryan/worst-designed-products-2019-cadbury-nike-adidas-google.html.

8. Interview with Jeff Layton, June 22, 2014.

Chapter 8

1. Kevin J. Ryan, "The Worst Designed Products of 2019."

2. Emma Green, "These Are the Americans Who Live in a Bubble," *Atlantic*, February 21, 2019. Accessed at https://www.theatlantic.com/politics/archive/2019/02/americans-remain-deeply-ambivalent-about-diversity/583123/; Maxine Najle and Robert P. Jones, "American Democracy in Crisis: The Fate of Pluralism in a Divided Nation," *PRRI*, February 19, 2019. Accessed at https://www.prri.org/research/american-democracy-in-crisis-the-fate-of-pluralism-in-a-divided-nation/.

3. Sheryll Cashin, *Loving*, p. 165.

4. Robin DiAngelo, *White Fragility: Why It's So Hard for White People to Talk About Racism* (Beacon Press, 2018), p. 31.

5. Mary Lee Talbot, "Irene Monroe Says White People Need to Talk About Race," *Chautauquan Daily*, August 14, 2018. Accessed at https://chqdaily.com/2018/08/irene-monroe-longing-for-justice-and-god-is-tied-to-longing-for-personal-healing/.

6. Dinitia Smith, "A Utopia Awakens and Shakes Itself; Chautauqua, Once a Cultural Haven for Religion Teachers, Survives," *New York Times*, August 17, 1998. Accessed at https://www.nytimes

.com/1998/08/17/arts/utopia-awakens-shakes-itself-chautau-qua-once-cultural-haven-for-religion.html.

Chapter 9

1. Que-Lam Huynh, Thierry Devos, and Laura Smalarz, "Perpetual Foreigner in One's Own Land: Potential Implications for Identity and Psychological Adjustment," *Journal of Social and Clinical Psychology* 30, no. 2 (2011), pp. 133–162. DOI: 10.1521/jscp.2011.30.2.133.
2. "Hana Tajima, The Muslim British-Japanese Designer Working with UNIQLO to Redefine the Hijab," Japan Trends, January 18, 2016. Accessed at https://www.japantrends.com/hana-tajima-muslim-british-japanese-designer-uniqlo/.
3. Dr. Darrius, "Detroit Blamed to 'Christmas in July' Island Chaos at Put-in-Bay," WJLB Detroit, July 23, 2018. Accessed at https://wjlbdetroit.iheart.com/content/2018-07-23-detroit-blamed-for-christmas-in-july-island-chaos-at-put-in-bay/; Susan Glaser, "'Overwhelmed' Put-in-Bay Struggles with Raucous Christmas in July Crowds," Cleveland.com, August 11, 2018. Accessed at https://www.cleveland.com/travel/2018/08/overwhelmed_put-in-bay_struggl.html.
4. Jon Stinchcomb, "27 People Arrested at Put-in-Bay 'Christmas in July' Weekend," *Port Clinton News Herald*, July 25, 2018. Accessed at https://www.portclintonnewsherald.com/story/news/local/2018/07/25/put-bay-christmas-july-result-27-arrests-75-citations/829762002/.
5. Michael Harrington, "Large Crowds Fight in Put-in-Bay," *Sandusky Register*, July 23, 2018. Accessed at https://sanduskyregister.com/news/17653/large-crowds-fight-in-put-in-bay/.
6. Dirk H. Hellhammer, Stefan Wust, Brigitte M. Kudielka, "Salivary Cortisol as a Biomarker in Stress Research," *Psychoneuroendocrinology* 34, no. 2 (February, 2009), pp. 163–171. DOI: 10.1016/j.psyneuen.2008.10.026.
7. "Timeline of Events in Shooting of Michael Brown in Ferguson," Associated Press, August 8, 2019. Accessed at https://apnews.com/9aa32033692547699a3b61da8fd1fc62.
8. Pamela Newkirk, *Diversity, Inc.*, p. 1.
9. https://chq.org/mirror?highlight=WyJtaXJyb3IiLCJwcm9qZWN0IiwicHJvamVjdCdzIiwibWlycm9yIHByb2plY3QiXQ.
10. See https://www.visitputinbay.org/safe-island-task-force/.

11. Andy Roberts, "PGA of America CEO: 'Golf Needs to Look More Like the Face of America,'" GolfMagic, August 9, 2018. Accessed at https://www.golfmagic.com/golf-news/pga-america-ceo-golf-needs-look-more-face-america.

12. Maria Pasquini "Alexis Ohanian Says He Stepped Down from Reddit Board to Help 'Make a Better World' for Daughter Olympia," *People*, June 7, 2020. Accessed at https://people.com/human-interest/alexis-ohanian-stepped-down-reddit-board-better-world-daughter/.

13. Kaya Yurieff, "Reddit Cofounder Alexis Ohanian Resigns from Board, Urges Seat Be Filled by Black Candidate," CNN Business, June 5, 2020. Accessed at https://www.cnn.com/2020/06/05/tech/alexis-ohanian-reddit/index.html.

14. Pamela Newkirk, *Diversity, Inc.*, p. 5.

15. Craig Shoup, "Rioting Charges Dropped against Men in Put-in-Bay Incident," *Fremont News Messenger*, June 8, 2020 (updated June 12, 2020). Accessed at https://www.thenews-messenger.com/story/news/local/2020/06/08/riot-charges-dropped-against-six-men-jailed-after-put-bay-incident/5322691002/.

16. Jonathan Monk, "Charges Dropped against 6 Men Arrested on Put-in-Bay; Sheriff Reflects on Issues in Justice System," WTOL 11, June 9, 2020. Accessed at https://www.wtol.com/article/news/local/protests/put-in-bay-weekend-charges-dropped/512-f43dec3d-0da2-4d20-a309-e8d2457ca3d4.

17. Allison Dunn, "Ottawa County Requests Federal Assistance after Viral Arrest Video," *Toledo Blade*, June 11, 2020. Accessed at https://www.toledoblade.com/local/police-fire/2020/06/11/Put-in-Bay-police-chief-resigns-after-viral-arrest-video/stories/20200611116.

18. "Put-in-Bay body camera June 6, 2020, video 1," *Sandusky Register*, June 10, 2020. Accessed at https://www.youtube.com/watch?v=sw5okn_1b_c.

19. Sheryll Cashin, *Loving*, p. 184

20. Susan Glaser, "'Overwhelmed' Put-in-Bay Struggles with Raucous Christmas in July Crowds."

21. "Put-in-Bay Police Chief on Leave, 2 Officers Resign after Violent Arrests of African American Visitors," Cleveland 19 News, June 11, 2020. Accessed at https://www.cleveland19.com/2020/06/11/put-in-bay-police-chief-leave-officers-resign-after-violent-arrests-african-american-visitors/.

22. Corinne Shutack, "97 Things White People Can Do for Racial Justice," Medium, August 13, 2017. Accessed at https://medium.com/equality-includes-you/what-white-people-can-do-for-racial-justice-f2d18b0e0234

23. Jonathan Holloway, "African American History: From Emancipation to the Present," Open Yale Courses, Spring 2010. Accessed at https://oyc.yale.edu/NODE/46.

24. Mike Jones, "Opinion: Roger Goodell's 'We, the NFL' Statement Was Good. But Owners' Actions Will Matter More," *USA Today*, June 6, 2020. Accessed at https://www.usatoday.com/story/sports/nfl/columnist/mike-jones/2020/06/06/roger-goodell-nfl-statement-good-owners-actions-protests-matter-more/3164736001/.

ACKNOWLEDGMENTS

I would like to thank many friends and family members who supported me during the writing of this book, especially Heather, Rose, Jessica, Beth, Jenna, Jiyun, Jenny, Meagan, Tom & Judy, Rami & Maria, Maia, Jane, Sapna, Liz, I-Hsing. Iara, Chris, Randy, Nicole, Erin, Tokiko, Ruth, Jason, Ben, Candy, Sara, and Tom. For their loving support in all that I do, I thank Charlene & Larry, Melissa & Gee, Jimmy & Jenn, Alec, Erin & Brian, Matt & Michelle, Sean & Natasha, Lee, Pete & Pidge, Mike & Cristina, Alex, Steve & Lori, Chloe Ann, Jennifer, Vivian & Chris, Matt & Carol, Nick, Amy & Vic, Margaret & Andrew, Jeannine & Gavin, Justine & Chris, Thom & Moira, Tanny & Helen, Neil & Katrina, Doug, Kermit & Cate, Eric & Oliver, Bruce & Roger, Sharon, Catherine, Dan, Lisa, Jerome, Susie, Alison and Maria.

I would like to thank many of my clients and colleagues and appreciate the stories they have shared with me over the years including Howard, Duncan, Wendy, Kate, Mimi, Jil, Mike, Koji, Masaharu, Tony, Keigo, Jerry, Pat, Jenn, Jose, Jean-Carlo, Elena, Hale, Maritza, Neha, Felicia, Kat, Bill, Lindsay, Chi, Joanna, Tim, Ann, Meghan, Debbie, Francine, Hironao, Kevin, Nicole, Melanie, Mits, Bernardo, Yanay, Jeff, Masa, LaVonda, Hiroyuki, Ben, Justin, Peter, Dawn, Leo, Doug, Filipa, Nyi Nyi, Shinji, Sheila, Takashi, Yanay, Norlito, Ricardo, Donnacha, Jason, Hiro, Lisa, Ruth, Jim, Yvette, Richard, Peter, Harly, Joseph, and Kumar.

For their support on this book, I would like to thank Lana Kitcher, Sara Kendrick, Linda Pattee, Pamela Nathenson at

World Connect, Jennifer McCarthy, Bobby Rahal, Bill Milani, Bruce Wexler, Cherrita Lee, Erica Theis, and Pete Diehl— genius creator of the TeamMachine.

And a very special thanks to my dear friends Laura & Eric for your continued friendship and for providing safe haven for my family as I finished writing this book.

As always, I offer deep gratitude to my parents, Brian & Sally, for their adventurous spirit and for modeling what WE-building looked like way before I knew what to call it. My work would not be possible without the inspiration and support of my family. Thank you, Declan, Jaden, and Mason, and my most heartfelt thanks to Patrick.

INDEX

ABOUT THE AUTHOR

LAURA KRISKA is an expert on cross-cultural relations with more than thirty years' experience bridging gaps in diverse workplaces. She has worked with Fortune 500 companies on four continents, helping thousands of professionals build trust across *Us versus Them* differences based on nationality, ethnicity, race, religion, age, or any factor of identity. Her WE-building framework provides practical and actionable insights for creating a more inclusive and productive world.

Born in Tokyo, raised in the Midwest, and now residing in New York City, Laura has been navigating culture gaps her whole life. She regularly conducts bilingual training sessions around the globe. Considered an authority on cultural integration, she is a regular lecturer and a TEDx speaker. She was the first American woman to work in Honda Motor Company's Tokyo headquarters. This experience is the basis of her first book, *The Accidental Office Lady*.

Follow her on Twitter: @laurakriska
www.laurakriska.com